WADSWORTH GUIDES TO LITERARY STUDY

Maurice Beebe, General Editor

The Brothers Karamazov and the Critics

БРАТЬЯ КАРАМАЗОВЫ

Edward Wasiolek

University of Chicago

Wadsworth Publishing Company, Inc.

Belmont, California

L.C. Cat. Card No.: 67-14512
Printed in the United States of America

PREFACE

The Brothers Karamazov is surely one of the world's great novels —for many, the greatest. Thinking of *The Brothers Karamazov*, the Russian critic Berdyaev exclaimed that no one was greater than Dostoevsky, not even Shakespeare. Freud put Dostoevsky—and he had *The Brothers Karamazov* in mind—in the company of Sophocles and Shakespeare. Jean-Paul Sartre found the core idea of existentialism in Ivan Karamazov's words "If there is no immortality, all is permitted." Psychologist, philosopher, political historian, theologian, and literary historian and critic have all paid tribute to Dostoevsky—and especially to *The Brothers Karamazov.*

The Brothers Karamazov is the climax to Dostoevsky's career, a culmination of all the vision, intelligence, and creative power that had developed without abatement in his long career. It is, like most of his great novels, very close to us today. "The Legend of the Grand Inquisitor" is astonishingly prophetic of twentieth-century political movements and deeply perceptive of the relationship of power and freedom. The four brothers are universal types—as recognizable in our world as they were in Dostoevsky's, and probably in Shakespeare's and Sophocles'.

The essays in this volume have been collected to help the student appreciate the complex beauty and power of *The Brothers Karamazov.* The selections are complete essays or complete chapters of books; there are no fragments, no ellipses.

The essays are distinguished and broadly representative in subject matter and method: Freud's essay is a psychological analysis of Dostoevsky the man and writer; Philip Rahv's and D. H. Lawrence's essays are specifically on "The Legend of the Grand Inquisitor"; Camus' essay is on Ivan's rebellion; Ernest Simmons' is a historical introduction to the novel; Ralph Matlaw examines the symbolic and mythic properties of the novel; Eliseo Vivas is concerned, among other things, with the relationship of craft and idea; Mark Kanzer gives us a Freudian view of a crucial scene; and my own selection takes up the novel as a whole. Also, freshly translated selections from the Dostoevsky letters and notebooks bearing on *The Brothers Karamazov* are presented here for the first time in English. Both were translated by the Editor.

This volume will hopefully have many uses. The practice of focusing upon a major text for an extended period of time is a valuable and educationally illuminating exercise in any literature course. Since material in this book lends itself to various levels of sophistication, it can be used in freshman English courses, introductory and advanced humanities courses, courses in critical method, and courses in Russian literature in translation.

All the selections have been reproduced as originally published with these exceptions: the spelling of names has been regularized throughout; some footnotes have been omitted, and the numbering of footnotes has been changed so as to be consecutive throughout each article. The titles of articles have in many instances been changed, although the original title for each selection is provided in a footnote. The original pagination of each article has been indicated in bracketed superscripts.

CONTENTS

BIOGRAPHICAL NOTE

The Man and His World

Dostoevsky's personality was often unattractive: he was nervous, intense, and at times intolerant. He whined constantly about money and conditions. Up to his middle years he was a passionate gambler, and more than once he begged and borrowed money to feed this passion. Once he even pawned the wedding ring of his pregnant wife so as to have one more turn at the roulette wheel.

His views on man seemed hardly more attractive: he believed man to be born sinful and weak, a prey to tumultuous passions more powerful than his will. Man's capacity for hurting himself and others and for telling lies to himself seemed to Dostoevsky measureless. His creatures are twisted and tortured, writhing in pain and reveling in it. Most readers are both attracted and repulsed by his world.

But there is another side to this picture. Dostoevsky's impulsive and passionate nature often found outlet in generous and good impulses. He cared very little about money, even though he complained constantly about not having enough. Although he had a neurotic need to be persecuted for debts, he tried honorably to discharge his obligations and once generously assumed—when in dire straits himself—the obligation of caring for his dead brother's widow, her five children, and the debts of his brother. He gave himself wholly to whatever he was doing and detested what to him were essentially Germanic traits of petty calculation and systematic planning of details. He loved children and lived in warm and selfless love with his second wife from 1867 until his death in 1881.

Dostoevsky's "ugly" universe is actually a realistic universe. Several generations of psychologists have now testified to his uncanny perception of man's real nature. Yet, he viewed man as essentially noble, as desiring dignity and freedom. And, most important and most debatable, Dostoevsky saw man as capable of *achieving* true dignity and freedom. Man can earn true freedom; and he earns it—if at all— by experiencing the tumultuous, suffering, and phantasmagoric universe that is Dostoevsky's world.

His Life and Work

When Dostoevsky completed *The Brothers Karamazov* in November of 1880—less than three months before his death—he was at the height of his creative powers and his literary reputation. Each monthly installment of *The Brothers Karamazov,* which came out in *The Russian Messenger* from 1878 to 1880, was greeted enthusiastically; and Dostoevsky was swamped with letters from readers who wrote to express their admiration or to find out what was going to happen next. *The Brothers Karamazov* is in scope and imaginative vision a fitting climax to his astonishing career.

Dostoevsky's literary career had begun thirty-two years before with the publication of his first novel, *Poor Folk,* in 1846. His works in the 1840s—*The Double, The Landlady, The Faint Heart, The Honest Thief, Mr. Prokharchin, Netochka Nezvanova*—are today, with the exception of *The Double,* important largely as sources for the themes and artistry that came later. These works are varied in theme, style, and intention and reveal to us a writer searching for idea and form. His work was interrupted by his arrest in 1849 as a member of a conspiratorial circle and his subsequent condemnation to eight years of imprisonment—four years of actual incarceration at Omsk and four years of involuntary service in the Siberian army, mostly at Semipalatinsk. Dostoevsky's attendance at the Petrashevsky Circle's meetings had been motivated largely by curiosity and the aimlessness of youth. He did nothing more serious against the government than read some forbidden books, listen to some inflammatory speeches, and give lip service to abstract, utopian, and socialist principles. The severity of the sentence, however, was warmly welcomed by Dostoevsky, who felt deeply the need for punishment. It was ten years before he returned to his beloved St. Petersburg and to active literary labor.

The years immediately following his return to St. Petersburg, 1859–1864, must be looked upon as transitional years in Dostoevsky's life and career. His work in these years is an uncertain mixture of pre-prison experimentation and post-prison maturity. The tragic world vision that was to characterize his work beginning with *Notes from the*

Underground seems to be held at comic distance in his first two works after imprisonment—*The Uncle's Dream* (1859) and *A Friend of the Family* (*The Village of Stepanchikovo*) (1859); is touched on in the thinly veiled autobiographical account of his prison experience in *The House of the Dead;* and is expressed inadequately in an inappropriate form in *The Insulted and the Injured* (1861). It was during these years that the great Dostoevsky was unconsciously forming.

His personal life during these years was a comic-tragedy of bewildering complexity. The journal (*Time*) that he edited with his brother Michael was besieged by creditors and then formally closed by the government in 1863 because of a bureaucratic error. Dostoevsky himself was threatened with imprisonment because of his personal debts. The wife he had married in Siberia was gravely ill with consumption, and Dostoevsky had fallen in love with a rather neurotic student, Paulina Suslova, half his age.

Throughout his life, Dostoevsky's solution to impossible conditions was to make them more impossible. In 1863, with a bankrupt journal, creditors threatening him with imprisonment, and a dying wife, he left Russia for the first time in order to meet his mistress in Paris. He stopped off to gamble in Germany and promptly obliterated his passion for Paulina Suslova with his passion for gambling. Eventually he met her in Paris and they spent some mutually frustrating months traveling about Europe together. He was decisively unimpressed by what he saw of the West.

Paradoxically, it was in 1863–1864, when Dostoevsky was undergoing the worst possible material and psychological problems, that his genius was being ignited. In 1864, at about the same time that his wife was dying, Dostoevsky was bringing to completion *Notes from the Underground*—a work that many consider one of the most important intellectual documents of the nineteenth century and that is customarily referred to as the prologue to the great novel-tragedies that were to follow. Two years later Dostoevsky published *Crime and Punishment* and the "great" Dostoevsky was definitively fixed in reputation. *The Idiot* (1868–69), *The Possessed* (1871–72), *The Adolescent* (1875), and *The Brothers Karamazov* (1878–1880) followed.

His personal life took a sharp turn for the better in 1867 with his marriage to Anna Grigorievna Snitkina, whom he had hired to take the dictation of his novel *The Gambler* (1866). She was a practical, efficient, well-organized person (of German descent), who loved Dostoevsky dearly but had scarcely the faintest idea of his creative and philosophical depths. Her prompt and efficient handling of his practical affairs undoubtedly relieved Dostoevsky of much strain and allowed him to give himself entirely to his work in the last fifteen years of his life.

To the very end of his life he was an enemy of every form of socialism and every form of rational limitation of men's lives and a champion of Russia, Christ, and the Orthodox church. His concern for the fate of Russia and its youth seemed to grow with the years, and his death in January 1881 was an occasion of great national mourning.

The Writing of The Brothers Karamazov

In the October 1877 issue of *The Diary of a Writer*, Dostoevsky announced to his readers that he was interrupting the publication of the monthly periodical in which he—not unlike a modern columnist—wrote on a great number of subjects: politics, culture, law courts, peasantry, the intelligentsia, Russian and foreign political life, religion, and the state of the contemporary Russian soul. In the last issue of *The Diary* in December, he explained that he was suspending publication in order to have time to write the artistic work that had formed itself almost unnoticed and involuntarily in his imagination during the past two years. The artistic work was *The Brothers Karamazov*.

The first explicit reference to work on *The Brothers* is dated March 16, 1878, when Dostoevsky wrote to V. V. Mikhaylov about his new novel.

I've got the main idea and will soon begin writing a large novel, in which, among others, children—especially young children from about seven to fifteen, will have a large part. They will be prominent in the novel. The observations of a person like you will be very valuable to me. Write to me *about children* whatever you know about them (incidents, habits, answers, words, traits, their family life, beliefs, crimes, innocence, nature, teachers, Latin language, and so forth, in short, whatever you know).

The actual writing of the novel began shortly after this. In Dostoevsky's notes—some of which are translated for the first time in this volume—one of the earliest entries (about April 1878) has the following schema:

Find out if you can lie down between the rails under a railway train when it passes by at full speed.
Find out if the wife of a condemned prisoner can marry someone else.
Does the Idiot have the right to keep a whole gang of foster children, have school, and so forth?
Get information about child labor in factories.
About secondary schools; visit a secondary school.

In addition to the fact that both the letter and the notes indicate quite strongly that children were very much on his mind when he began the novel, the early notes also show us that Dostoevsky's thinking about the novel was quite advanced when he actually began to write. It seems quite clear that he had been thinking about the novel and accumulating material for quite some time before 1878. In a letter to *The Russian Messenger* in 1880, he himself spoke of having worked on the novel for three years.

In one sense, much of the novel had been tentatively explored in expository form in *The Diary of a Writer* in 1876–1877. For example, in the very first issue of *The Diary*, in 1876, we find the following: "I always looked with interest at children, but I now observe them in a special way. I've had an ideal for a long time to write a novel about present-day Russian children, present-day fathers, and about their interrelationships." In *The Diary*, Dostoevsky also discussed the celebrated Kroneberg case in which a father was acquitted by the courts for mistreating his seven-year-old daughter. As in *The Brothers*, the girl was locked in the outhouse at night for failing to ask to go to the bathroom. Another case that Dostoevsky discussed at length in *The Diary* was the Kornilova affair concerning a mother who threw her stepdaughter from the fifth floor. And in significant respects, "The Legend of the Grand Inquisitor" had already taken form in issues of *The Diary* during 1876. Early in the year, Dostoevsky discussed a hypothetical future society based on advanced scientific knowledge and the denial of human freedom. In the May issue of *The Diary*, he returned to the same theme and used for the second time the Biblical phrase "stones turned into bread." When a reader wrote to ask him what he meant by this expression, he answered in a letter on June 7, 1876, with the following:

When the devil tempted Christ, three colossal universal ideas were brought together; eighteen centuries have passed and there are still no more difficult and wiser questions than these. And they are questions that we are still trying to answer today.

I mean by "stones turned into bread" our present social question of *environment*. I'm not speaking of the future; it has always been that way.

Continuing, Dostoevsky recreated the argument of the devil in words that are remarkably similar to those the author used two years later in expressing the Grand Inquisitor's arraignment of Christ:

Why go to the poor, ravaged by hunger and oppression, looking more like beasts than like people, and preach to these hungry people to abstain from sins and strive for humility and virtue. Wouldn't it be better to *feed* them first? That would be more humane. . . . You, after all, are the Son of God; the whole world has waited for you impatiently. Act like one who is superior in mind and justice and give them all food. *Make them secure;* give them a social system so that bread and order will be theirs forever. And then ask them not to sin. Then if they sin, they will be ungrateful, but now they sin from hunger. It is sinful to demand such things from them.

You are the Son of God—therefore you can do all things. Look at all the stones. All you have to do is command it and the stones will turn into bread.

Command it so that henceforth the earth bears fruit without labor. Teach the people the knowledge to arrange things so that life will be henceforth secure. Don't you believe that the worst sins and miseries of mankind come from hunger, cold, poverty, and from the impossible struggle for existence?

And Dostoevsky adds: "Here is the first idea which the evil spirit posed for Christ. Agree that it is hard to come to terms with it."

As we see from the letters published in this volume—especially those to the assistant editor of *The Russian Messenger*—Dostoevsky felt deep commitment to the task he had set for himself. Again and again he depicts himself as fearful that his artistic powers are not great enough to encompass what his heart and vision wish to express. When he sent in the Epilogue to *The Brothers Karamazov* in November 1880, he was exhausted, exhilarated, and in such poor health that he was to die three months later. According to his wife's reminiscences, however, he was already planning a sequel to *The Brothers Karamazov*, in which Alyosha was to have the chief role. Death robbed us of this sequel, but it was generous enough to permit him to finish what Freud has called "the most magnificent novel ever written."

БРАТЬЯ КАРАМАЗОВЫ

1. THE WRITER

Selections from the Letters

No. 1—To N. M. Dostoevsky

May 16, 1878

My dearest brother Nikolay. Our Alyosha died today from a sudden stroke of epilepsy; he had never suffered from it before. Yesterday, he was still having a good time, running about, singing, and today he lies dead. The attack began at 9:30 in the morning and by 2:30 in the afternoon our little Alyosha was dead. We are burying him Thursday in the Great Okhtensky Cemetery. Goodbye, Kolya, shed a tear for little Alyosha; you often caressed him (do you remember how he mimicked a drunken man, Van'ka the fool?). It is unbearably sad.

No. 2—To S. A. Iur'ev

July 11, 1878

I received your letter the day before yesterday, on June 9. I first heard of you and began to respect you when you began to edit *The Conversation*. At that time, too, I heard from others that you had a good opinion of me. I would be very happy to make your acquaintance. In your letter you mention that I have preserved my opinion of you "even though we haven't seen each other for such a long time." But did we ever see each other and were we ever personally acquainted? You won't believe how often such reminiscences weigh heavily on me. The point is that I've suffered from epilepsy for twenty-five years, which I picked up in Siberia. This disease has robbed me little by little of ability to remember faces and events to such a degree that I (liter-

Translated by the Editor from the fourth volume of A. S. Dolinin's *F. M. Dostoevsky, Pis'ma* [*Letters*], 4 vols. (Moscow-Leningrad, 1928, 1930, 1934, 1959).

ally) have forgotten even all the plots and details of my novels. Since I haven't republished some of them since they were first published, I have completely forgotten them. For this reason, please don't be angry that I have forgotten the time and circumstances of our first acquaintanceship and meeting. I, and others, often have this trouble. If you would be so kind, please recall for me at least the occasion, time, and circumstances of our former acquaintanceship.

And about the novel; I'll tell you the full truth in answer to your flattering invitation: I have begun to write my novel, but it's a long way from being finished; I've just begun it. It's always been that way with me; I begin a long novel (NB they run about 640–720 pages) about the middle of summer and finish about half of it by the New Year. In January the first part usually appears in this or that journal. After that I continue to publish the novel with few breaks in the journal during the whole year up to December inclusively, and I always finish the novel in the year in which it began to appear. Up to now I haven't carried over a novel into the next year.

After long collaboration with *The Russian Messenger*, I accepted Nekrasov's invitation and published my novel *The Adolescent* in his journal, even though *The Russian Messenger* had wanted the novel. At the time, however, I informed M. N. Katkov that I considered myself primarily his collaborator. Concerning the novel I'm now writing, I have already entered into informal relations with Katkov and have already accepted a 2,000-ruble advance from him (as has always been my custom). Things are not conclusively settled for reasons which I can't go into here, but which in essence are extraneous and have nothing to do with the literary essence of the novel. These extraneous matters, however, will take form in September or October of this year and can only be settled then.

Therefore, I can give you a completely definite answer to your invitation to publish my novel in *Russian Thought* only in October, if you will be in Moscow about that time. Only then will I know where I will publish the novel.

As for your journal *Russian Thought*, I was delighted to hear of its beginning, as I remember with delight *The Conversation*. I will always consider myself flattered to be of use to your journal when I am able.

If you find it necessary to get in touch with me about any matter, I will be here in Old Russia up to August 25.

No. 3—To N. A. Liubimov

May 10, 1879

I've sent off to you today forty pages (minimum) of the text for *The Brothers Karamazov* for the forthcoming May issue of *The Russian Messenger*. This is one half of Book V entitled "Pro and Contra." The second half of Book V will be sent (in good time) for the June issue, and will consist of forty-eight pages. I have found it necessary then to divide Book V into two issues of *The Russian Messenger*. Even if I tried my utmost, I could not finish it before May (the packing and moving to Old Russia put me behind); consequently, I wouldn't receive the proofs, and they are terribly important for me. Book V is in my view the culminating point of the novel, and it ought to be brought to an end with extreme care. As you will see from the enclosed text, I want to depict the most extreme blasphemy and the seeds of destructive ideas in our time among our youth, which have torn themselves away from reality. I am now preparing to express also a refutation of this blasphemy and anarchy in the last words of the dying Elder Zossima, one of the characters in my novel. Since the difficulty of the task I've undertaken is apparent, you will surely understand, my respected Nikolay Alekseevich, that I would rather extend the material over two issues rather than spoil the culminating chapter by hurrying. . . .

In the text I am sending you I represent the basic convictions of one of the important characters in the novel. These convictions represent precisely what I understand to be the *Synthesis* of contemporary Russian anarchism; the negation not of God, but of his creation. All of socialism originated and began with the negation of the meaning of historical reality and ended in a program of destruction and anarchy. Anarchists were in many cases people sincere in their convictions. My hero puts forth the theme, which *in my opinion* is irrefutable: the senselessness of children's suffering, and deduces from this the absurdity of all historical reality. I don't know whether I've handled it well, but I do know that my character is real in the highest degree. (In *The Possessed* I was criticized for creating many fantastic characters, but later—believe it or not—they were all justified by reality and consequently they were realistically conceived.) K. P. Pobedonostsev told me, for example, of two or three cases of anarchists who were arrested and who were strikingly like those described by me in *The Possessed*. Everything my hero says in the text I have sent you is based on reality. All the anecdotes about children actually happened; they were reported in our newspapers and I can show you where. I've thought up nothing. The whole story of the General who set his dogs on a child is a real event; it was published last winter in *Arkhiv*, I think, and reprinted in many newspapers. My hero's blasphemy will be solemnly refuted in the next issue (June). I am working on it now with fear, trembling, and awe. I consider my task (the destruction of anarchism) a civil feat. Wish me luck, most respected Nikolay Alekseevich.

I'm looking forward to the proofs with the greatest impatience. Address: Old Russia, F. M. Dostoevsky.

In the text I've sent there is not a single indecent word. There is the fact of the little five-year-old girl who is smeared with *excrement* by those who were bringing her up, because she didn't ask to go to the bathroom at night. But I beg you not to eliminate this word. I took this from the recent trial record. All the newspapers (Two months ago, for example, *Meklenburg*, and *Voice*) kept the word *excrement*. It must not be softened, Nikolay Alekseevich, it would be too, too unfortunate. We aren't writing for ten-year-old children. Besides, I am convinced that even without my plea, you would keep my text as it is. . . .

No. 4—To N. A. Liubimov

June 11, 1879

The day before yesterday I sent to the editorial office of *The Russian Messenger* the continuation of *The Karamazovs* (the ending of Book V "Pro and Contra") for the June issue. I bring to an end there what "proud and blasphemous lips speak." One of the most impassioned of contemporary negaters declares himself openly to be on the devil's side, and he affirms that the devil is better for the happiness of people than is Christ. This is a stirring lesson for our foolish but terrifying Russian socialism (terrifying because our youth believes in it): Bread, the tower of Babel, the complete enslavement of the freedom of conscience—that's what the desperate nihilist and atheist ends up with! The difference is that our socialists (and as you well know, they are not only the underground nihilists) are consciously crafty and liars, who do not admit that their ideal is the enslavement of man's conscience and the lowering of humanity to the level of cattle. But my socialist (Ivan Karamazov) is a sincere person, who admits quite openly that he agrees with the views of "The Grand Inquisitor" about mankind and who maintains that Christ's faith has demanded more of man's nature than it can give. This question is posed in the section: "Do you, future saviors of mankind, feel contempt or respect for mankind?"

And they do and say all this as if in the name of love of humanity: "The law of Christ is hard and abstract, and weak people cannot bear it." And in place of the law of Freedom and Enlightenment, they present man with the law of chains and enslavement by bread.

The death of the Elder Zossima and his conversations with friends at his death bed will take place in the next book. This will not be a sermon, but an account of his own life. If it comes off, I will have done a good thing: I will have forced others to admit that the pure ideal Christian is not an abstraction, but is someone concrete, real, possible, and there for everyone to see. I will also make my point that Christianity is the only refuge of the Russian land from all its evils. I pray to God that the work comes off; it's going to be a thing of deep feeling; if only I have enough inspiration. Most important, the theme is such that it hasn't occurred to any of our current writers or poets; consequently, it is *original*. I'm writing the whole novel for this section; if only it comes off! That's what's troubling me! I'll get it to you for the July issue, certainly no later than the 10th of July. I'll do my best to meet this deadline.

I received your letter, most respected Nikolay Alekseevich, about the money you sent, and I'm waiting impatiently for the thousand you promised. I find myself to be almost penniless, and I would prefer not to borrow. Therefore, I *beg you* most earnestly to send me that thousand rubles as quickly as possible, if possible *without delay*, because I really need them. . . .

No. 5—To N. A. Liubimov

August 7, 1879

I am hurrying to send out to you the whole of Book VI of *The Karamazovs* for publication in the August issue of *The Russian Messenger*. I have called Book VI "The Russian Monk." This is a bold and provocative title, for all our unsympathetic critics will cry out: "Who is the Russian Monk that one dares put him on such a pedestal?" But all the better if they cry out, right? (And I know that they will not restrain themselves) I believe that I have not sinned against reality: The picture is true not only as an ideal, but also true as reality.

But I'm not sure that it will come off. I've been able to say only a tenth of what I've wanted to say. Still, I look on Book VI as the culminating point of my novel. By themselves many of the counsels of the Elder Zossima (or more correctly, his manner of expressing them) go with his character, that is, with the way I have artistically depicted him. Even though I share his thoughts completely, as he expresses them, I would have expressed them in a different form and in different words, if I were personally to express them. He *could not* express them in any other language or *spirit* than in those that I gave him. Such, for example, his thoughts about the following: about what a monk is, about masters and servants, or about whether one person can be the judge of another person. I took his person and figure from old Russian monks and holy men, just as I took their deep humility, their infinite and naive expectations about the future of Russia, and its moral and even political predestination. Didn't the holy metropolitans Sergey, Pyotr, and Aleksey always have similar views about Russia?

I beg you most earnestly (I plead with you), most respected Nikolay Alekseevich, to give my proofs to a reliable proofreader, since I cannot, because of my absence, correct them myself. I beg you particularly to turn your attention to the 10th to the 17th half pages inclusively of the proofs (the sub-chapter under the rubric: *About the holy writing in the Elder Zossima's life*). This chapter is deeply felt and poetic; I took the prototype from some of the teachings of Tikhon Zadonsky and the simplicity of explanation from the book of wanderings of the Monk Parfeni. Look it over yourself, most respected Nikolay Alekseevich. Be a father to me. After the proofs have been examined, tell Mikhail Katkov about this. I would like to have him read them and give me his opinion, for I think highly of his opinion.

I am hoping that you as editor will not find anything in this book that has to be crossed out or corrected; there's not a word that needs to be changed, I swear it!

I also beg you to keep all the divisions into chapters and sub-chapters as I have made them. A sort of extraneous manuscript is included here (Aleksey Karamazov's notes), and the manuscript is interpreted by him in his own way. I wish, by the way, to lodge a complaint: in the July issue, my rubrics for the chapter "The Grand Inquisitor" were not only tampered with, but everything was printed without breaks, ten pages running. I found this very irritating, and I register here with all due respect my complaint.

I will send out to you the next book, the seventh, under the title "Grushenka" about the 10th of September without fail. This will bring to an end Part II of *The Karamazovs* this year. I intend to publish Book VII in two issues of *The Russian Messenger,* in September and October. There will be only thirty-two pages for the September issue, not more. But what's to be done? There are two separate episodes in Book VII, sort of like two separate stories. With the end of Part II, the *spirit* and *meaning* of the novel will have been expressed. If it doesn't come off, then it will be my fault as an artist. As I have already written you, I'm putting off until next year the third part of the novel, which will be no longer than Part I. My health has interfered! Part II will therefore be sort of disproportionately long. But what's to be done! That's the way it turned out.

I thank you most kindly for fulfilling my request about sending money to my wife in Old Russia; she has already informed me that this has been done.

Let me hurry to make one more request in good time: Don't forget, most respected Nikolay Alekseevich, to have the August issue of *The Russian Messenger* sent to Old Russia! I will be home precisely at the time it comes out.

No. 6—To K. P. Pobedonostsev

August 13, 1879

. . . your opinion of what you have read of *The Karamazovs* pleased me very much (about the force and vividness of the writing). And you bring up a *very essential* point: that I have not yet answered all those atheistical propositions and that they have to be answered. I am frankly quite worried and upset about this. For I intend to give the answer to all this negative side in Book VI, "The Russian Monk," which will appear August 31, 1879. I tremble for it on this account: Will it be enough of an answer? Especially because my answer is not a direct one, that is, it does not answer the propositions expressed (by the

Grand Inquisitor) point by point, but is indirect. I give here something directly contradictory to the world view expressed before, but I do it not point by point, but sort of by way of artistic representation. And this is what troubles me. That is, will it be understood, and will I succeed in attaining my end even to some extent? . . .

No. 7—To N. A. Liubimov

September 16, 1879

I am sending you with this letter Book VII of *The Karamazovs* for the September issue. . . .

I beg you, Nikolay Alekseevich, not to eliminate anything from this book. There's no need because everything is proper. Only one little word might be disturbing (about the dead body): *stank*. But Father Ferapont says this word and he can't speak in any other way: and even if he could say *smelled,* he would not say it; he would say *stank*. Please let this pass, for the *sake of Christ*. There's nothing else in the book. . . . The last chapter (which I'll send out shortly) *Cana of Galilee*—is the most essential in the whole book, and perhaps even in the novel. With this chapter I am finished with the monastery: there won't be anything more about the monastery. This part ends with the next book (the October issue) and then there will be an interruption, as I've already informed you.

P.S. Most respected Nikolay Alekseevich, I beg you particularly to go over the proofs of the legend of the onion very carefully. This is a precious story; I copied it from the words of a peasant woman, and, consequently, it's been *written down for the first time*. At least I've never heard of it before now.

No. 8—To E. N. Lebedeva

November 8, 1879

The servant Smerdyakov killed the old man Karamazov. All the details will be made clear in the subsequent course of the novel. Ivan Karamazov took part in the murder only obliquely and from a distance; he took part only in that he refrained from (intentionally) talking sense to Smerdyakov when he talked to him before leaving for Moscow and of expressing to him clearly and categorically his disgust at the projected crime (which Ivan saw and knew clearly would happen). Therefore, he more or less permitted Smerdyakov to commit the crime. The granting of permission to Smerdyakov was necessary, and it will be explained later why. Dmitry was completely innocent of the murder of his father.

When Dmitry Karamazov leaped off the fence and began to wipe the blood from the head of the hurt old servant and said these words to

him: "The old man fell into misfortune," etc., he more or less told the
reader already that he was not the murderer of his father. If he had
killed his father and ten minutes later Grigory, then he wouldn't have
climbed down from the fence to the felled servant only to convince
himself that an important witness to his crime was dead. In addition,
he feels a kind of sympathy for him, and says the poor man got hurt
and so forth. If he had killed his father, then he would not stand over
the body of the servant with words of pity. It is not only the plot of the
novel that is important for the reader, but also some knowledge of
man's soul (psychology), and every author has the right to expect this
from his readers.

In any case your interest in my work is flattering.

No. 9—To N. A. Liubimov

November 16, 1879

I sent you yesterday the ending of Book VIII of *The Karamazovs*,
which you have undoubtedly already received. I beg your forgiveness
for being late once again. There appeared suddenly a number of new
characters, and even though they appeared only for a moment, it was
necessary to sketch them as fully as possible, and thus the book turned
out to be longer than I at first planned, and it took longer to write.
Consequently, the delay was completely unexpected for me also. I beg
you most earnestly, most respected Nikolay Alekseevich, for proofs as
fine as those I've seen up to now.

I wrote you previously that I would finish in November and would
cease until next year, but circumstances have taken a different form,
for I will send you a ninth new book for the December issue, and this
book will bring to an end this part. This ninth book appeared suddenly
and unexpectedly for me also: The point is that at first I wanted only
to restrict myself to the *judicial* investigation at the trial. But taking
counsel of a procurator (one with a big practice) I saw suddenly that a
whole terribly interesting and terribly defective part of our criminal
proceedings (a weak spot of our criminal proceedings) would in that
way disappear from my novel. This part of the process is called "The
Preliminary Investigation," with its old routine and its latest abstrac-
tions among our young jurists, investigators, etc. Therefore, in order to
complete this part, I will write a ninth book with the title "Preliminary
Investigation," which I will get to you in December and earlier if
possible. I will also note more strongly still the character of Mitya
Karamazov. He purifies his heart and conscience under the threat of
misfortune and false incrimination. He will accept in his soul the
punishment not because of what he did, but because of being evil
enough to have wanted to do the crime. He will be falsely condemned
for the crime because of a judicial error. His character is completely
Russian: when the thunder doesn't roll, the peasant doesn't cross

himself. His moral purification begins during the very first hours of the preliminary investigation, which I'm planning in the ninth book. This is all precious to me as the author. . . .

No. 10—To N. A. Liubimov

August 10, 1880

Together with this letter I have dispatched to the editorial office of *The Russian Messenger* for the August issue: The ending of Book XI of *The Karamazovs*, 72 half-pages of letter paper.

I beg you most earnestly to send me in good time the proofs. I won't keep them more than a minute.

The twelfth and last book of *The Karamazovs* will arrive at your office definitely about the 10th or the 12th of next (September) month. It will also be about the same length. After that there will remain the Epilogue, which will be about twenty-four pages in length; I'll get that to you for the October issue.

Now, about what I've just sent.

I consider the sixth, seventh, and eighth chapters to be the best done. I don't know how you'll look on the ninth chapter, most respected Nikolay Alekseevich. Perhaps you'll think it too unusual. But in truth I had no desire to be unusual. I ought to tell you that I have checked for a long time with the opinions of more than one doctor. They affirm that "brain fever" can be preceded by hallucinations as well as nightmares. My hero, of course, sees hallucinations also, but he mixes them up with his nightmares. We have more than a physical (diseased) trait, when a man begins to fail at times to distinguish between reality and phantoms (which has happened to every man at least once in his life). Denying the reality of the spirit world, he insists on the reality of the spirit when it appears. Tortured by lack of faith, he (unconsciously) still wants the spirit to be real and not something fantastic.

But I'm prattling. You'll read it and see for yourself, most respected Nikolay Alekseevich. But forgive me my *devil:* He's only a petty devil, and not Satan with "his singed wings." I don't think the chapter will be too boring, even though it is rather long. I don't think that anything will be censored except perhaps two little words: *"hysterical yelps* of the cherubs." I beg you to let these pass. After all, it's the devil talking, and he can't talk in any other way. If it's impossible to let them pass, then put in their stead "joyous cries." But wouldn't it be better to have "yelps"? The other will be rather prosaic and won't fit the tone.

Nor do I think that anything the devil says need be censored. The two stories *about the confessional box*, though a bit reckless, are definitely not dirty. Doesn't Mephistopheles lie once in a while in both parts of *Faust?*

I consider that the tenth and last chapter put forth the state of Ivan's soul sufficiently, and the nightmare of the ninth chapter also. I have verified (I repeat again) the medical state by consulting medical opinion.

Even though I myself think that this ninth chapter could be inserted or taken out, I would not now renounce it because I wrote it for some reason *with pleasure*.

Brain fever strikes my hero precisely at the moment when he is giving testimony at the trial. (That's in the twelfth, forthcoming book.)

And so I have expressed to you all my doubts, most respected Nikolay Alekseevich. I will await the proofs with the utmost impatience. . . .

Selections from the Notebooks

No. 1—The Meeting in the Elder's Cell

The Elder returns to the cell. The conversation goes on without interruption.

They tell the Elder what they have been talking about: Is there anything on earth that compels man to love mankind?

Or:

Is there a law of nature to compel man to love mankind?

"That is a law of God. There is no law of nature, isn't that so?"

He (the murderer) [Ivan] affirms that there is no law and that people love only because of their faith in immortality.

The Elder: "You are either blessed or very unhappy if you so believe."

The murderer: "Why unhappy?"

The Elder: "In case you don't believe in immortality."

The murderer: "Yes, you've guessed it."

"You haven't yet decided, and your sorrow lies in your indecision."

Ilinsky comes in, *bows*.

Miusov: "I most emphatically don't agree. Love for mankind lies in man himself, as a law of nature."

Everyone is quiet. "No point in trying," the murderer says.

Translated by the Editor from A. S. Dolinin's *F. M. Dostoevsky, materialy i issledovaniya* [*Archival Materials*] (Leningrad, 1935). The headings have been inserted by the Editor.

Miusov: "In that case, if there is no immortality?"
"How can you define where the limit is?"
"The limit is reached when I do harm to mankind."
"Well, why put yourself out?"
"Well, in order to live more comfortably. If people can't live by love, they will live by reason."
"If everything is to be based on reason, nothing would occur."
"In that case, one can do whatever one wants."
"Yes."
The landowner [Fyodor Karamazov]: "Teach me to love. What do I have to do in order to achieve salvation?"
"Don't lie. Property. Face."
"Learn to love. Nose."
With relatives.
"I know that he will not return from the dead. Karl Moor."

"If there is no God and immortality of the soul, then there cannot be any love for mankind."
. . . .

NB   All the objects and everything in the world for man are incomplete; nevertheless, the meaning of all things in the world are not given to man.
The earth ennobles. Only the possession of the earth ennobles one. Without the earth the millionaire is a proletariat. And what is a proletarian? He is still a swine. So as not to be a swine one must be reborn, but only the earth can bring one to rebirth. He has to become a possessor of the earth.
. . . .

Mention in passing about the normality of the pagan criminal code. There is no difference between state and pagan codes. If the church permits a pagan court, then it rejects its own destiny. Not by struggle, by way of an ideal. . . . Not a defined position in the state, but including the whole state within itself. If that is impossible now, it is, nevertheless (desirable); it ought to be made the goal of the further development of Christian society.
The union of society not in the state, but the union of society for the elimination of the state, for the transformation of the state into the church.
Miusov then objects: "That's criminal."
The murderer: "Not punishment, but excommunication."
Lafargue.
The Elder: "That is the way it is. Yes, it is almost occurring right now. However incompatible these two principles may be, truth comes about at times through conflict (which one, etc.)."

Question: Has the church come to an end as a Christian society on earth, has it reached its ideal and its final form, or does it continue to develop in consonance with its heavenly goal? The dogmatic side of faith is not taken into account, but only the moral state of man and society at a given moment."

No union of society can and ought not acquire power—hold sway over the civil and political rights of its members.

The church is not a kingdom of this world.

If it is not of this world, then it can't be on this earth at all. This is an unworthy play on words for a churchman and in the world of the church. I read this passage in the book of this churchman, whom you are arguing against, and I was surprised by it. It is not so recorded in God's book. It is not right to play on words in that fashion. Christ came to us precisely to establish his church on earth; the heavenly kingdom, to be sure, is in heaven, but you enter there only through the church. Unworthy plays on words and riddles are therefore not appropriate. The church does in truth reign and should and will reign. And I believe it will reign on this earth, for we have signs and promises of that.

. . . .

Miusov: "That is ultramontanism!"

The Elder: "We don't have any mountains here."

The Elder: "A blessed idea, if you yourself believe in it."

Miusov: "Why do you think that he does not believe? He's gone farther than ultramontanism; he assures us that there is no reason to love, and that the only reason people love is because they believe in the immortality of the soul."

The Elder threw a look at him: "Verily, you are blessed if you so think."

The murderer winces, talks unwillingly.

Miusov argues heatedly that people can achieve salvation without religion.

The Elder: "I don't mean to transform love into suffering."

"You are either happy or you are suffering if you don't believe. The process is not finished in you."

The old man gets up and goes off to the people. (The whole scene in a happy and even playful tone, as if they were trying each other.)

He returned, argument. Landholder on his knees.

Teach me to achieve salvation.

Don't lie.

Property.

Love. Nose.

He himself.

Relatives.

This relative—Karl Moor.

Miusov to the Elder. "All of you are sort of joking."

The Elder with a quiet smile. No. I am speaking seriously, for Russia, thank God, still believes.

. . . .

1. You impressed me just now with your remark: "Not to be ashamed of myself so much because everything comes from that. With this remark you more or less saw through me completely, read what was inside of me. That's just the way everything strikes me when I visit people. I feel I am baser than they and that they are all seeing me as a clown. Well, when I see how they feel, then I really do play the role of a clown. I'm not afraid of your opinion, because you are all, to the very last one, more stupid and base than I am! That's why I'm a clown, from shame and from mistrust and the desire to brawl. If I were only sure when I walked into a room that everyone took me to be the best and smartest of men, then, Lord, what a good man I would be!

No. 2—Alyosha and Dmitry

Can it be that she can love someone like me? (NB   comparison with Ivan).
"And I think that she does love someone like you."
"She likes her virtue and not me."
"Don't worry; she is sincerely good and noble."

"Why have I been with father for three weeks?"
"I know, really, that I don't have a right to anything."
"I would throw him over, but I've got to give back those 3,000."

Ilinsky to Alyosha (in passing)
He keeps sending Ivan to Chermashnya. He's waiting for her?
"To Chermashnya?"
There will be galoshes. Run after water. No, it's really over! He said fatally.

I know, 3,000 from Smerdyakov.

"Tell her that I told you to say goodbye by bowing."

Perhaps I'll murder.

"If she loves you, then she will forgive you."
"She wants to save me."

Ivan—the learned one.
Ilinsky thoughtfully.
"I don't measure up to their little fingers, but"

"If she comes to my father, then it will be the end of my phantom. How will I be able to marry after that?"

"I'll kill, perhaps, and then kill myself."

Alyosha: "Oh, Dmitry, how unhappy you are!"

"Do you think that my mother was his also? What do you think?"

No. 3—Ivan and Alyosha: Pro and Contra Section

The mother of the child who was torn apart.
The rock of faith.

"Do you understand me, Alyosha?"

"I understand you very well."

"I didn't see Dmitry."

"(He was very upset), about Smerdyakov."

"Smerdyakov interests you."

"Yes."

"Brother, are you really leaving tomorrow?"

"I don't know. A little while ago about Katerina Ivanovna. Still about Katerina Ivanovna. I will go away."

"And Dmitry and father."

"What am I, my brother's keeper?" (Cain's answer.)

"Are you determined or not?"

"Determined and not."

Not so long ago (at Katerina Ivanovna's) we were all so young, and giving each other talkings-to.

"Brother, if you leave, then Dmitry"

"My brother's keeper (I want to live myself)."

"Brother, you will really leave tomorrow?"

"I'm wasting my time; I've finished with that love. That was a stupid thing. Once, Alyosha, they used to turn my head for a whole half-year, but this one is a student."

Important

Katerina Ivanovna in delirium.

"What's there. Were you there?"

"Everything's fine there."

His face darkened. Then immediately he laughed.

"I have cured myself (of love)."

"I'm going to kiss my graves."

"I won't pay what this future harmony costs. Oh, if it costs so much, I won't allow it. Small children are more precious to me, and I beg in advance to be released from this harmony. I am returning my ticket."

"That's revolt," said Alyosha.

"Revolt. I would prefer your calling it something else. Can one live in revolt, when it is not a question of not wanting to accept, but of being unable to accept. Can you accept it? Answer."

(He is silent)

"Can you understand how parallel lines can meet? Can you understand how a mother can embrace the general and forgive him?"

"No, I still cannot. Still cannot."

"Let's go. It's late (account)."

"How is it that you can love the sticky little leaves. How do you want to live?"

"In the Karamazov fashion."

"That is, everything is permitted."

"Everything permitted."

"I would like to annihilate completely the idea of God. If not in the Karamazov fashion, a shade of honor is enough up to thirty."

"And then?"

"Lose yourself in the stink of sensuality, or ambition, or cruelty, or get a passion for cards, or . . ."

"Or?"

"Or, destroy yourself?"

"I thought that you could lose yourself in gambling, learning to love chess, becoming a banker, and playing the stock market, becoming a courtier. But I've come to the conclusion that all that would be impossible for me. The idea will not die. Life, even if as a worm. Only one thing, only one, will do: beastly sensuality with all its consequences of cruelty, crime, all the way to the Marquis de Sade. That will keep one going for a while. But to do it, you will have to keep the fires of the blood burning all your life. But if you can do that, it's disgusting, and you ought, therefore, to shoot yourself. I've come to the conclusion that up to thirty the very force of life will keep you going; up to then you will be fascinated with what's in the cup, that is, with deceptions; therefore, destroy yourself. I'll live like that up to thirty; I'm pinning my hopes on the baseness of my character, and I'll tell you quite frankly: If I were put in prison, or had to serve as a lackey, or become a slave and I was fed each day with blows, I would still continue to thirst for life. I'm relying on the baseness of my nature."

"How do you want to live?"

"In the Karamazov manner (everything permitted)."

"You can't live in sensuality. It's impossible for you."

"Immerse myself in sensuality, in beastly raptures, like my father. Yes, it's very dirty. Better to *destroy* myself."

"Would you agree to that?" Architect. Building.
"Goodbye."
"Goodbye, Ivan. I love you Ivan."
"And I love you too."

Ivan. "We know, after all, that he didn't find anything there. Stupid attempt. It's even insulting for me. Well, what?"
Inquisitor. You are truth itself. You can't lie.
Don't curse.
We are aware (3,000).

"You think I'm for the poor, for the peasant, the worker. They smell, are coarse, drunk. I wish the best for them, but I don't understand how Christ could have agreed to love them. I don't understand Christ's love."

Child.
"If you were creating the world, would you create it on the basis of one child's tear?"
Somewhere in a tavern, they were talking rubbish. Only in Russia is that possible.
"Even if everything was fully illuminated, would you agree?"
"I still could not!"

The General.
Shoot
"Oh, if you really say to shoot him. Listen, take a look at Louis XVII."
"Solely, therefore, so as to formulate one question. Would you agree to create it in that way? With the goal, finally, of making people happy, give them peace?"
"And for that, all that would be necessary definitely would be the torture of only one little being, one that would beat its breast and cry for God. The tears of a child (I'm talking only about a child). If you're honest, the world is worth the little fist of a child. If you were to create the world, would you create it at the cost of a child's tear?"
"No."

"Let's grant that the compensations of eternal harmony are incomprehensible to you. That's why I don't accept the world. I'm talking only of children. Granted, I'm just an insect, I ought not to agree out of love for mankind, I ought not. The price is too high. I give back my entry ticket."
"Life is base. Our minds have invented the retribution of God, but immortality, if I'm dead, is base."

"Don't come any more; go to your Zossima."
"Is your father Seraficus alive?"
"He's alive and I wrote down his last words."

No. 4—The Grand Inquisitor

Chop off everyone's heads.
The Inquisitor: "What do we need that for? We are more humane than you. We love the earth."
Inquisitor: "I love humanity more than you."
. . . .

Believe what the heart says.

Inquisitor: "Can that be just? Let it be just, but I don't accept it."

The secret that there is no truth, no God, the God that you preached.
. . . .

"Why have you come to interfere in our work. I'll have you burned."

Inquisitor. "From love of humanity I say to you, to you who loved him more than yourself. You alone can understand me, and, therefore, I'm revealing to you our secret. And tomorrow before daylight, I will have you burned."
The more stupid the quicker one reaches one's goal. Stupidity is always the shortest route. I sacrificed my own dignity.

"But I don't accept it, because no matter how great the idea is, it is not worth this suffering."
"Angels will sing. If the mother embraces the torturer of her son, if she forgives him, then that means that something has happened which is surely higher than all those misfortunes. Still, I don't want it. It's revolt."
Here.
"If I'm asked to take part, I can't take part. Forgive me."
Evening party.
. . . .

Portrait.
"Why have you come to us?"
"Why have you come to interfere with our work?"
"Don't say anything; I know what you will say; but listen to me. First of all, I will burn you tomorrow."
"I have only one word to say to you: you have been disgorged

from hell and are a heretic, and the very people who fell on their knees before you will rake up the coals around you tomorrow."

"Have you seen the people? What more did you want? You said that you wanted to make them free, and have you seen these free people? Did you see them? We have sacrificed much for this matter and we were forced to do it in your name; fifteen centuries of pieces, but now we've made it strong."

"Why are you interfering with us, why are you destroying what we've built?"

"No, if there's someone who has earned the pyre, it's you."

"Man is born a rebel."

"The most righteous flee from us into the desert. We honored them as holy ones, but they acted like rebels, for they did not dare run away from us."

"Can a free man be happy?"

Stones into bread.

All the wise men of the earth could not have invented wiser questions than those written in those lines.

"Feed first and then ask."

"He tried your inner faith. You did not give in, but can everyone be like you? Can they live on faith alone, and then how will the rest be protected from rebellion?"

Kingdom.

"You refused the kingdom of this earth, and we have been forced to assume it. And if it costs blood and whole generations, you alone will be guilty."

"They sing of you as without sin, but I say to you that you are guilty."

"And we still have a long time to wait before we create the kingdom of this earth."

"A whole swarm of locusts will come out of the earth, and will cry that we are in slavery, that we corrupt young girls, but they will become subdued. It will end by their calming down and the best of them will join us in accepting suffering for power. But they, cursed ones, do not know what we are taking upon ourselves; we are taking upon ourselves knowledge and suffering."

. . . .

Alyosha: "I imagined that you would do it differently; you are arraigning only the Catholic priesthood."

Ivan: "My poem is stupid. But wouldn't you agree that my Inquisitor is half right?"

Alyosha: "You think so, think so? You don't believe in God?"

Ivan: "He has irrefutable authority. 14,000 and those what?"

Alyosha: "Perhaps for you; not irrefutable. You don't believe in God. What does his secret consist of? Can one bring happiness to people with the old man's idea? Perhaps one can."

The old man remains with his idea. But you? I remain also with the idea of the old man, for he loves humanity more. Can one love idiots? Perhaps one can. You don't believe in God. Sticky leaves. "What secret," asked Alyosha. You justify.

The second temptation. "Yes, you would not have hurt so much as your foot."

"You should have done as the Proud Spirit. True, you understood that you would have hurt yourself."

"But you rejected the authority of the Miracle. And how we have been forced to fight to correct you, and if there is one person who is sinful, it is you."

"You proclaimed that people had dreamed for a long time of being free." Centrifugal force, doesn't belong to the earth, *freedom from miracles*.

"You did not descend from the cross and you are God. You asked too much of man. People need miracles, that is, authority. Miracles and mystery. Yes, mystery. Now about mystery. With us man will die of disease."

"We have the task of finding in man and in the suffering he undergoes that common and irrefutable something before which he can bow down. Unless he has this, man will not be at peace and will not be able to construct any kind of society. This secret is based on that coarse imperfection of the way he has been constructed. Man is born free and his first concern after receiving the gift of freedom is to find someone to give it to as quickly as possible. As a consequence, he creates Gods for himself as he has during all of history. Whoever knows this secret of mankind's existence, knows how to subjugate mankind, and whoever can does subjugate him."

"You were given an absolute banner against which man alone or together with the whole world would not think of rebelling. But you rejected it in the name of freedom."

"The question of conscience is personal, that is, how to come to terms with your conscience. The social and state question—the absolute and oldest of all questions—is whom to bow down to. For men will never be at peace by themselves, and never will they find unity as a whole."

If they do not know whom to bow down to.

"In accepting bread, you would have answered this human question of whom to bow down to."

"You should have come to them so that they cowered before you, and then you would have proclaimed to them a hitherto unheard of freedom."

The third secret: the necessity of universal union, for no matter how strong nations may be, they dream of universal unity.

. . . .

"Man can be at peace with his conscience only when his freedom is taken away. For people look for peace more than for anything else. You proclaimed that life is struggle, and forever took away peace from them. Instead of firm, clear, and simple principles, you took everything away."

"And the second thesis, the second secret of man's nature is based on the need for man to bring peace to his conscience by knowing the distinction between good and evil. Whoever teaches, whoever shows the way, he is the prophet."

"He who comes, like you, to possess the souls of people and have them follow you must bring peace to the conscience of man, and must give men a clear and firm understanding of what is evil and what is good. And when you took on such a great task, you didn't know—oh, you did not know that you will never give peace to man's conscience and will never give peace and joy to his spirit until you take away his freedom."

"But could your banner of heavenly bread really have united all the people in poverty in indisputable harmony? But the strengths of mankind are various. There are the strong and the weak. There are those who by their very nature cannot live on heavenly bread, for it is not for such; such are endless in number, like the sands of the sea. How will you unite them in worship when the majority do not even understand what is meant by that? Instead of the universal banner of harmonious worship, there has arisen the banner of strife, quarrels, and eternal wars; it would not be such with the banner of earthly bread. But look."

"The overwhelming majority of people are not capable of religion, and, therefore, his religion cannot be called a religion of love. He came only for the chosen few, for the strong and mighty. And those, who have suffered his cross, will not find anything that was promised, just as he did not find anything after his cross. Such is your Sinless One, who has been put forth. But the idea of slavery, of subjugation and mystery, the idea of the Roman Church, and perhaps of the Masons, is much better for the happiness of the people, even though based on general deception. That's the meaning of your Sinless One."

"Because of universal worship, they destroyed each other with the sword, created Gods and tried to force the rest of the world to bow down and worship their Gods. They called to one another: give up your Gods, and bow down before ours; otherwise death to you and your Gods. And so will it be to the end of the world. If the Gods were to disappear from the world, it would still be the same. If the Gods were to disappear from the earth, they would still fall down before idols."

In the desert B. All these things will be pointed out to you.

"Who to bow down before? There is no concern that is more enduring and more torturous for mankind than, finding himself free, to find out as soon as possible whom to bow down to. Man is born free and his greatest concern after receiving freedom is to give it to someone. He wants to give away this gift of freedom, which has been so torturous, as soon as possible. But man seeks to bow down before something that is so indisputable, so completely indisputable that everyone together would agree to bow down with him. For the concern of these pitiful creatures is not only to find me or someone else to bow down to, but to find someone that all would believe in and all would bow down before, all without fail together. This need for common worship has been one of the greatest sufferings of each individual personally and of humanity as a whole from the beginning of time. Because of this, man has created Gods for himself during the whole course of history. You knew, you must have known this basic secret of mankind's nature, yet you rejected the only absolute banner, which was offered to you, by which you could have forced all to bow down before you without argument. The banner of earthly bread and you rejected it in the name of freedom and heavenly bread. Now look!

Look now what else you did when the second question was posed to you.

And everything again in the name of freedom! I say to you that there are no more torturous cares than to find someone to whom to give as quickly as possible this gift of freedom with which the unfortunate creature is born. But only he who can bring peace to the consciences of men can possess their freedom; this was the point of the second thesis, the second question, the second suggestion which was given to you. With bread you were given an indisputable banner: give man bread and man will bow down before you, because there is nothing more indisputable than bread; but if at the same time someone possesses his conscience, he will then throw up your bread and follow him who will explain to him what is good and what is evil and who by those definitions seduces his conscience. You were right in that. For the secret of human existence consists not only in being able to live, as animals live, but in knowing why one lives. Man will not want to live without a clear idea of why he is living, but will rather kill himself than remain on earth, even though he may be surrounded by bread. That's the way things are, but look what happened. Instead of possessing the freedom of people so as to take it from them, you increased it, made it much greater! Either you have forgotten what peace is; even death is preferable for man than freedom and especially free choice in the knowledge of good and evil. Look, look, even the rebels against us look only for tranquillity. Why do the godless love materialism and materialistic teaching so much? Precisely because by such teaching everything comes to an end quickly, everything passes without leaving a trace, and consequently everything ends in annihilation and death. That is, they look for tranquillity with the smallest freedom. There is nothing more tempting for man than freedom of conscience, and nothing more tormenting. And look, instead of firm foundations for the calming of mankind's conscience, once and for all—you chose all that is unusual, puzzling, and indefinite, chose everything that is beyond the strength of people, and increased their agitation, and you acted therefore as if you did not love them at all. You, who came to give your life for them. Instead of relieving the people of freedom, you increased it and burdened them with torments and hopes of an eternal spiritual kingdom. With torments, I say, for despite the fact that they are unbearable, there is nothing more seductive for man.

You desired a free love from man so that, attracted and captivated, he would follow you freely. He was supposed to decide what was good and evil with a free heart, having only the example of your image before him. But didn't you know that he would finally place in doubt and reject even your image and your truth, if he were crushed by such a frightful burden as freedom of choice? They will cry out now, finally, that truth cannot be in you, because it was impossible to leave them in more confusion and torment than you have done, you, who have given them so much upset and so many unresolved tasks. You therefore have constructed the very foundation of the destruction of your kingdom; don't blame anyone else any longer. Yet, what was proposed to you? The rational spirit showed you first of all how the people were weak, ignoble, and ungrateful. He showed you three powers, the only three on earth, which have the eternal capacity of conquering and soothing the consciences of these weak rebels for their own happiness. These three strengths are miracle, mystery, and authority. You rejected all three and put forth your example instead."

No. 5—Ivan and Smerdyakov

Smerdyakov: "I told Ilinsky that she will come without fail."
"Why did you say that?"
He wants to kill.
"I'll become sick from fear. And he will knock without me."
"And suppose Grushenka is not there?"
"What about the money?"
"He won't take it."
"You don't know him."

"Go away."

"How can I go?"

"I'm only concerned that later they don't suspect that I took the money."

"Who will touch you?"

"You for example."

At night after the conversation with Smerdyakov.

At first: he was laughing at me. Yes, he was laughing.

And later at night, he jumps up. "Does he really think, scoundrel, that it will be pleasant for me that my father will be killed? Yes, that's exactly what he's thinking." (His familiarity is insulting.)

(The important thing is not clear; bring up the important point.)

"The devil take it! Perhaps it really will be agreeable for me. Ha! Ha! Perhaps he really thinks that I'm in it together with Dmitry? Perhaps something good will come of it. Besides it's nonsense; the scoundrel is simply afraid of everything so as not to get mixed up in it."

"The devil take it, perhaps he wants to do the killing."

Ivan still (in conversation with Smerdyakov).

"All that's nonsense; it cannot be that my brother Dmitry Fyodorovich has planned to kill with premeditation. If such a sin were to happen, it would happen by chance in a quarrel, when he would be taking Grushenka away."

Smerdyakov: "The sum that they may look for is 3,000."

Ivan: "Nonsense."

"He, he needs money very much."

Ivan: "Nothing will happen."

Smerdyakov. "Of course, every reasonable man ought to think that way."

"As the saying goes, it is interesting to talk with a clever man."

No. 6—Smerdyakov's Simulated Attack

After saying goodbye to his sons, Fyodor remained very content. For two whole hours he almost felt himself to be happy, when suddenly something very irritating and very inconvenient for everyone occurred in the house, plunging Fyodor Karamazov into great uneasiness. For some reason Smerdyakov went to the cellar and fell from the top step. It was lucky that at the time Marfa Ignatyevna, Grigory's wife, happened to be in the yard. She did not see him fall, but she heard his cry, a very strange cry, but known to her as the cry of an epileptic falling into a fit. Whether the attack occurred when he was going down the stairs, and he fell as a consequence immediately into unconsciousness, or, the opposite, his attack—as a well-known epileptic —occurred from the fall and concussion was impossible to know. But he was found at the bottom of the cellar, writhing and trembling, flailing about with foam in his mouth. They thought at first that he had broken or hurt something, but "God spared him" as Marfa Ignatyevna expressed it. Nothing of that kind took place. Only it was difficult to take hold of him and carry him out of the cellar. They called in some neighbors and one way or another got him out. Fyodor Karamazov witnessed this whole ceremony; he even helped and was clearly very frightened and somewhat distraught. The sick man, however, did not regain consciousness; although his attacks would subside for a while, they would then begin again. Everyone concluded that the same thing that happened last year when he fell accidentally from the attic would happen again. They remembered that at that time, they applied ice to his temples. They found some ice in the cellar and Marfa Ignatyevna took charge of this. Fyodor Karamazov decided about evening to send for Dr. Hertzenstube (if he can't help at night then tomorrow, but he came rather quickly). Having examined the patient carefully (he was a very careful and attentive doctor, middle-aged and respectable old man), he concluded that the attack was very serious and dangerous. Although he, Hertzenstube, still did not understand it all, he would recommend new remedies in the morning if the present ones did not help. They placed the sick man in the wing with Grigory and Marfa Ignatyevna. Then Fyodor Karamazov had one misfortune after another that day. Marfa Ignatyevna prepared his dinner, and the soup, compared to Smerdyakov's, came out tasting like slop, and the chicken turned out to be so dry that it was impossible to eat. Marfa Ignatyevna answered her master's bitter reproaches by saying that the chicken had been very old anyway and that she had not been trained as a cook. Toward evening, Fyodor had something else to worry about: he learned that Grigory, who had been ailing for two days, suddenly took to his bed almost completely because of his lumbago. Fyodor finished his tea as quickly as possible and locked himself in his house. He was in a frightful state, trembling with expectancy. The point was that he was almost sure that Grushenka would come that night; at least she had hinted at it. Yesterday morning Smerdyakov had assured him that she would come. His heart was beating; he walked around the room listening to noises. He had to keep his ear sharply cocked; Dmitry was probably tracking her and might come. When she knocks at the window (Smerdyakov had assured him that he had told her how and where to knock), then he had to open the door immediately so as not to keep her waiting for nothing in the entry, and, God forbid, so as not to frighten her away.

It was troublesome for Fyodor, but his heart had never bathed itself in a sweeter hope. After all, she was sure, almost sure, to come; you could count on it this time.

No. 7—The Trial

A man who gives away his last 5,000 and has a knavish thirst for 3,000. All that presented the matter in a new light. About the 3,000 sent by post. I didn't really give it to him to send by post: I sort of felt that he needed money for some affair and I didn't know how to propose lending it to him more delicately. He was tormenting himself in vain. I always was very sure that he would manage to send those 3,000 as soon as he got the money from his father. I knew that he was fighting with his father, and I have always been convinced that he had been hurt by his father. I don't remember his making any threats against his father. At least he never said anything in my presence, no threats. He was firmly convinced that he would receive the money. And if he had come to me, I would have quickly calmed his fears. But he didn't come to me. And I . . . I was in such a situation that I could not call him to me. All the more so, I had no right to be demanding since I had received a monetary favor from him of greater dimensions before, and I took it despite the fact that I had no way of knowing that I would ever be in a position to pay my debt back to him.

She had been betrothed to Mitya up to the point that he left her. Whom he left her for—the procurator did not touch on this question out of consideration for her. They began to question her, among other things, about the three thousand.

It was not here, but in the beginning of our acquaintanceship. Fetyukovich approached this cautiously, sensing something favorable. (NB Remarkable that although he had been sent for by them, he didn't know anything about the episode of the 5,000 rubles that Mitya had given her.)
"Yes, it didn't take place here. It took place before, there . . ."
"No, never will I be able to forget that minute."
Enthusiasm and hidden sobs rang out.
The confession was in any case something new.

There was some question about whether it was very honorable, and whether in any case that is the way an innocent girl should have acted.
But from the first words Katerina Ivanovna announced firmly in answer to one of the questions given to her

Everything took place because of me; he fell in love with me and left his lady. She tried to treat me to chocolate, to seduce me. She has very little true shame; that's what.
The judge said suggestively

. . . .

"I wanted to save him. He tormented me. He took my money looking me straight in the eyes."

NB   (muddled)

"Oh, he laughed at me because of the bow down to the ground. I hated him."

Mitya. Remembering. Well, what now, lost.

"You've destroyed me, Katya." Katya's testimony.

Stepmother.

Mitya exclaims bitterly.

Hysterics.

Grushenka.

They took her away.

The doctor entered.

Continuation.

The debate begins at 8 o'clock.

2. THE CRITICS

A Historical and Analytic
Introduction to *The Brothers*
Karamazov

ERNEST SIMMONS

In Russia *The Brothers Karamazov* is regarded as Dostoevsky's greatest novel. His most matured art, his wisdom, ideas, faith, and doubts find their fullest expression in this book. Nowhere else has he so successfully and so characteristically abstracted mind and will and passion from their background of names and clothes and exhibited them in such pure, disembodied states of being. Nowhere else has the white-hot intensity of his ideological world glowed so brightly or has he spiritualized ideas so arrestingly and so profoundly. All that life meant for him—its experiences, symbols, and vision—is reflected in these extraordinary characters. If the final test of a great novel is the enduring sense of having undergone a vital and lasting experience in the reading of it, then *The Brothers Karamazov* easily takes a place among the few supreme novels of world literature.

In a sense Dostoevsky had been preparing for this task throughout most of his creative life. Certain ideas that went into the novel may well have flashed across his imagination while he was in prison in Siberia. The thematic continuity of his works, beginning with *Notes from the Underground,* and the character-types, starting with his

From Ernest J. Simmons, "The Karamazovs," in *Dostoevsky: the Making of a Novelist* (New York: Random House, 1940). Vintage Russian Library, V-736. Chapter XXI in its entirety. Permission granted by the author.

27

earliest productions, achieve their fullest development in *The Brothers Karamazov*. That source of so much of his later fiction, the plan of 'The Life of a Great Sinner,' contributes its increment; and the boys' club, which figured so prominently and to no purpose in the various drafts of *The Idiot*, becomes an important feature. Finally, certain articles in *The Diary of a Writer* contain much material that has a direct bearing on the subject-matter and ideas of the novel.

On the evidence of a few jottings in his notebook, it has been inferred that Dostoevsky conceived the character of Smerdyakov in 1876, which would suggest that the plan of the novel was surprisingly well advanced at a very early date. The most recent editor[263] of the manuscript notes to the novel, however, convincingly establishes the fact that the reference to Smerdyakov really belongs to 1878. In the last issue of *The Diary of a Writer* (December 1877), Dostoevsky frankly tells his readers that he is discontinuing the publication in order to devote himself to an artistic work that had been 'imperceptibly and involuntarily composing itself' in his mind over the past two years. In the same month he writes to a friend: 'There is a novel in my head and heart and it begs to be expressed.'[1] As early as the summer of this same year, he had visited haunts of his childhood, the villages of Darovoe and Chermashnya, with the express intention of refreshing his memory on material for the novel. Clearly, then, the period of preliminary planning of *The Brothers Karamazov* belongs to the year 1877, although he very likely conceived the idea of the novel the year before.

With no other time-consuming occupation, the planning went forward rapidly in the early months of 1878. In March, Dostoevsky wrote to a pedagogical friend to request detailed information about the behaviour of school children, although these facts were not necessary until the second half of the book. In the spring, however, the sudden death of his young son interrupted the work. With the hope of assuaging his grief, his wife sent him on a trip to the monastery of Optina Pustyn, celebrated for the piousness of its elder, Father Amvrosi. He stopped off at Moscow and easily persuaded Katkov to give him an advance on the projected novel. Then he continued to the monastery in the company of his intimate friend, the philosopher Vladimir Soloviev, to whom he confided the plot of *The Brothers Karamazov*. At the monastery he talked with the elder who consoled him on the loss of his child in words which Dostoevsky recalled when writing the effective consolation of Zossima to the poor peasant woman bereaved of her child. Indeed, Optina Pustyn and Father Amvrosi provided special details for the monastic scenes and the characterization of Zossima in the novel.

Upon his return to Staraya Russa, Dostoevsky once more set to

---

[1] A. S. Dolinin, *F. M. Dostoevsky, Pis'ma* (*Letters*), Vol. III, No. 612 (Moscow-Leningrad, 1934), p. 284.

work. The first instalment was ready before the end of the year, and it appeared in the *Russian Messenger* in January 1879. The remainder, however, progressed very slowly. The immediate and enthusiastic public responses to the early sections supported his own conviction of the significance of the work and encouraged him to take the utmost care with the succeeding parts. It was his most deliberately and slowly written novel, as though he felt that his immortality depended upon this work alone. Only after three years[264] of effort did he finish it—the last chapter was completed in November 1880—and his faith in the performance was amply justified, for *The Brothers Karamazov* raised him to the heights of national fame.

Despite the long period of deliberation over the various details, the plot of the novel seems to have occurred to Dostoevsky pretty much in its entirety. It is better constructed than most of his plots, and even includes carefully designed periods of relief from the intensity of the main theme. Although it is his longest novel, the bare outlines of the plot may be summed up in a few sentences. It is a story of crime in which Dmitry Karamazov and his father are rivals for the love of Grushenka. Smerdyakov, an illegitimate son, murders the father, and Dmitry is accused of the crime and convicted on circumstantial evidence. Into this sordid tale, however, Dostoevsky has introduced a titanic struggle of love and hate, with all its profound psychological and spiritual implications, and the whole is cast against the background of the life of a town and a monastery. The last two novels had reflected a steadily growing interest in religious problems. In *The Brothers Karamazov* the Church and God become the very foundation upon which he erects the huge superstructure of the work. Throughout, the whole novel is pervaded with a search for faith—for God. This search for God is the central 'idea' of the novel.

It is surprising how often Dostoevsky draws upon actual happenings for the element of crime in his fiction. Behind the murders in *Crime and Punishment, The Idiot,* and *The Possessed* are real crimes which he had read about in newspapers. These are the 'fantastic facts' of his theory of realism; from such realized facts come the ideas that take on flesh and blood when embodied in his characters. It is now fairly certain that the dominant theme of murder in the plot of *The Brothers Karamazov* was not an imaginary situation. In the manuscript notes to the novel, Dmitry, upon his first appearance, is referred to as 'Ilinsky,' and he is frequently indicated by this name in succeeding notes. Dostoevsky's use of the names of real people in the notes to designate characters who have been modelled on them was pointed out in the case of *The Possessed* in which the name Granovsky was often employed for Stepan Trofimovich, and Nechaev for Pyotr Verkhovensky. The name Ilinsky, it seems, was also that of a real person. In *The House of the Dead* Dostoevsky describes one of the convicts as 'a certain parricide, formerly a nobleman and a public functionary. He

had given great[265] grief to his father—a true prodigal son. The old
man endeavoured in vain to restrain him by remonstrance on the fatal
slope down which he was sliding. As he was loaded with debts, and his
father was suspected of having, besides an estate, a sum of ready
money, he killed him in order to enter more quickly into his inheritance.' (Chapter II) Towards the end of the book (Chapter VII)
Dostoevsky takes an occasion to remark that he has received news from
Siberia that this supposed parricide had been falsely accused and
unjustly condemned. From an account by Dostoevsky's wife, it appears
that the man's real name was Ilinsky. On the basis of this clue, a recent
investigator made a detailed comparison and is able to offer convincing
evidence to the effect that Ilinsky in *The House of the Dead* was
unquestionably the immediate inspiration for the characterization of
Dmitry Karamazov. From the account in *The House of the Dead*, it is
clear that Ilinsky made a deep impression on Dostoevsky, and the
man's innocence no doubt fostered his interest in the case. In appearance, background, and behaviour Ilinsky has much in common with
Dmitry. More important, perhaps, is his reputed crime of parricide and
the judicial error that resulted in his conviction, facts which are strikingly similar to those in the plot of the novel. As a final bit of evidence
in support of this identification, it should be noted that the town of
Tobolsk, where Ilinsky was alleged to have committed the crime, is the
very town first mentioned in the manuscript notes as the scene of the
action of the novel. (Dostoevsky finally changed the name in the
printed text.) Once again, then, Dostoevsky appears to have had
recourse to the facts of real life instead of literary imaginings for the
central theme of the plot of a novel.

Although both the murder as the central theme and the ideological
direction seem to have been settled upon at the outset, Dostoevsky
experienced his usual difficulty with the events and their relation to the
characters, which as yet were only vaguely imagined. On the very first
page of the notes, definitely dated April 1878, and amid reminders to
buy boots and tobacco, is the observation: 'Memento (for a novel)—
To find out whether it is possible to lie between the rails under a train
when it is going at full speed.' This note, of course, refers to the
episode of Kolya Krasotkin, which was not actually written up until
two years later and appeared only in the tenth book of the novel.
Further references to children in the early notes suggest that he had
intended to introduce them at the beginning and had designed a more
significant role for them than they[266] have in the printed work. It is
very likely that his unknown plan for a novel about 'Fathers and
Children,' which he was contemplating even before he began to write
A Raw Youth in 1874, influenced this initial design for the opening of
The Brothers Karamazov.

Once the actual writing began, however, Dostoevsky displayed a
mastery over his rich material which was unusual in the early stages of

his novels. With exceptional brevity, and representing something of a departure from his customary dramatic method of starting a work *in medias res*, nearly all the chief characters are presented in the first thirty-five pages, including the principal facts in their lives up to the point where their story begins. And within the brief scope of this concise exposition, the potential psychological development of each of these characters is at least suggested.

Like the great characters of previous masterpieces, the chief men and women of *The Brothers Karamazov* are cast in the form of embodied ideas. Nothing in human experience as we know it will satisfactorily explain the exaggerated motives and actions of old Karamazov, Dmitry, Ivan, Alyosha, Smerdyakov, Zossima, Grushenka, and Katerina Ivanovna. Nor is this exaggeration the kind that we expect in fiction or which is traditionally warranted in art. The ordinary meaning of realism is not broad enough to justify such creations. Yet these characters are real and vital. They win our sympathy, and we have little difficulty in identifying ourselves with this or that aspect of their natures. Many factors contribute to this realism in the apparently unreal. Like symbols in a modern allegory of life, the characters are personifications of ideas, but personifications treated so realistically that we effect a willing suspension of disbelief and accept them as living human beings. We never seem to think of Dostoevsky's characters absolutely in terms of themselves, in terms of their physical and surface characteristics. We think of them rather in terms of the ideas which they personify. They are not so much men and women as human souls, who live in a region of experience from' which all the circumstances of ordinary life appear to have been eliminated, and in which only the soul survives. In this sense, artistic reality tends to approximate more and more closely to spiritual reality or to ideas of spiritual reality.

The father of this strange Karamazov brood has left his mark on each of his sons. Despite their striking individual differences, they are all Karamazovs by virtue of something deeper than the normal ties of kinship. The Karamazov taint is carnal sensuality, which in its less vicious manifestations Dostoevsky describes as a zest for[267] living. It is the dominating characteristic of the father; it helps to wreck the life of Dmitry; it is always just below the surface in Ivan; and at odd moments it even rears its ugly head in the saint-like nature of Alyosha. Dostoevsky was interested in the subject of heredity, and this aspect of the novel may well have been influenced by Zola's *La Fortune des Rougon*, which he had no doubt read. The children of the lust-loving father in Zola's novel also inherit the traits of their parent. Dostoevsky, however, would have little sympathy for the scientific materialism behind Zola's understanding of heredity. The inherited trait of the Karamazov sons does not lend itself to any physiological explanation. The moral transports of Dmitry, the questing rationalism of Ivan, and

Alyosha's spiritual rapture defy scientific analysis. All of them are philosophers, as Dmitry remarks, and the animal instincts in them constantly struggle with the moral and spiritual side of their natures. They are all deeply imbued with a Schiller-like moral consciousness. Indeed, the ecstasy of love in Schiller's *Hymn of Joy* is one of the basic elements of the whole ideological conception of the novel, and the father and his two sons in *Die Räuber*, if we may judge from the frequent reference to them, were very much in Dostoevsky's mind in the characterizations of old Karamazov, Dmitry, and Ivan.

Although old Karamazov is a monster of lust and debauchery, it would be a mistake to regard him in this light only. He possesses a natural cunning and is by no means devoid of a subtle comprehension of the deeper motives of human behaviour, both in himself and in others. In his youth he made a living by playing the buffoon in the families of nobles, and he continues to play the buffoon with enjoyment but often with manifest design. Like Foma Fomich, in *The Village of Stepanchikovo*, who had also earned his keep as a hired jester, old Karamazov courts insult because he derives a pleasure from personal affront. On the other hand, he takes a cynical delight in baiting his real or imaginary enemies. By means of shady dealings, he has obtained some wealth, but his money makes him greedy for more. He is generous with himself, however, and his chief pleasure in life is to indulge his carnal appetites. Occasionally he is troubled by a stab of conscience, and at moments he reveals even a sentimental affection for his dead wives and his sons. In his cups, he may display the furtive spirituality of a repentant drunkard and go so far as to entertain the idea of the existence of God. None of his associates, however, is misled by these fugitive good impulses. The old cynic is utterly a sensualist, corrupt and immoral to the core. The dark[268] Karamazov strain rules his life and finally leads him to his death.

Of the sons, the notes indicate that Alyosha took shape earliest in Dostoevsky's imagination. He describes him in the novel as 'the future hero of my story,' and various hints in the notes, as well as the evidence of Dostoevsky's wife, make it clear that he intended to continue the development of Alyosha in one or more sequels. Presumably he was to marry Liza, live through a period of sinning, during which he would come in contact with a variety of people, including revolutionary terrorists, and finally achieve salvation through suffering. Alyosha was obviously destined to undergo the holy pilgrimage of the hero in the plan of 'The Life of a Great Sinner.' In the end, however, Dostoevsky's death prevented the fulfilment of the vast design of his great unwritten masterpiece which had nurtured so much of his fiction.

These plans for the future development of Alyosha no doubt account for the sense of incompleteness of the characterization in the novel. However, the part he has to play is important and well sustained. His mother was a deeply religious, passive, and long-suffering woman, and these traits are inherited by Alyosha. The scene in which she holds him up as an infant before the ikon is a symbolic dedication of Alyosha to God. The 'idea' he embodies is that of the religious spirit brought into contact with sin in which faith triumphs over unbelief. Although he represents the Christian ideal, there is nothing of the pale mystic about him, or of the seminarist engrossed in theological studies and smelling of the lamp. He is a novice at the local monastery, but his elder bids him take off his cassock and go out into the world and experience life. The red-cheeked, handsome Alyosha does not demur, for he believes that 'everyone should love life above everything in the world.' There is even latent in him the dark Kara-mazov strain. In this true son of God, who carries in his heart the secret of renewal for all, Dostoevsky is clearly building a nature that will wrestle with the devil and not lose his soul.

In one of the early notes, not repeated in the novel in any form, Alyosha is referred to in a paraphrase of a line from the Second Part of *Faust:* 'The highest beauty is not external but within.' Like Prince Myshkin, Alyosha possesses this 'highest beauty,' which is a moral beauty. There are striking resemblances between the two characters which are further supported by the fact that Dostoevsky often refers to Alyosha in the notes as 'The Idiot.' He has the[269] intuitive wisdom of Myshkin and his selfless compassionate heart and radiant personality. Further, his part in the novel resembles somewhat that of Myshkin in *The Idiot.* He moves through the pages morally influencing the characters and events, without ever playing much of an active role. Like all the Meek characters, he is passive, submissive, ever ready to turn the other cheek, and Christ-like in his capacity for suffering. With his intuitive wisdom he understands the tempestuous passions around him, but his virginal soul is unscorched by their hot flame. His love for Liza recalls that of Myshkin for Aglaya Epanchina, for his feelings hardly transcend the emotion of pity and the desire to contribute to the spiritual and moral health of this strange young girl.

In Alyosha, however, one may detect slight deviations from the hitherto uniform pattern of the Meek characters. The variations, no doubt, were intended as a psychological basis for the greater change to come in his role of hero in the projected sequel. Thus, the dark Karamazov strain in him, which was to run its full course in the continuation, leads him to the edge of sin on several occasions. In his love for Liza, Alyosha at least once displays a feeling foreign to the Meek type. Even his religious faith is momentarily shaken by the incident of the stinking corpse and nearly overthrown by the arguments of Ivan. Such weaknesses in his moral armour, however, are quickly mended; his mission in the novel is to influence all by his sublime faith in life. He is the only one of the three brothers who is able to love life more than the meaning of life. For him alone is reserved the ecstasy of the 'living life,' mentioned by Versilov in *A Raw Youth*. In the famous scene which signalizes his recovery of faith, he experiences this higher synthesis of life as he leaves the monastery to go out into the night:

The earth's silence seemed to melt into the silence of the heavens, the mystery of the earth was one with the mystery of the stars. Alyosha stood, gazed, and suddenly, as though his strength failed him, he threw himself down on the earth. He did not know why he embraced it. He could not have told why he longed so irresistibly to kiss it, to kiss it all. But he kissed it weeping, sobbing and bathing it with his tears, and vowing passionately to love it, to love it for ever and ever. . . . There seemed to be threads from all those innumerable worlds of God linking his soul to them, and it was trembling all over 'in contact with other worlds.' He longed to forgive everyone and for everything and to beg forgiveness, Oh, not for himself, but for all men, for all and for everything. (Part VII, Book III, IV) [270]

Although incomplete, the picture of Alyosha is impressive. Had Dostoevsky lived to continue it in the sequel, the dream of most of his creative life—to portray a good man on his pilgrimage through sin and suffering to salvation—might have been fulfilled in a characterization of extraordinary grandeur.

Like his younger brother, Dmitry loves life, but the meaning of life continually puzzles him. He occupies the central position in the novel and perhaps ought to be considered the hero, for the story of *The Brothers Karamazov* is essentially the story of Dmitry. In him the Karamazov taint of carnal sensuality is most pronounced. There is a suggestion of dualism in his actions, but simplicity and deep feeling are the essence of his nature, qualities which make for a unified apprehension of life in Dostoevsky's scheme of things. Dmitry acts on instinct, and his emotions provide always the clearest image of his nature. There is poetry in his soul which is reflected in his impulsive behaviour and colourful language. His whole life is like an epic in which the turbulent action is relieved by occasional lyric flights.

Dmitry can be introspective, but he thoroughly distrusts the rational approach to human experience. The only problem that seems to torment his generous mind is the struggle of the good and beautiful with the forces of evil in the heart of man. In those remarkable chapters, 'The Confession of a Passionate Heart,' he bares his soul to Alyosha in a self-revelation of love and hate. In telling of his strange adventure with Katerina Ivanovna, he is concerned solely with the state of his feelings over the way that proud woman humbled herself before him. He will have nothing of any rationalization of his actions. 'To hell with all who pry into the human heart!' he exclaims. Yet he cannot evade the problem of the Karamazov vileness in his nature which contends with his yearning for the good and the beautiful. He deplores the thought that a man of lofty mind begins with the ideal of the Madonna and ends with the ideal of Sodom. What is still worse, he feels, is that both ideals coexist in the mind of man.

> Yes, man is broad, even too broad. I'd have him narrower. The devil only knows what to make of it! What represents itself to the mind as shameful is beauty to the heart. Is there beauty in Sodom? Believe me, it is found in Sodom for the immense majority of people. Did you know that secret? The awful thing is that beauty is a mysterious as well as a terrible thing. God and the devil are fighting there and the battlefield is the heart of man. (Part I, Book III, iii) [271]

The Karamazov devil conquers in the heart of Dmitry. He possesses those qualities, however, which Dostoevsky associated with the good man who can be saved. All the evil in him is ameliorated by his capacity to suffer and to repent. Like Zossima, who bows down before him as one condemned to suffer, he perceives, if only vaguely, that the individual must share the guilt and suffering of others. He does not offer any extenuation for the purely circumstantial part he played in the murder of his father, for he admits to a certain moral blame, to the feeling that he wanted to kill the old man. With Katerina Ivanovna he displays the same generous instinct. He had once loved her, but her proud nature and actions had turned his love into hate. After all, she lacked the very love which comes from the heart, the kind of love that Grushenka could give him and which he himself gave in return. Yet, after her most damaging evidence at the trial, he freely forgave her.

There is nothing in the novel comparable to the cumulative emotional effect and infinite pathos of the scene of Dmitry in the tavern. All the burning lust which had sent him on that wild ride to Grushenka is suddenly extinguished by the awful charge of parricide. The insistent cross-examination of the magistrate grips the attention as the soul of Dmitry is revealed with all its dross and all its innate nobility, the nobility of the natural man who acts from impulse and feeling. It is at this point, rather than at his trial, that he emerges as a great tragic figure.

Dmitry casts out the devil of evil by suffering and throws in his lot with God. With all his humility, however, he despairs of the fortitude he will require in Siberia, and his newly found faith wavers. Still, in the end, he is willing to take up his cross, for he is conscious of his baseness, of having sullied his own honour which he values above everything. As he is about to be committed to prison, he makes public testimony of his faults and admits that the tragedy which has befallen him is perhaps a necessary blow to arouse him to the need of reforming his ways. And he concludes: 'I accept the torture of accusation, and my public shame. I want to suffer, and by suffering I shall purify myself. Perhaps I shall be purified, gentlemen? But listen, for the last time, I am not guilty of my father's blood!' (Part III, Book IX, ix)

Dmitry Karamazov is one of the greatest of all Dostoevsky's

characters. He has that broadness, that wide heart which Dostoevsky admired so much in real life. Dmitry must have appealed to him as one of the most typical Russians that he ever created.[272] For many readers, too, Dmitry has come to typify the Russian nature—its expansiveness, generosity, impulsiveness, innate nobility, and capacity for suffering, a man whose offences are inevitably the defects of his virtues.

Unlike either of his brothers, Ivan is more concerned with the meaning of life than with life itself. He puts life on the operating table, dissects it, and comes away disillusioned, without ever seeming to realize that life is to be lived. For many readers Ivan will always remain the most absorbing character in the novel; for many critics he is not only the most brilliant mouthpiece of Dostoevsky's ideas, but the very mental image of the man who created him. The 'idea' that Ivan embodies is that of the purely rational being whose reason leads him into evil and to a denial of God. He is not, however, a mere allegorical personification of an abstract idea. The problem that tortures his soul is not apprehended in a cold, lifeless fashion. It is a live coal thrust into his heart, and the consequent sufferings of Ivan are dramatized against a background of pulsing life.

So different in many respects from the other members of the family, it might seem that Ivan has nothing in common with the Karamazovs. Even the father, who sees his own image in Dmitry, declares to Alyosha: 'But I don't recognize Ivan, I don't know him at all. Where does he come from? He is not one of us in soul.' (Part II, Book IV, ii) The father, however, is not correct. Ivan is a Karamazov, but an educated and rationalizing one. In him the Karamazov taint takes the form of intellectual evil. Dmitry admits that he was quite capable of murdering his father. In a sense, Ivan does murder him, for he deliberately plants the idea in Smerdyakov's head, knowing full well that his devotee will carry it out. In the notes, Dostoevsky actually designates Ivan as the murderer, indicating conclusively the full import of his moral guilt. No, Ivan is a true Karamazov, and his theory that 'all is permitted' is virtually an intellectual justification of the Karamazov lust for life.

Ivan is the last of Dostoevsky's remarkable series of Doubles, and in him is expressed most fully the philosophical development of the split personality. His ambivalence takes the highest form of the cosmic struggle of man with God, which had been foreshadowed by Terentev in *The Idiot* and Kirilov in *The Possessed*. In this struggle he is concerned precisely with those factors which were at the bottom of Dostoevsky's own search for faith—the problem[273] of sin and suffering and their relation to the existence of God. Ivan passionately and obstinately searches for a way out of his dilemma, and with a seriousness that indicates that upon the results of his quest will rest his desire to live or not to live. The famous section 'Pro and Contra,' in which this philosophical and religious struggle is waged, is the true culmination of the novel, not only the greatest scene that Dostoevsky ever wrote, but certainly one of the most remarkable in literature. The whole ideological conception of the novel, as well as the resolution of Ivan's struggle, is centred in this section, and the subject deserves a separate chapter.

There is another Karamazov, although an illegitimate one—Smerdyakov. More in the spirit of a practical joke rather than of wanton lust, old Karamazov had begotten him of a vagrant idiot girl and brought him up as a servant in his own house. Smerdyakov is a macabre study in the psychology of human degeneracy. Although a bastard, he is tarred with the Karamazov brush. With his foppish manners, low cunning, and pretensions to learning, there can be little doubt that Dostoevsky designed him as a parody of Ivan. The intellectual Ivan is his hero, and he poll-parrots his very arguments about the existence of God. In his smug bourgeois ambitions and offensively rebellious nature, Ivan considers him raw material for revolution—a bitter thrust against the radicals on Dostoevsky's part. The mere hint of his hero takes root in his shrewd mind; he murders old Karamazov and robs him of the money he had put aside to bribe Grushenka into submission. In those three unforgettable visits after the murder, Smerdyakov holds up to Ivan the mirror of his moral and intellectual depravity. Ivan is appalled at the image of himself, and it loses nothing of its verisimilitude as the revelation of this aping lackey. No villain of Dostoevsky is quite so repulsive as Smerdyakov, and none is described with such psychological mastery.

Although the Karamazov family holds the centre of the stage, there is a profusion of secondary characters who are nearly all sharply conceived and treated with a richness of detail unusual in the minor figures in Dostoevsky's novels. The three principal female characters are thoroughly in the tradition of the Doubles and among the best-drawn women in this group. Like previous female Doubles, their whole action in the novel centres in the emotion of love.

In the portrayal of Katerina Ivanovna, there is a considerable psychological advance over the other 'infernal women' of Dostoevsky. [274] Her dual nature becomes apparent from that day when Dmitry gallantly refused to take advantage of her voluntary submission after he had given her the money to save her peculating father from disgrace. Her love for the large-souled Dmitry takes the usual form of a struggle between pride and submissiveness. All her behaviour is dictated by this ambivalence. She desires to torture Dmitry and to be tortured by him. Her cruelty and denial had turned his love to hate. She has very much the same feeling for Ivan, but a Double himself, he fully appreciates her split personality. He clearly perceives that she continually lacerates herself in welcoming Dmitry's insults, and that her submissiveness and self-abasement have their roots in her towering pride. Even Alyosha understands perfectly that she must ultimately dominate the man she loves. She might have dominated Dmitry if it had not been for Grushenka; but she can never dominate Ivan, whose own dualism comprehends this same incorrigible pride. 'She loved neither of them—neither Ivan nor Dmitry,' Alyosha concludes. And in the absolute sense, this is true. Subtly probing all the refined nuances of her ambivalent emotions, Dostoevsky reveals in Katerina Ivanovna a woman caught between the grinding stones of her dualism, between pride and submissiveness, between love and hate.

Grushenka is a more elementary type of the female Double. In her appearance, background, and actions she resembles Nastasya Filipovna in *The Idiot*. Like her, Grushenka has suffered a deep moral hurt in her youth and the fact has profoundly affected her outlook on life. It is difficult, however, to accept the violent change in her nature after she entices Alyosha to her house. Apparently Dostoevsky was similarly troubled by this abrupt transformation. The seventh book, which contains the attempted seduction, and is entitled 'Alyosha' in the novel, he had called 'Grushenka' in the notes. It is clear from this fact, and from the notes themselves, that he had originally attached much more significance to this turning point in Grushenka's life and had intended to devote considerably more space to the scene between her and Alyosha. Some of the themes in the notes are not worked up in the novel, notably a few which suggest that Alyosha was more sorely tempted by her charms than appears to be the case in the final version. Compared to the notes, this section in the novel is condensed, the effects toned down, and the vital spiritual change in Grushenka hinted rather than analysed in detail, which seems to have been his initial intention. Of course, the sudden softening of her nature, the [275] emergence of an unexpected virtue and spirituality, may be psychologically justifiable on the basis of Alyosha's recognition of her true moral dignity—a situation comparable to that in *The Idiot* when Myshkin recognizes the moral dignity of Nastasya Filipovna. After this reformation in Grushenka, however, the further development of her character is quite consistent. Although the dual emotions of love and hate rule over her behaviour throughout most of the novel, like Dmitry, generosity, a wide soul, and a capacity to suffer seem to effect a synthesis in the contending forces of her nature. In the end, like Sonya Marmeladova, she is prepared to travel the prisoner's road to Siberia with the man she loves.

That strange girl, Liza Khokhlakova, whose mother provides the comic relief of the novel, reveals a nature in which emotional ambivalence dangerously approaches a pathological state. Self-abasement and the desire to suffer lead her to a point where she deliberately courts self-destruction. 'I should like someone to torture me,' she says to Alyosha, 'to marry me and then torture me, deceive me and then go away. I don't want to be happy.' Then she admits that she wishes to suffer, to kill herself. Finally, she tells Alyosha of her dream of the child crucified on the wall, and how pleasant this would be if she could see it and eat pineapple compote while listening to the groans. Such manifestations reveal the excessively morbid nature of Liza. She is capable at once of self-renunciation and mockery, of tenderness and torture, and of answering with ridicule a love self-affirmed. Her confused relations with Alyosha and Ivan indicate clearly the split nature of her personality. She likes Ivan because she imagines that she will suffer and be tortured in loving him; and she is attracted to Alyosha because she feels that she can tyrannize over him and make him suffer.

The notes show that a more important place in the novel was originally designed for Rakitin, that seminarist who seems as much out of place in the monastery as the saint-like Alyosha would be in a brothel. His ideological contrast to Alyosha and his scorn for the Russian masses are more emphasized in the notes. It is very likely that Dostoevsky was parodying a real figure in this characterization. Several have been suggested by critics, but the most plausible is the editor of *National Notes*, A. A. Kraevsky, who had rejected the first version of *Crime and Punishment*. Like Kraevsky, Rakitin has essentially no concern with humanity or its morality. He is the type of liberal Westerner that Dostoevsky loathed. Like Alyosha[276] and Ivan, he occupies himself with higher questions of religion and philosophy, but he has nothing of Alyosha's love for humanity and is incapable of the intellectual heights of Ivan. To his liberalism he adds a touch of socialism, but only to a degree in which it seems advantageous and not dangerous. Dostoevsky no doubt intended him to represent the new democratically-minded youth of the day, who treated the weighty problems of history, religion, and society so superficially. Really all Rakitin wants is a career, and he cavalierly contemplates one in the Church or in journalism. He rather favours the idea of going up to St. Petersburg and working on a fat periodical, and he imagines that he will eventually become the editor and supply it with liberal tendencies of slight socialistic leanings, because such a practice seems to be in vogue. His place in the novel is as a contrast to the Karamazov brothers; his shallow comprehension of life is opposed to their intense and profoundly serious searchings into the meaning of life. Ivan thoroughly understands Rakitin and hates him as an enemy who adulterates his own ideas.

As a kind of subplot, but artistically interwoven into the fabric of the novel, is the theme of Captain Snegiryov and his family and the gang of boys under the leadership of Kolya Krasotkin. The captain and his family are surrounded with a halo of suffering, and Dostoevsky spares no detail in his effort to lay bare the tragedy of their lives in all its senselessness. The contrast between this wretched family, whose misfortunes are beyond its control, and the Karamazovs, whose tragedy arises from their own folly, was an intentional part of the total design. Little Ilyusha's behaviour over the beating of his father by Dmitry is infallibly true psychologically and emotionally, and the narrative at this point is wonderfully effective. The whole relationship between father and son is handled with delicateness and an uncanny understanding of a child's sense of dignity and of the fitness of things in a child's world.

Although Dostoevsky makes it amply clear that Kolya Krasotkin is a most unusual boy and a born leader among his comrades, this prodigy nevertheless strains the reader's credulity. To be sure, he is one of Dostoevsky's 'thinking children,' and his grave and mature language is quite in keeping with his mature actions. Yet, his trenchant observations on life and psychological wizardry exaggerate nature's most extravagant gifts to her fourteen-year-old sons. If disbelief is suspended and interest sustained, it is because of an unfailing human affection for the natural-born hero. Kolya is a boy-hero, and the extraordinary things he does seem to make little[277] difference provided he does them heroically. In general, Dostoevsky's treatment of the whole group of children is remarkably effective. Another author might have lathered the beautiful death scene of Ilyusha with mawkish sentimentality, but Dostoevsky never once goes beyond the limits of sheer human sentiment.

The swift tempo of the previous novels is deliberately toned down in *The Brothers Karamazov*. There are suggestions of the measured tone and epic sweep which Dostoevsky had formerly contemplated as the narrative method of his unwritten masterpiece, 'The Life of a Great Sinner.' Comic and digressive elements provide relief from the series of intense dramatic scenes which are among the most brilliantly imagined and artistically executed in the whole range of his fiction. With impressive cumulative effect everything leads up to the trial scene, which is handled in a consummate fashion. No novelist has ever surpassed Dostoevsky at this sort of thing. For years he had followed court trials with almost a morbid curiosity, and he had amassed a surprising amount of technical knowledge on judicial procedure. In letters to the associate editor of the *Russian Messenger*, N. A. Liubimov, we are informed of his infinite care about these technical matters. He seeks advice on legal points from lawyers and expert medical opinion about the hallucinations of Ivan. Not only does he fill in the background of Dmitry's trial with patient attention to all the details, but the examination and testimony are contrived both to advance the action and to bring out the further psychological development of the characters. The legal evidence connected with the murder of old Karamazov is complex, and Dostoevsky handles it with subtlety. His ability to place himself in the position of all the witnesses and the two lawyers, and in an entirely objective manner to present the conditioned reasoning of each speaker, as this reasoning in every instance would be limited by the speaker's imperfect knowledge of the facts in the case, is

little short of amazing. It is all a triumph of the dramatic method in
dealing with a complexity of material over which a lesser artist would
have stumbled many times.

The novel ends on the glad note of resurrection, when Alyosha
informs Kolya and his young playmates that the dead will rise again
and joyfully tell over to one another everything that has happened.
Whether he has in mind the resurrection of the fallen Dmitry to a new
life, it is hard to say. From the notes, one gathers that Dostoevsky
originally intended at the end to effect a general reconciliation, at least
between Dmitry, Grushenka, and Katerina Ivanovna. Such[278] a
denouement, however, would have been quite unsuitable artistically,
and he wisely abandoned it. The novel concludes with the ultimate
fate and future relations of Dmitry and Grushenka merely suggested,
with the dualism of Ivan and Katerina Ivanovna unresolved, and with
the future story of Alyosha still to be written.[279]

Dostoevsky and Parricide

SIGMUND FREUD

Four facets may be distinguished in the rich personality of
Dostoevsky: the creative artist, the neurotic, the moralist and the
sinner. How is one to find one's way in this bewildering complexity?

The creative artist is the least doubtful: Dostoevsky's place is not
far behind Shakespeare. *The Brothers Karamazov* is the most magnificent novel ever written; the episode of the Grand Inquisitor, one of the
peaks in the literature of the world, can hardly be valued too highly.
Before the problem of the creative artist analysis must, alas, lay down
its arms.

The moralist in Dostoevsky is the most readily assailable. If we
seek to rank him high as a moralist on the plea that only a man who
has gone through the depths of sin can reach the highest summit of
morality, we are neglecting a doubt that arises. A moral man is one
who reacts to temptation as soon as he feels it in his heart, without
yielding to it. A man who alternately sins and then in his remorse

From *Collected Papers of Sigmund Freud* (1959), Vol. V, pp. 222–242. Edited
by Ernest Jones. Reprinted by permission of the publisher, Basic Books, Inc.,
Publishers, New York.

erects high moral standards lays himself open to the reproach that he has made things too easy for himself. He has not achieved the essence of morality, renunciation, for the moral conduct of life is a practical human interest. He reminds one of the barbarians of the great migrations, who murdered and did penance for it, till penance became an actual technique for enabling murder to be done. Ivan the Terrible behaved in exactly this way; indeed, this[222] compromise with morality is a characteristic Russian trait. Nor was the final outcome of Dostoevsky's moral strivings anything very glorious. After the most violent struggles to reconcile the instinctual demands of the individual with the claims of the community, he landed in the retrograde position of submission both to temporal and spiritual authority, of veneration both for the Tsar and for the God of the Christians, and of a narrow Russian nationalism—a position which lesser minds have reached with smaller effort. This is the weak point in that great personality. Dostoevsky threw away the chance of becoming a teacher and liberator of humanity and made himself one with their gaolers. The future of human civilization will have little to thank him for. It seems probable that he was condemned to this failure by his neurosis. The greatness of his intelligence and the strength of his love for humanity might have opened to him another, an apostolic, way of life.

To consider Dostoevsky as a sinner or a criminal rouses violent opposition, which need not be based upon a philistine assessment of crime. The real motive for this opposition soon becomes apparent. Two traits are essential in a criminal: boundless egoism and a strong destructive impulse. Common to both of these, and a necessary condition for their expression, is absence of love, lack of an emotional appreciation of (human) objects. One at once recalls the contrast to this presented by Dostoevsky—his great need of love and his enormous capacity for love, which is to be seen in manifestations of exaggerated kindness and caused him to love and to help where he had a right to hatred and revenge, as, for example, in his relations with his first wife and her lover. That being so, it must be asked why there is any temptation to reckon Dostoevsky among the criminals. The answer is that it comes from his choice of material, which singles out from all others violent, murderous and egoistic characters, thus pointing to the existence of similar tendencies in his own soul, and also from certain facts in his life, like his passion for gambling and his[223] possible admission of a sexual assault upon a young girl.[1] The contradiction is

---

[1] See the discussion on this point in Fülöp-Miller and Eckstein (1926). Stefan Zweig (1920) writes: 'He was not halted by the barriers of bourgeois morality; and no one can say exactly how far he transgressed the bounds of law in his own life or how much of the criminal instincts of his heroes was realized in himself.' For the intimate connection between Dostoevsky's characters and his own experience, see René Fülöp-Miller's remarks in the introductory section of Fülöp-Miller and Eckstein (1925), which are based upon Nikolai Strakhov.

resolved by the realization that Dostoevsky's very strong destructive instinct, which might easily have made him a criminal, was in his actual life directed mainly against his own person (inward instead of outward) and thus found expression as masochism and a sense of guilt. Nevertheless, his personality retained sadistic traits in plenty, which show themselves in his irritability, his love of tormenting and his intolerance even towards people he loved, and which appear also in the way in which, as an author, he treats his readers. Thus in little things he was a sadist towards others, and in bigger things a sadist towards himself, in fact a masochist, that is to say the mildest, kindliest, most helpful person possible.

We have selected three factors from Dostoevsky's complex personality, one quantitative and two qualitative: the extraordinary intensity of his emotional life, his perverse instinctual predisposition, which inevitably marked him out to be a sado-masochist or a criminal, and his unanalysable artistic endownment. This combination might very well exist without neurosis; there are people who are complete masochists without being neurotic. Nevertheless, the balance of forces between his instinctual demands and the inhibitions opposing them (plus the available methods of sublimation) would even so make it necessary to classify Dostoevsky as what is known as an 'instinctual character'. But the position is obscured by the simultaneous presence of neurosis, which, as we have said, was not in the circumstances inevitable, but which comes into being the more readily, the richer the complication which has to[224] be mastered by the ego. For neurosis is after all only a sign that the ego has not succeeded in making a synthesis, that in attempting to do so it has forfeited its unity.

How then, strictly speaking, does his neurosis show itself? Dostoevsky called himself an epileptic, and was regarded as such by other people, on account of his severe seizures, which were accompanied by loss of consciousness, muscular convulsions and subsequent depression. Now it is highly probable that this so-called epilepsy was only a symptom of his neurosis and must accordingly be classified as hystero-epilepsy, that is, as severe hysteria. We cannot be completely certain on this point for two reasons, first, because the anamnestic data on Dostoevsky's alleged epilepsy are defective and untrustworthy, and secondly, because our understanding of pathological states combined with epileptiform seizures is imperfect.

To take the second point first. It is unnecessary here to reproduce the whole pathology of epilepsy, for it would throw no decisive light on the problem. But this may be said. The old *morbus sacer* is still in evidence as an ostensible clinical entity, the uncanny disease with its incalculable, apparently unprovoked convulsive seizures, its changing of the character into irritability and aggressiveness, and its progressive lowering of all the mental faculties. But the outlines of this picture are quite lacking in precision. The seizures, so savage in their onset, accompanied by biting of the tongue and incontinence of urine and working up to the dangerous *status epilepticus* with its risk of severe self-injuries, may, nevertheless, be reduced to brief periods of absence, or rapidly passing attacks of vertigo or may be replaced by short spaces of time during which the patient does something out of character, as though he were under the control of his unconscious. These seizures, though as a rule determined, in a way we do not understand, by purely physical causes, may nevertheless owe their first appearance to some purely mental[225] cause (a fright, for instance) or may react in other respects to mental excitations. However characteristic intellectual impairment may be in the overwhelming majority of cases, at least *one* case is known to us (that of Helmholtz) in which the affliction did not interfere with the highest intellectual achievement. (Other cases of which the same assertion has been made are either disputable or open to the same doubts as the case of Dostoevsky himself.) People who are victims of epilepsy may give an impression of dullness and arrested development, just as the disease often accompanies the most palpable idiocy and the grossest cerebral defects, even though not as a necessary component of the clinical picture. But these seizures with all their variations, also occur in other people who display complete mental development and, if anything, an excessive and as a rule insufficiently controlled emotional life. It is no wonder in these circumstances that it has been found impossible to maintain that 'epilepsy' is a single clinical entity. The similarity that we find in the manifest symptoms seems to call for a functional view of them. It is as though a mechanism for abnormal instinctual discharge had been laid down organically, which could be made use of in quite different circumstances—both in the case of disturbances of cerebral activity due to severe histolytic or toxic affections, and also in the case of inadequate control over the mental economy and at times when the activity of the energy operating in the mind reaches crisis-pitch. Behind the dichotomy we have a glimpse of the identity of the underlying mechanism of instinctual discharge. Nor can that mechanism stand remote from the sexual processes, which are fundamentally of toxic origin: the earliest physicians described copulation as a minor epilepsy, and thus recognized in the sexual act a mitigation and adaptation of the epileptic method of discharging stimuli.

The 'epileptic reaction,' as this common element may be called, is also undoubtedly at the disposal of the neurosis whose essence it is to get rid by somatic means[226] of quantities of excitation which it cannot deal with psychically. Thus the epileptic seizure becomes a symptom of hysteria and is adapted and modified by it just as it is by the normal sexual process of discharge. It is therefore quite right to distinguish between an organic and an 'affective' epilepsy. The practical significance of this is that a person who suffers from the first kind has a disease of the brain, while a person who suffers from the second kind is a neurotic. In the first case his mental life is subjected to an alien disturbance from without, in the second case the disturbance is an expression of his mental life itself.

It is extremely probable that Dostoevsky's epilepsy was of the second kind. This cannot, strictly speaking, be proved. To do so we should have to be in a position to insert the first appearance of the seizures and their subsequent fluctuations into the thread of his mental life; and for that we know too little. The descriptions of the seizures themselves teach us nothing and our information about the relations between the seizures and Dostoevsky's experiences is defective and often contradictory. The most probable assumption is that the seizures went back far into his childhood, that their place was taken to begin with by milder symptoms and that they did not assume an epileptic form until after the shocking experience of his eighteenth year—the murder of his father.[2] It would be very much to the[227] point if it could be established that they ceased completely during his exile in Siberia, but other accounts contradict this.[3]

The unmistakable connection between the murder of the father in *The Brothers Karamazov* and the fate of Dostoevsky's own father has struck more than one of his biographers, and has led them to refer to 'a certain modern school of psychology.' From the standpoint of psycho-analysis (for that is what is meant), we are tempted to see in that event the severest trauma and to regard Dostoevsky's reaction to it as the turning-point of his neurosis. But if I undertake to substantiate this view psycho-analytically, I am bound to risk the danger of being unintelligible to all those readers who are unfamiliar with the language and theories of psycho-analysis.

We have one certain starting-point. We know the meaning of the

---

[2] See René Fülöp-Miller (1924). [Cf. also the account given by Aimée Dostoevsky (1921) in her life of her father.] Of especial interest is the information that in the novelist's childhood 'something terrible, unforgettable and agonizing' happened, to which the first signs of his illness were to be traced (from an article by Suvorin in the newspaper *Novoe Vremya*, 1881, quoted in the introduction to Fülöp-Miller and Eckstein, 1925, xlv). See also Orest Miller (1882), 140: 'There is, however, another special piece of evidence about Fyodor Mikhailovich's illness, which relates to his earliest youth and brings the illness into connection with a tragic event in the family life of his parents. But, although this piece of evidence was given to me orally by one who was a close friend of Fyodor Mikhailovich, I cannot bring myself to reproduce it fully and precisely since I have had no confirmation of this rumour from any other quarter.' Biographers and scientific research workers cannot feel grateful for this discretion.

[3] Most of the accounts, including Dostoevsky's own, assert on the contrary that the illness only assumed its final, epileptic character during the Siberian exile. Unfortunately there is reason to distrust the autobiographical statements of neurotics. Experience shows that their memories introduce falsifications, which are designed to interrupt disagreeable causal connections. Nevertheless, it appears certain that Dostoevsky's detention in the Siberian prison markedly altered his pathological condition. Cf. Fülöp-Miller (1924, 1186).

first attacks from which Dostoevsky suffered in his early years, long
before the incidence of the 'epilepsy.' These attacks had the significance of death: they were heralded by a fear of death and consisted of
lethargic, somnolent states. The illness first came over him, while he
was still a boy, in the form of a sudden, groundless melancholy, a
feeling, as he later told his friend Soloviev, as though he were going to
die on the spot. And there in fact followed a state exactly similar to real
death. His brother Andrei tells us that even when he was quite young
Fyodor used to leave little notes about before he went to sleep, saying
that he was afraid he might fall into this death-like sleep during the
night and therefore begged that his burial should be postponed for five
days. (Fülöp-Miller and Eckstein, 1925, lx.) [228]

    We know the meaning and intention of such death-like seizures.
They signify an identification with a dead person, either with someone
who is really dead or with someone who is still alive and whom the
subject wishes dead. The latter case is the more significant. The attack
then has the value of a punishment. One has wished another person
dead, and now one *is* this other person and is dead oneself. At this
point psycho-analytical theory brings in the assertion that for a boy this
other person is usually his father and that the attack (which is termed
hysterical) is thus a self-punishment for a death-wish against a hated
father.

    Parricide, according to a well-known view, is the principal and
primal crime of humanity as well as of the individual. (See my essays
on *Totem and Taboo*, 1912–13.) It is in any case the main source of the
sense of guilt, though we do not know if it is the only one: researches
have not yet been able to establish with certainty the mental origin of
guilt and the need for expiation. But it is not necessary for it to be the
only one. The psychological situation is complicated and requires
elucidation. The relation of a boy to his father is, as we say, an
'ambivalent' one. In addition to the hate which seeks to get rid of the
father as a rival, a measure of tenderness for him is also habitually
present. The two attitudes of mind combine to produce identification
with the father; the boy wants to be in his father's place because he
admires him and wants to be like him, and also because he wants to
put him out of the way. This whole development now comes up
against a powerful obstacle. At a certain moment the child comes to
understand that an attempt to remove his father as a rival would be
punished by him with castration. So from fear of castration, that is, in
the interests of preserving his masculinity, he gives up his wish to
possess his mother and get rid of his father. In so far as this wish
remains in the unconscious it forms the basis of the sense of guilt. We
believe that what we have here been describing are the normal
processes, the [229] normal fate of the so-called 'Oedipus complex';
nevertheless it requires an important amplification.

    A further complication arises when the constitutional factor we call bisexuality is comparatively strongly developed in the child. For then, under the threat to the boy's masculinity by castration, his inclination becomes strengthened to deflect in the direction of femininity, to put himself instead in his mother's place and take over her role as object of his father's love. But the fear of castration makes *this* solution impossible as well. The boy understands that he must also submit to castration if he wants to be loved by his father as a woman. Thus both impulses, hatred of the father and being in love with the father, undergo repression. There is a certain psychological distinction in the fact that the hatred of the father is given up on account of fear of an *external* danger (castration), while the being in love with the father is treated as an *internal* instinctual danger, though fundamentally it goes back to the same external danger.

What makes hatred of the father unacceptable is *fear* of the father; castration is terrible, whether as a punishment or as the price of love. Of the two factors which repress hatred of the father, the first, the direct fear of punishment and castration, may be called the normal one; its pathogenic intensification seems to come only with the addition of the second factor, the fear of the feminine attitude. Thus a strong bisexual predisposition becomes one of the pre-conditions or reinforcements of neurosis. Such a predisposition must certainly be assumed in Dostoevsky, and it shows itself in a viable form (as latent homosexuality) in the important part played by male friendships in his life, in his strangely tender attitude towards rivals in love and in his remarkable understanding of situations which are explicable only by repressed homosexuality, as many examples from his novels show.

I am sorry, though I cannot alter the facts, if this exposition of the attitudes of hatred and love towards[230] the father and their transformations under the influence of the threat of castration seems to readers unfamiliar with psycho-analysis unsavoury and incredible. I should myself expect that it is precisely the castration complex that would be bound to arouse the most universal repugnance. But I can only insist that psycho-analytic experience has put these relations in particular beyond the reach of doubt and has taught us to recognize in them the key to every neurosis. This key, then, we must apply to our author's so-called epilepsy. So alien to our consciousness are the things by which our unconscious mental life is governed!

But what has been said so far does not exhaust the consequences of the repression of the hatred of the father in the Oedipus complex. There is something fresh to be added: namely that in spite of everything the identification with the father finally makes a permanent place for itself in the ego. It is received into the ego, but establishes itself there as a separate agency in contrast to the rest of the content of the ego. We then give it the name of super-ego and ascribe to it, the inheritor of the parental influence, the most important functions. If the father was hard, violent and cruel, the super-ego takes over those

attributes from him and, in the relations between the ego and it, the
passivity which was supposed to have been repressed is re-established.
The super-ego has become sadistic, and the ego becomes masochistic,
that is to say, at bottom passive in a feminine way. A great need for
punishment develops in the ego, which in part offers itself as a victim
to fate, and in part finds satisfaction in ill treatment by the super-ego
(that is, in the sense of guilt). For every punishment is ultimately
castration and, as such, a fulfilment of the old passive attitude towards the father. Even fate is, in the last resort, only a later father-
projection.

The normal processes in the formation of conscience must be
similar to the abnormal ones described here. We have not yet succeeded in fixing the boundary line[231] between them. It will be
observed that here the largest share in the event is ascribed to the
passive component of repressed femininity. Moreover, it must be of
importance as an accidental factor whether the father, who is feared in
any case, is also especially violent in reality. This was true in Dostoevsky's case, and we can trace back the fact of his extraordinary sense of
guilt and of his masochistic conduct of life to a specially strong
feminine component. Thus the formula for Dostoevsky is as follows: a
person of specially strong bisexual predisposition, who can defend
himself with special intensity against dependence on a specially severe
father. This characteristic of bisexuality comes as an addition to the
components of his nature that we have already recognized. His early
symptom of death-like seizures can thus be understood as a father-
identification on the part of his ego, permitted by his super-ego as a
punishment. 'You wanted to kill your father in order to be your father
yourself. Now you *are* your father, but a dead father'—the regular
mechanism of hysterical symptoms. And further: 'Now your father is
killing *you*.' For the ego the death symptom is a satisfaction in phantasy of the masculine wish and at the same time a masochistic satisfaction; for the super-ego it is a punishment satisfaction, that is, a
sadistic satisfaction. Both of them, the ego and the super-ego, carry
on the role of father.

To sum up, the relation between the subject and his father-object,
while retaining its content, has been transformed into a relation
between the ego and the super-ego—a new setting on a fresh stage.
Infantile reactions from the Oedipus complex such as these may
disappear if reality gives them no further nourishment. But the characteristics of the father remain the same, or rather, they deteriorate with
the years, and so too Dostoevsky's hatred for his father and his death-
wish against that wicked father were maintained. Now it is a dangerous
thing if reality fulfils such repressed wishes. The phantasy has become
reality and all defensive[232] measures are thereupon reinforced.
Dostoevsky's attacks now assumed an epileptic character; they still
undoubtedly signified an identification with his father as a punishment,

but they had become terrible, like his father's frightful death itself. What further content they had absorbed, particularly what sexual content, escapes conjecture.

One thing is remarkable: in the aura of the epileptic attack, one moment of supreme bliss is experienced. This may very well be a record of the triumph and sense of liberation felt on hearing the news of the death, to be followed immediately by an all the more cruel punishment. We have divined just such a sequence of triumph and mourning, of festive joy and mourning, in the brothers of the primal horde who murdered their father, and we find it repeated in the ceremony of the totem meal. If it proved to be the case that Dostoevsky was free from his seizures in Siberia, that would merely substantiate the view that his seizures were his punishment. He did not need them any longer when he was being punished in another way. But that cannot be proved. Rather does this necessity for punishment on the part of Dostoevsky's mental economy explain the fact that he passed unbroken through these years of misery and humiliation. Dostoevsky's condemnation as a political prisoner was unjust and he must have known it, but he accepted the undeserved punishment at the hands of the Little Father, the Tsar, as a substitute for the punishment he deserved for his sin against his real father. Instead of punishing himself, he got himself punished by his father's deputy. Here we have a glimpse of the psychological justification of the punishments inflicted by society. It is a fact that large groups of criminals long for punishment. Their super-ego demands it and so saves itself the necessity for inflicting the punishment itself.

Everyone who is familiar with the complicated transformation of meaning undergone by hysterical symptoms will understand that no attempt can be[233] made here to follow out the meaning of Dostoevsky's attacks beyond this beginning.[4] It is enough that we may assume that their original meaning remained unchanged behind all later accretions. We can safely say that Dostoevsky never got free from the feelings of guilt arising from his intention of murdering his father. They also determined his attitude in the two other spheres in which the father-relation is the decisive factor, his attitude towards the authority of the State and towards belief in God. In the first of these he ended up with complete submission to his Little Father, the Tsar, who had once performed with him in *reality* the comedy of killing which his seizures

---

[4] See *Totem and Taboo* (1912–13). The best account of the meaning and content of his seizures was given by Dostoevsky himself, when he told his friend Strakhov that his irritability and depression after an epileptic attack were due to the fact that he seemed to himself a criminal and could not get rid of the feeling that he had a burden of unknown guilt upon him, that he had committed some great misdeed, which oppressed him. (Fülöp-Miller, 1924, 1188.) In self-accusations like these psychoanalysis sees signs of a recognition of 'physical reality,' and it endeavours to make the unknown guilt known to consciousness.

had so often represented in *play*. Here penitence gained the upper hand. In the religious sphere he retained more freedom: according to apparently trustworthy reports he wavered, up to the last moment of his life, between faith and atheism. His great intellect made it impossible for him to overlook any of the intellectual difficulties to which faith leads. By an individual recapitulation of a development in world-history he hoped to find a way out and a liberation from guilt in the Christ ideal, and even to make use of his sufferings as a claim to be playing a Christ-like role. If on the whole he did not achieve freedom and became a reactionary, that was because the filial guilt, which is present in human beings generally and on which religious feeling is built, had in him attained a super-individual intensity and remained insurmountable even to his great intelligence. In writing this we are laying ourselves open to the charge of having abandoned the impartiality of analysis and of subjecting Dostoevsky to judgements that can only be[234] justified from the partisan standpoint of a particular philosophy of life. A conservative would take the side of the Grand Inquisitor and would judge Dostoevsky differently. The objection is just; and one can only say in extenuation that Dostoevsky's decision has every appearance of having been determined by an intellectual inhibition due to his neurosis.

It can scarcely be owing to chance that three of the masterpieces of the literature of all time—the *Oedipus Rex* of Sophocles, Shakespeare's *Hamlet* and Dostoevsky's *The Brothers Karamazov*—should all deal with the same subject, parricide. In all three, moreover, the motive for the deed, sexual rivalry for a woman, is laid bare.

The most straightforward is certainly the representation in the drama derived from the Greek legend. In this it is still the hero himself who commits the crime. But poetic treatment is impossible without softening and disguise. The naked admission of an intention to commit parricide, as we arrive at it in analysis, seems intolerable without analytical preparation. The Greek drama, while retaining the crime, introduces the indispensable toning-down in a masterly fashion by projecting the hero's unconscious motive into reality in the form of a compulsion by a destiny which is alien to him. The hero commits the deed unintentionally and apparently uninfluenced by the woman; this latter element is however taken into account in the circumstance that the hero can only obtain possession of the queen mother after he has repeated his deed upon the monster who symbolizes the father. After his guilt has been revealed and made conscious, the hero makes no attempt to exculpate himself by appealing to the artificial expedient of the compulsion of destiny. His crime is acknowledged and punished as though it were fully conscious—which is bound to appear unjust to our reason, but which psychologically is perfectly correct.

In the English play the presentation is more indirect; the hero does not commit the crime himself; it is carried[235] out by someone else, for whom it is not parricide. The forbidden motive of sexual rivalry for the woman does not need, therefore, to be disguised. Moreover, we see the hero's Oedipus complex, as it were, in a reflected light, by learning the effect upon him of the other's crime. He ought to avenge the crime, but finds himself, strangely enough, incapable of doing so. We know that it is his sense of guilt that is paralysing him; but, in a manner entirely in keeping with neurotic processes, the sense of guilt is displaced on to the perception of his inadequacy for fulfilling his task. There are signs that the hero feels this guilt as a super-individual one. He despises others no less than himself: 'Use every man after his desert, and who should 'scape whipping?'

The Russian novel goes a step further in the same direction. There also the murder is committed by someone else. This other person, however, stands to the murdered man in the same filial relation as the hero, Dmitry; in this other person's case the motive of sexual rivalry is openly admitted; he is a brother of the hero's, and it is a remarkable fact that Dostoevsky has attributed to him his own illness, the alleged epilepsy, as though he were seeking to confess that the epileptic, the neurotic, in himself was a parricide. Then, again, in the speech for the defence at the trial, there is the famous joke at the expense of psychology—it is a 'knife that cuts both ways': a splendid piece of disguise, for we have only to reverse it in order to discover the deepest meaning of Dostoevsky's view of things. It is not psychology that deserves to be laughed at, but the procedure of judicial enquiry. It is a matter of indifference who actually committed the crime; psychology is only concerned to know who desired it emotionally and who welcomed it when it was done. And for that reason all of the brothers, except the contrasted figure of Alyosha, are equally guilty, the impulsive sensualist, the sceptical cynic and the epileptic criminal. In *The Brothers Karamazov* there is one particularly revealing scene. In the course of his talk with Dmitry, Father Zossima[236] recognizes that Dmitry is prepared to commit parricide, and he bows down at his feet. It is impossible that this can be meant as an expression of admiration; it must mean that the holy man is rejecting the temptation to despise or detest the murderer and for that reason humbles himself before him. Dostoevsky's sympathy for the criminal is, in fact, boundless; it goes far beyond the pity which the unhappy wretch might claim, and reminds us of the 'holy awe' with which epileptics and lunatics were regarded in the past. A criminal is to him almost a Redeemer, who has taken on himself the guilt which must else have been borne by others. There is no longer any need for one to murder, since *he* has already murdered; and one must be grateful to him, for, except for him, one would have been obliged oneself to murder. That is not just kindly pity, it is identification on the basis of a similar murderous impulse—in fact, a slightly displaced narcissism. (In saying this, we are not disputing the ethical value of this kindliness.) This may perhaps be quite generally the mechanism of kindly sympathy with other people, a mechanism which one can discern with especial ease in the extreme case of the guilt-ridden novelist. There is no doubt that this sympathy by identification was a decisive factor in determining Dostoevsky's choice of material. He dealt first with the common criminal (whose motives are egotistical) and the political and religious criminal; and not until the end of his life did he come back to the primal criminal, the parricide, and use him, in a work of art, for making his confession.

The publication of Dostoevsky's posthumous papers and of his wife's diaries has thrown a glaring light on one episode in his life, namely the period in Germany when he was obsessed with a mania for gambling (cf. Fülöp-Miller and Eckstein, 1925), which no one could regard as anything but an unmistakable fit of pathological passion. There was no lack of rationalizations for this remarkable and unworthy behaviour. As often[237]happens with neurotics, Dostoevsky's burden of guilt had taken a tangible shape as a burden of debt, and he was able to take refuge behind the pretext that he was trying by his winnings at the tables to make it possible for him to return to Russia without being arrested by his creditors. But this was no more than a pretext; and Dostoevsky was acute enough to recognize the fact and honest enough to admit it. He knew that the chief thing was gambling for its own sake—*le jeu pour le jeu*.[5] All the details of his impulsively irrational conduct show this and something more besides. He never rested until he had lost everything. For him gambling was another method of self-punishment. Time after time he gave his young wife his promise or his word of honour not to play any more or not to play any more on that particular day; and, as she says, he almost always broke it. When his losses had reduced himself and her to the direst need, he derived a second pathological satisfaction from that. He could then scold and humiliate himself before her, invite her to despise him and to feel sorry that she had married such an old sinner; and when he had thus unburdened his conscience, the whole business would begin again next day. His young wife accustomed herself to this cycle, for she had noticed that the one thing which offered any real hope of salvation—his literary production—never went better than when they had lost everything and pawned their last possessions. Naturally she did not understand the connection. When his sense of guilt was satisfied by the punishments he had inflicted on himself, the inhibitions upon his work became less severe and he allowed himself to take a few steps along the way to success.[6]

[5] 'The main thing is the play itself,' he writes in one of his letters. 'I swear that greed for money has nothing to do with it, although Heaven knows I am sorely in need of money.'

[6] 'He always remained at the gaming tables till he had lost everything and was totally ruined. It was only when the damage was quite complete that the demon at last retired from his soul and made way for the creative genius.' (Fülöp-Miller and Eckstein, 1925, lxxxvi.)

What part of a gambler's long-buried childhood is it[238] that forces its way to repetition in his obsession for play? The answer may be divined without difficulty from a story by one of our younger writers. Stefan Zweig, who has incidentally devoted a study to Dostoevsky himself (1920), has included in his collection of three stories *Die Verwirrung der Gefühle* (1927) one which he calls 'Vierundzwanzig Stunden aus dem Leben einer Frau' ['Four-and-Twenty Hours in a Woman's Life']. This little masterpiece ostensibly sets out only to show what an irresponsible creature woman is, and to what excesses, surprising even to herself, an unexpected experience may drive her. But the story tells far more than this. If it is subjected to an analytical interpretation, it will be found to represent (without any apologetic intent) something quite different, something universally human, or rather something masculine. And such an interpretation is so extremely obvious that it cannot be resisted. It is characteristic of the nature of artistic creation that the author, who is a personal friend of mine, was able to assure me, when I asked him, that the interpretation which I put to him had been completely strange to his knowledge and intention, although some of the details woven into the narrative seemed expressly designed to give a clue to the hidden secret.

In this story, an elderly lady of distinction tells the author of an experience she has had more than twenty years earlier. She has been left a widow when still young and is the mother of two sons, who no longer need her. In her forty-second year, expecting nothing further of life, she happens, on one of her aimless journeyings, to visit the Rooms at Monte Carlo. There among all the remarkable impressions which the place produces, she is soon fascinated by the sight of a pair of hands which seem to betray all the feelings of the unlucky gambler with terrifying sincerity and intensity. These hands belong to a handsome young man—the author, as though unintentionally, makes him of the same age as the narrator's elder son—who, after losing everything, leaves the Rooms in the depth of despair,[239] with the evident intention of ending his hopeless life in the Casino gardens. An inexplicable feeling of sympathy compels her to follow him and make every effort to save him. He takes her for one of the importunate women so common there and tries to shake her off; but she stays with him and finds herself obliged, in the most natural way possible, to join him in his apartment at the hotel, and finally to share his bed. After this improvised night of love, she exacts a most solemn vow from the young man, who has now apparently calmed down, that he will never play again, provides him with money for his journey home and promises to meet him at the station before the departure of his train. Now, however, she begins to feel a great tenderness for him, is ready to sacrifice all she has in order to keep him and makes up her mind to go with him instead of saying goodbye. Various mischances delay her, so that she misses the train. In her longing for the lost one she returns once more to the Rooms and there, to her horror, sees once more the hands which had first excited her sympathy: the faithless youth had gone back to his play. She reminds him of his promise, but, obsessed by his passion, he calls her a spoil-sport, tells her to go and flings back the money with which she has tried to rescue him. She hurries away in deep mortification and learns later that she has not succeeded in saving him from suicide.

The brilliantly told, faultlessly motivated story is of course complete in itself and is certain to make a deep effect upon the reader. But analysis shows us that its invention is based fundamentally upon a wishful phantasy belonging to the period of puberty, which a number of people actually remember consciously. The phantasy embodies a boy's wish that his mother should herself initiate him into sexual life in order to save him from the dreaded injuries caused by masturbation. (The numerous creative works that deal with the theme of redemption have the same origin.) The 'vice' of masturbation is replaced by the mania for gambling; and the[240] emphasis laid upon the passionate activity of the hands betrays this derivation. The passion for play is an equivalent of the old compulsion to masturbate; 'playing' is the actual word used in the nursery to describe the activity of the hands upon the genitals. The irresistible nature of the temptation, the solemn resolutions, which are nevertheless invariably broken, never to do it again, the numbing pleasure and the bad conscience which tells the subject that he is ruining himself (committing suicide)—all these elements remain unaltered in the process of substitution. It is true that Zweig's story is told by the mother, not by the son. It must flatter the son to think: 'if my mother only knew what dangers masturbation involves me in, she would certainly save me from them by allowing me to lavish all my tenderness on her own body.' The equation of the mother with a prostitute, which is made by the young man in the story, is linked up with the same phantasy. It brings the unattainable within easy reach. The bad conscience which accompanies the phantasy brings about the unhappy ending of the story. It is also interesting to notice how the *façade* given to the story by its author seeks to disguise its analytic meaning. For it is extremely questionable whether the erotic life of women is dominated by sudden and mysterious impulses. On the contrary, analysis reveals an adequate motivation for the surprising behaviour of this woman who had hitherto turned away from love. Faithful to the memory of her dead husband, she had armed herself against all similar attractions; but—and here the son's phantasy is right —she did not, as a mother, escape her quite unconscious transference of love on to her son, and fate was able to catch her at this undefended spot.

If the mania for gambling, with the unsuccessful struggles to break the habit and the opportunities it affords for self-punishment, is a repetition of the compulsion to masturbate, we shall not be surprised to find that it occupied such a large space in Dostoevsky's life.[241] After all, we find no cases of severe neurosis in which the autoerotic satisfaction of early childhood and of puberty has not played a part; and the relation between efforts to suppress it and fear of the father are too well known to need more than a mention.[242]

The Two Dimensions of Reality in *The Brothers Karamazov*

ELISEO VIVAS

1

A novelist of the amplitude and depth of Dostoevsky is likely to be used by his many critics each for his own special purpose. Dostoevsky has been used by the founder of psychoanalysis and by innumerable amateur Freudians as an interesting pathological specimen—which of course he was. He has also been considered as forerunner of Freud in his own right, as social or political thinker, as religious prophet and as theologian. To each of these fields Dostoevsky contributed interesting speculations, often original and important. But he was and always remained a novelist, although he used the newspaper article and on occasion the lecture platform as vehicle of expression.

To say, however that Dostoevsky was a novelist is not to say that his ends were "aesthetic." Dostoevsky was not an artist because of the manner in which he handled his subject matter.[47] Henry James was unfair to him; it would be difficult, with the single exception of *The Possessed,* to suggest improvements in the architecture of his major novels, and this accords with the fact, known from external sources, that he thought long and deeply over their composition before he began them. But he never enjoyed the leisure required to bring his work to perfection. He was, nevertheless, an artist in the immediate, concrete manner in which he seized the subject matter of experience. His lack of interest in nature has often been noticed. It is as if he had

Eliseo Vivas, "The Two Dimensions of Reality in *The Brothers Karamazov,*" in *Creation and Discovery* (New York: Noonday Press, 1955), pp. 47–70. Reprinted by permission of the author.

an eye capable exclusively of spiritual vision and for which, therefore, the inanimate ambient world could become visible only insofar as it is helped to disclose the fluid dynamism of the psychic. He saw human beings as concrete, actual agents of action, agonists of the drama of actual life. If we contrast him with Kafka, who in some respects is not unworthy of being put on the same plane as the Russian, we see the difference between an eye which is primarily dramatic and one which is metaphysical. Kafka's world is a dynamic world, but its denizens are not genuine human beings but metaphysical hypostatizations representing certain aspects of the spiritual life. And for this reason what Kafka has to say about the soul does not refer to its concrete workings but to its dialectical tensions. As psychologist—in the sense in which the term can be used to refer to a man like Dostoevsky—Kafka was negligible, for we do not learn anything from his novels which we did not already know from either Kierkegaard or Freud. We learn something else no less valuable, but we do not learn anything new about what is behind our social masks. (From Kafka himself, considered as pathological specimen, we may, using his books as diagnostic evidence, learn about a modern neurosis—but for that we do not need Kafka, and the evidence he furnishes is neither reliable nor complete.)

These remarks are not intended to deny that Dostoevsky had a deep interest in social, ethical, and theological "problems." Indeed it is not difficult to isolate from his writings—or even from his novels alone —a body of doctrine to which we can be reasonably certain that he subscribed. But this doctrine, however truly espoused by him, is not representative of his total vision of the world, since it neglects the context of concrete circumstance which[48] is an essential element in the definition of its meaning for him. It is true, of course, that Dostoevsky had strong convictions. He was, for instance, a committed Christian and a political conservative. But to take his Christianity without the careful qualifications forced on us by the dramatic manner in which he conceived human destiny would be to view it falsely; his faith is not a purely intellectual, logically simple, structure; it is an extremely complex and internally heterogeneous mass of living insights —affective, moral, and intellectual—in tension, and ordered not after the manner of the philosopher but of the dramatist. When therefore one asks oneself what were Dostoevsky's views on Christianity, one has to consider (simplifying for the sake of the illustration) not only what we can find out about one character or a class of characters, but what he tells us in the novels as a whole. But what he tells us is a story, in which one character acts and talks in one way and another in another, each in terms of his own convincing logic and psychology. In this picture we will have to choose the truth, as Dostoevsky saw it, from the error. But this distinction cannot be made in the same sense in which one finds it made in a theological or an ethical treatise. Thus for instance, the reader, in putting Zossima and his beliefs and commitments at the center of the picture, will also have to remember that Dostoevsky was able to make the predicament of Shatov perfectly convincing through his conversation with Stavrogin (*The Possessed,* Part II, Chapt. 1, vii). The latter presses Shatov for a confession, to which Shatov can only answer: "I . . . I will believe in God." But Shatov insists on his faith in "The body of Christ, in Russian Orthodoxy," and asserts, at the same time, and not unaware of his difficulty, that "the object of every national movement, in every people and at every period of its existence is only the seeking for God, who must be its own God." We cannot avoid the conviction that Shatov's predicament was something which Dostoevsky had thought through passionately, and must be reckoned with in formulating his "views." But even if we reject the validity of Shatov's views, we cannot leave out of account the fact that it was in the teeth of the latter's assertions that Dostoevsky held his truth. From internal evidence alone one can formulate in abstract terms the philosophy of a good many novelists and among these of[49] some very great ones. But the error of some of the efforts to interpret the meaning of Dostoevsky's novels lies in the assumption that there are "doctrines" or "views" to be found in them—systematic structures of abstract thought involving major affirmations and denials—when what they contain is a dramatic organization of life, which includes characters most of whom are deeply interested in ideas.

All of this is to say that Dostoevsky fulfills the primary function of the artist, which so very few artists fulfill to the same extent. What he does is to organize or, better, to inform experience at the primary level and by means of animistic and dramatic categories. He does not undertake the philosopher's task, which is to abstract from experience already dramatically informed a formal structure in order to test its capacity to meet the exigencies of logical coherence and clarity of the rational intellect. What he does is to make life, insofar as man can do it, to be a poet and to give experience the form and intelligibility required by the whole mind, by the intellect and by the will. Without this primary organization life would either be chaos or instinctual routine. Men can live without philosophy, and not unsuccessfully, and history and anthropology show that for the most part they do. But without poetry human life is not possible.

I have labored this point because critics of Dostoevsky often undertake to give us systematic accounts of ideas and doctrines which Dostoevsky never could have entertained. Consider for instance Berdyaev's analysis. It is certainly one of the most searching, yet the total picture that we gather from it is that Dostoevsky was a theologian —which he was and was not; he was, since he could not view the human drama except as against the far horizon of eternity; but he was not, since a writer who sides with a character who says that the formula that twice two makes four does not meet with his acceptance —a thinker who distrusted the intellect as deeply as Dostoevsky did—is not a man who could have systematized his views, even if he had tried.

It has been said that Dostoevsky organized his works in terms of "an idea," but if what I have said is valid this statement cannot stand. Nor can we say, with another of his critics, that Dostoevsky dramatized his ideas. It is closer to the truth to say[50] that in his books, which are pure stories, the story is the idea. However the word "idea" is not being used here in its ordinary sense, but as it is employed in musical aesthetics. His stories, however, pure drama though they are, exhibit two levels or aspects of human reality: the psychological and the metaphysical. The first we have the right to expect of any serious novelist; only, psychologically Dostoevsky gives us considerably more than we are usually given by even the greatest of poets. The second very few readers demand and when they do very seldom get; indeed a number of his readers—particularly the "enlightened," "modern" ones—find it embarrassing and superfluous. When we look at the relationship between these levels we find that the philosophical informs (in the technical Aristotelian sense) the psychological and the latter in turn informs the story. The matter of the story (the object of imitation, in terms of Aristotelian aesthetics) is human experience. But Dostoevsky has informed it twice through his creative activity; and we, his readers, are able with his aid to grasp the constitution of human experience at a depth inpenetrable to all but the greatest poets.

2

The fresh and profound insights which Dostoevsky added to our knowledge of the human soul have been discussed thoroughly and admirably by many of his critics. All that needs to be done, therefore, is to remind the reader summarily of them; effort can be more profitably put into an analysis of the means through which these insights find expression. Thus, it is a commonplace that Dostoevsky anticipated Freud; that he was cognizant of the fact and understood the role of the unconscious; that he had a lucid knowledge of the duality exhibited by the human psyche and of its consequences; that he understood adequately the function of dreams; that he knew how shame leads a man to frustrate the actions through which he attempts to appease it, and how pride is the expression of insecurity and shame; how cruelty constitutes self-castigation, and how injured vanity takes revenge through love. In short, all the insights that have become commonplaces since Freud were clearly his own; nor can I think[51] of any important phenomenological datum furnished by the Viennese scientist which had escaped the observation of the Russian novelist.

But no abstract catalogue of "insights" can do justice to the breadth and depth of Dostoevsky's knowledge of the man that flourished in Europe and Russia in the Nineteenth Century and whose descendants have merely refined his neuroses. To do justice to his contribution we must view it not merely as the product of his psychological acumen but as the product of his art. In the vast canvas of his major novels—and this is particularly true of the greatest of them, *The Brothers*—one finds a series of "studies" of the various modalities through which certain types of human beings express themselves. The "type" however is gathered by us inductively from his unique specimens and it is not the former but the latter that interest Dostoevsky; nevertheless it is our intuition of the type in the individuals that makes them intelligible, while the individuals enable us to intuit the type, through the interrelationships of a complex system of similarities and contrasts which in this essay we cannot explore exhaustively but must be content to illustrate succinctly.

For illustration let us consider a type of individual with whom Dostoevsky was profoundly preoccupied and which, for lack of a better designation, we shall call "the liberal." In *The Brothers* there are at least five or six fairly complete "studies" of this type: Ivan, Smerdyakov, Miusov, Rakitin, and Kolya. But we could increase the number by adding some of the lesser characters. A liberal is, in religious matters, either an unbeliever or an agnostic; politically he is a reformist or a socialist; intellectually a "European" or Europeanized; and morally for Christian love he substitutes secular meliorism. Let us start with Ivan. What we know of him directly, by listening to him talk and observing his relation to his brothers and to his father, his feeling for Katerina Ivanovna, his conversations with Smerdyakov, and his illness, is far from exhausting the knowledge imparted about him, which comes to us also indirectly through what we learn of Smerdyakov, Rakitin, and Miusov—to mention only these. But young Kolya, too, throws a good deal of light on Ivan. Smerdyakov is, if you will allow the expression, an abyss of shallowness, a pure, corrupted[52] rationalist whose shallow intelligence has nothing to express but his pomaded lackey's vanity and trivial, upstart ambition, while Ivan is intelligent and, in an ordinary sense, sincere. But it is impossible to claim a complete understanding of Ivan until we have seen what can happen to his ideas when they are vulgarized by his bastard stepbrother and are put to the test pragmatically. Because Ivan, an intellectual, will not find out what is "the cash value" of his ideas, the visits to the sick lackey before the latter's suicide are a revelation to him of what he himself truly is and of how he, no less than Dmitry, is as much involved in the murder as the "stinking scoundrel." But neither Ivan nor Smerdyakov is fully intelligible until we have considered Rakitin, the theological student. Here is another upstart, trying to conceal his lowly origin; he is dishonorable, egotistical, unscrupulous and evil; he is vain and clever and he is self-deceived. He says he is a liberal and looks toward Europe for the salvation of Russia, but he is a dishonorable scoundrel interested in no one but himself, lacking the greatness and depth which Ivan in a measure has while possessing advantages which Smerdyakov lacks. He is not a physical murderer, but he is much more of a murderer than the brothers Karamazov: they murdered a depraved buffoon, but he murders innocent and naïve souls with the poison of his ideas. Dmitry fears him instinctively and he has already begun to corrupt young Kolya. In the United States today he would have proclaimed himself a "scientific humanist." This is why, with a wisdom which transcends his own intellectual shortcomings, Dmitry calls him a "Bernard," intuitively grasping the evil inherent in Rakitin's trust in science. Rakitin is both a contrast to and a mirror image of Ivan. The latter is honorable and his atheism is anguished. The former is a clever and shallow cad. But this is not all, for Ivan's advanced ideas must be considered by contrast with Miusov, the Europeanized Russian liberal who liked to give the impression that he had had his turn on the barricades in Paris. Ivan is not irredeemable, because he never loses his roots in the Russian soil, while Miusov has lost touch with his native Russia. With his wealth, family background, worldly sophistication, there is nothing inside the polished shell. He thinks of himself as a humanitarian but of course he really isn't, as his treatment of his nephew shows.[53] Now each of these characters throws light on the others, and placed in order from Ivan through Miusov, Rakitin, Smerdyakov, and Kolya (who is a boyish Ivan who has not yet lost the lovableness of childhood) they give us a complete picture of the anti-religious, rationalistic "liberal" in his various modalities. Several other series of contrasting modalities of the same type are "studied," for instance that of the monks, with Zossima, Paissy, Ioseff, Ferapont, and the monk from Obdorsk revealing the nature of Christian love, Christian renunciation of the world, and the pathological manifestations to which religion can give rise.

However it is not possible to understand an individual or a type through behavioral observation alone. We have to look into those secret crevices of the soul which ordinarily the individual does not suspect he has. In *The Brothers* we become acquainted with Ivan in the ordinary manner—see him act, hear him express his attitudes and his ideas. In the famous chapters 4 and 5 of Book V, entitled "Rebellion" and "The Grand Inquisitor," we see the depth of his concern for the religious problem and are given a first look into the nature of his difficulties. But Dostoevsky goes not only beyond Ivan's observed behavior, into his intellectual and moral structure, but into the unconscious double, which the Freudian would call the Id. This dimension of the personality had begun to be suspected in Dostoevsky's day, but not until Dostoevsky himself clarified it does literature begin fully to explore it. Freud's influence of course has made it the ordinary possession of literate men. (It is merely a matter of accuracy to remember, however, that Dostoevsky has not been the only writer before Freud who was aware of the fact that the human soul has a third, hidden dimension. Shakespeare, to take a trite example, used a somnambulistic dream to reveal a hidden sense of guilt. Nor was Freud the first psychologist to look into unconscious motives; Nietzsche used the method frequently and with tremendous success.) But Dostoevsky's grasp of hidden motives and of instinctual processes which express themselves deviously differs in a very important respect from that exhibited by contemporary novelists who go to Freud for their knowledge of the human soul. Dostoevsky conceives the soul as fluid and he presents it, so to speak, directly for his reader's inspection. Freudians have taught us to conceive[54] of the soul as a stiff mechanism made up of instincts and forces and energies which constitute a lumbering and creaking machine. Again, they have made current the doctrine that the phenomena which are not directly observable can be discovered only by inference. The reading of dreams, the analysis of the true meaning of everyday errors, the discovery of our hidden desires and intentions behind our ostensible discourse and behavior, thus become a silly and rather mechanical puzzling out of facile charades. And the result is that the conception of character of the novelist who has learned his human nature from Freud and not in the world, as Dostoevsky did, becomes the game of planting symbols according to a simple mechanical formula. In Freud, taken within the context of his therapeutic objectives, his analytic technique and his hypothetical constructions have a pragmatic justification. But when these constructions are used by amateurs for *their* purposes, what in the hands of the therapist is a source of insight degenerates rapidly into a shallow technique of obfuscation.

Dostoevsky reveals Ivan's unconscious through the use of a Freudian device—the hallucination or delirium which Ivan undergoes when he is ill and in which he meets the Devil who, he tells us twice, is himself. Through this "visit" we find out that the man who is preoccupied with the relation between Church and State, and who clearly grasps the consequence of the denial of freedom to man in favor of happiness, is really, at bottom, a man whose soul is ripped by a contradiction of which he is perfectly aware, but which he is not able to resolve. For while Ivan cannot believe in God he believes nevertheless in evil; but he goes beyond the Manicheans, for he gives evil the primacy. The Devil says to Ivan:

> I . . . simply ask for annihilation. No, live, I am told, for there'd be nothing without you. If everything in the universe were sensible, nothing would happen. There would be no events without you, and there must be events. So against the grain I serve to produce events and do what's irrational because I am commanded to. . . .

Of course the primacy of evil is qualified by the fact that the Devil accomplishes the creative task in obedience to a command, but nevertheless it is he who is the cause of events.[55]

In this same paragraph the "visitor" says to Ivan, "You are laughing—no, you are not laughing, you are angry again. You are forever angry, all you care about is intelligence. . . ." This is a very important remark to which we shall have to return. Let us however follow the conversation a few minutes longer. Ivan, "with a smile of hatred," asks:

> "Then even you don't believe in God?" . . .
> "What can I say—that is, if you are in earnest . . ."
> "Is there a God or not?" Ivan cried with the same savage intensity.
> "Ah, then you are in earnest! My dear fellow, upon my word I don't know. There! I have said it now!"
> "You don't know, but you see God? No, you are not some one apart, you are myself, you are I and nothing more! You are rubbish, you are my fancy!"
> "Well, if you like, I have the same philosophy as you, that would be true. *Je pense, donc je suis,* I know that for a fact, all the rest, all these worlds, God and even Satan—all that is not proved, to my mind. . . ."

Thus it turns out that Ivan, who believes in the primacy of evil, when you press him, does not know, is an absolute solipsist, and cannot discover proof of the world, of God, or even of Satan. The reason for his plight has already been given to us by his double: all he cares about is intelligence. And intelligence by itself is the source of all evil, and ultimately of despair. This is one of the things that Dostoevsky knew with the same certainty that Ivan knew that he was because he thought.

Through the delirium Dostoevsky has shown us the depths of Ivan's personality, but without the need to refer us to the Freudian code-book. Other devices which Dostoevsky employs in order to reveal the depths of the soul are not as easy to explain in general terms. One of the ways in which he does it is by having one character explain or reveal the meaning of another's actions; another is by having a character behave differently before each of the other characters with whom he has intercourse. Thus, Kolya, that delightfully lovable mischief-maker, is quite a different person with his fellows than he is with Alyosha or with the two children of the doctor's wife to whom his mother rented rooms.[56] This device gives us the complexity of a person. But usually in order to reveal the duality of the soul Dostoevsky conducts the dramatic narrative on two planes, in such wise that while a character, let us say, is protesting love for another, he is revealing hatred. As illustration take the manner in which Fyodor immediately upon entering the Elder's cell reveals through his buffoonery his deep shame.

> "Precisely to our time," cried Fyodor Pavlovitch, "but no sign of my son Dmitry. I apologize for him, sacred Elder!" (Alyosha shuddered all over at 'sacred elder.')

Before the guests have had time to take in the room, we, the readers, are plunged into the scene, shameful and comic, in which Fyodor's buffoonery discloses what it intends to cover, a sick soul consumed with the need to castigate itself. Or let us recall the chapter entitled "A Laceration in the Drawing Room," although almost any other episode chosen at random would serve as well. In this chapter Katerina Ivanovna, Mme. Hohlakov, Ivan, and Alyosha discuss Katerina's feeling for Dmitry. In this conversation Katerina tells the others that she does not know if she still loves Dmitry but that she feels pity for him and does not intend to abandon him even if he abandons her for Grushenka. She will not get in his way, she says, she will go to another town, but she will watch over him all her life. In the long run, she is certain to be able to show him that she loves him like a sister who has sacrificed her life to him. The moment that she begins to discuss Dmitry the reader begins to suspect that she is not quite sincere. The lack of sincerity is suggested by Dostoevsky himself through an explanation which he makes of the word "laceration" used by Madame Khokhlakova during the scene with Grushenka the preceding day. The word "sacrifice" used by Katerina Ivanovna gives her away completely, for her statement contrasts sharply with the picture already presented of her return of the money given her by Dmitry, the way in which she declares her love to Dmitry and asks him to marry her, telling him that she will be his chattel, when we have already seen how proud she really is. Dmitry earlier had told us that she loved her own virtue, not him. Now it becomes clear that Katerina Ivanovna is really[57] after revenge. In order to make Dmitry pay for the humiliations he has inflicted on her she is quite willing to put herself to a great deal of pain and sacrifice. This is fully confirmed by Alyosha's explosion when he tells her in a tone entirely out of harmony with his usual gentleness that she does not love Dmitry and wants to hurt him, and that she loves Ivan and wants to hurt him also. Later, at the trial, after Katerina Ivanovna has given evidence in Dmitry's favor, she becomes hysterical and gives the President of the Court the letter that convicts Dmitry, thus giving full reign to a hatred which until then she had tried to conceal from herself but which Dostoevsky had already clearly revealed to the reader. But no sooner is Dmitry sentenced than she repents and seeks his love, in an oblique way again.

3

Dostoevsky, of course, is not equipped to give a scientific explanation of those aspects of the personality which he discovered, nor is he interested in doing so. But he does more than give a mere phenomenological description of psychological processes. Indeed what gives his novels their depth and makes him one of the great thinkers of the modern world is that while positive science and naturalistic philosophy were straining to reduce man to purely naturalistic terms and to deny his metaphysical dimension in empirical terms, Dostoevsky was rediscovering that dimension in empirical terms which gave the lie to the modernists by reinvoking ancient truths whose old formulation had ceased to be convincing. With Kierkegaard, therefore, he was one of a small number of men who helped us forge the weapons with which to fend off the onrush of a naturalism bent on stripping us of our essentially human, our metaphysical, reality.

The reason that Dostoevsky is able to make these discoveries is not hard to find. It is well known that he started as a liberal and in "the house of the dead" gave up his youthful faith and turned toward orthodoxy. In Siberia he seems to have found, as many had found earlier and others have found since under adversity, that certain radical crises of the human spirit are neither intelligible nor manageable by means of any form of naturalistic philosophy.[58] Dostoevsky's shift has frequently puzzled his readers. How was it possible for him, they have asked, to come out of prison with a heart free of resentment at the cruel mockery of the execution and the horror of the four years of prison? But no one can claim to be a serious reader of Dostoevsky who does not know the answer to this question. His books are the answer—if we remember that below their psychological is to be found a metaphysical level. Dostoevsky exhibits a fact that to the average Christian seems ridiculous: that the guilt of one man is the guilt of all. We see in his pages how concern with iniquity expresses itself in a liberal and in a Christian way. The former repudiates self-guilt, and this leads to cannibalism; the latter accepts it and seeks to dissolve evil in selflessness and love. This is one insight which is clear and at which Dostoevsky arrived because he was a religious man and not a naturalist.

Dostoevsky's turn toward political conservatism and religious orthodoxy has been taken by many of his critics as evidence that he was wrong about social and religious questions in spite of his great powers as an artist and his psychological acuity. One of his critics, Simmons, dismisses his philosophy because it implies the denial of progress. His critics pretend to admire his art but deplore the content of his philosophy, obviously blind to the organic connection between his skill as artist, his perspicacity as psychologist, and his metaphysical insight. But one has not begun to understand him until one has grasped how, as Dostoevsky deepened his insight into human nature, he came more and more clearly to see that man's plight, his unhappiness, his divided soul, his need for self-laceration, his viciousness, his pride and his shame, his ills in short, flow from the same fountain-head, his unbelief. But unbelief is lack of love which in turn is hell. Dostoevsky progressively gains a firmer grasp of this insight through his creative work and in his last novel he is finally able successfully to bring into a comprehensive dramatic synthesis all his views of man and of his relations to his fellows and to the universe. At the heart of all questions, he comes to see, is the question of God, which is the question of love. Early in *The Brothers* he tells us that if Alyosha decided that[59]

God and immortality did not exist he would at once have become an atheist and a socialist. For socialism is not merely the labor question, it is before all things the atheistic question, the question of the form taken by atheism to-day, the question of the tower of Babel built without God, not to mount to Heaven from earth but to set up Heaven on earth.

This is to say that the labor question as it has been formulated since his day is the critical mode through which contemporary secularism manifests itself. For what socialism seeks is the recognition and institutionalization—achieved in Russia with the revolution—of a historical process already fully manifest in bourgeois society since the Seventeenth Century, but which the bourgeoisie has resisted acknowledging explicitly: Socialism would have man define his destiny exclusively in historical terms and denies the validity or necessity of metaphysical agencies. This process, which Dewey has called "the conclusion of natural science," would uproot as obstructive vestiges all religious institutions and beliefs and would substitute for them a conception of human destiny defined in terms of secular meliorism. This problem poses itself in Dostoevsky's mind in terms of a comprehensive metaphor possessing two conflicting terms, "Russia *versus* Europe." "Europe" promised happiness, but Dostoevsky saw that the price of an exclusively secular happiness was freedom. On this side one had only the choice between the Grand Inquisitor and the nihilism of Shigalyov and Pyotr Stepanovitch (in *The Possessed*), for whom is substituted the even more vicious and convincing figure of that "Bernard," Rakitin (in *The Brothers*). On the other side one had "Russia," and the term, Dostoevsky believed passionately, had to be accepted, so to speak, "as was" and without bargaining. The pictures of Shigalyov and Rakitin need not give us pause, however, even if we find that we cannot accept them as probable, since for these elements of the metaphor we can substitute at discretion the more up-to-date picture of the commissar with his automatic always at the back of the head of anyone who challenges his will. The truth of the insight is what matters; and at this moment history threatens to give us a complete and irrefutable demonstration of it. Confronted with such an either-or Dostoevsky chose "Russia" in the belief that the Russian[60] people would never accept atheistic socialism because they were too deeply and genuinely Christian. If we take the metaphor as intended we cannot fairly maintain that Dostoevsky was wrong. Indeed he came very close to the truth. But we must add in the same breath that one element of the metaphor's tenor, "Russia," was not in his day to be found and never will be either in history or in geography. The other element of the tenor, "Europe," includes "the state" which is force, with its instruments, mysticism, miracle, and authority;

justice without love, which involves blood; equality in things; and the multiplication of desires. Those at the controls of such a society are condemned to isolation and spiritual suicide and the ruled are sentenced to envy or murder. In contrast "Russia," which in justice to Dostoevsky we should remember he conceived as an ideal not yet adequately actualized, includes the church after it has absorbed the state, the denial of desires, the brotherhood of all living beings, spiritual dignity, justice in Christ and instead of pride and envy, humility and recognition of one's own sinfulness, and hence one's responsibility for the sins of all other men. The first term, "Europe," is of course exaggerated, and the second an improbable idealization. And if the reader should inquire by what means did Dostoevsky identify church bureaucracy and worldliness with Europe-Rome and what permitted him to clear the Russian hierarchy of all charges, so as to make it the potential kingdom of heaven on earth, the answer, unsatisfactory to us who do not love Russia and do not hate Europe as he did, runs something like this: Dostoevsky knew that the City of God is not of this world, but the route to it must be through "Russia" and not through "Europe," since the latter has been corrupted beyond redemption by the Grand Inquisitor, the Bernards and the socialists—who are three peas from the same pod. That a man who finds the ethical essence of Christianity in love could so inordinately hate Rome-Europe, or indeed could without shame exhibit the sores of his anti-Semitism, is something which no admirer of his ought to conceal or should try to apologize for. There is wisdom enough in him to make up for his ugly defects.

The question of God, however, is not a question that Dostoevsky settles easily by falling back on simple faith. Dostoevsky, who can[61] easily be convicted of blindness to the evils of his own state and church, refuses flatly to compromise with the facts of individual experience, untoward as he knows them to be to his religious beliefs. Referring to *The Brothers* he is quoted as having said:

Even in Europe there have never been atheistic expressions of such power. Consequently, I do not believe in Christ and His confession as a child, but my hosanna has come through a great furnace of doubt.

In his notebook, and referring to criticisms of *The Brothers*, he writes

The villains teased me for my ignorance and a retrograde faith in God. These thickheads did not dream of such a powerful negation of God as that put in "The (Grand) Inquisitor" and in the preceding chapter. . . . I do not believe in God like a fool (a fanatic). And they wished to teach me, and laughed over my backwardness! But their stupid natures did not dream of such a powerful negation as I have lived through. It is for them to teach me!

But we do not need this statement in order to discover how prolonged and anguished was his struggle with the religious question. All we need in order to make the discovery is a hasty reading of *The Brothers.* It has often been said of Milton that he did better by his Satan than by his God; and similarly it has been argued that Dostoevsky's good and saintly characters, Prince Myshkin in *The Idiot,* Father Tihon in *The Possessed,* and Father Zossima, are far more tenuous than the human devils that abound in his books. There is, I believe, some truth in this observation. But the statement is partly false if it is forgotten that Dostoevsky believed that genuine goodness can only be reached by those who plunge down to the bottom and there, in their darkest hour, somehow find God. This was his own personal experience and it was borne out by observation. If this is true, it is Zossima, and not Prince Myshkin (in *The Idiot*), who is the truly good man. But it cannot be denied that none of his good or saintly characters—Sonia in *Crime and Punishment,* Myshkin, and even Zossima—is endowed with as dense and authentic a humanity as his evil characters. Dostoevsky was aware of this criticism, which is not difficult[62] to answer. The reason why they are not, is that genuine goodness and saintliness are harmonious, unassertive and hence undramatic, dull, affairs. But this is not a comment on them or on Dostoevsky but on us, his readers.

Be that as it may, in the portraits of his great sinners and criminals Dostoevsky did not study merely the effects of vice but the effects of disbelief. He traces the effect of vice, pride, and hatred on the disintegration of the personality and he is most successful in drawing men in whom vice is connected with their repudiation of their condition as creatures and with their consequent effort to set themselves up wittingly or unwittingly as gods. And he shows how men who do not believe in God end up by believing in their own omnipotence. At the root of this transposition we find pride, which would not have welled up and flooded one's consciousness had he been able to grasp clearly the fact that he is a creature, which is to say, finite and dependent. But this kind of pride is in turn traced by Dostoevsky to the misuse of reason, the belief that science and the intelligence are enough for the development of human life. In the early *Notes from the Underground* he stated fully what for lack of a more adequate term we must refer to as his anti-intellectualism. From that book on, the worst evil of his characters is in one way or another connected with the belief in the self-sufficiency of the intellect. There is of course evil in the sensual animalism of Fyodor Karamazov, but there is greater evil in Rakitin. And the greatest responsibility for the crime must be assumed by Ivan, the source of whose corruption we have already looked at.

But Dostoevsky is not a propagandist and much less a dogmatist. He is, in the most important sense of that word of many meanings, a genuine philosopher, for he really inquired, questioned, sought the truth, instead of seeking bad reasons for what he already believed on faith (if I may be allowed to spoil Bradley's famous epigram). It would not be inexact to say that Dostoevsky was forced against his will by the facts that his experience disclosed to him into the conviction that atheism is fatal practically and false theoretically. But he would never allow any argument or any fact to involve him in the denial of an aspect of experience which presented itself to him as authentic.[63]

But then, how can one believe in God?—How, that is, if one is not a peasant woman of simple faith but has the brains, the education, and the range of experience of an Ivan? One cannot, is Ivan's answer, so long as the evil of the world remains to give the lie to God. It is known that Dostoevsky called chapters 4 and 5 of Book V of *The Brothers*—to which we have already referred—"the culminating point of the novel." The first of these chapters contains Ivan's case against God. I call it "Ivan's dossier," because he introduced his case by saying to Alyosha that he is "fond of collecting certain facts and anecdotes copied from newspapers." This is data one cannot neglect, if one is going to attempt an explanation of the ways of God to man. There is the case of Richard, the Swiss savage, burnt at the stake in Geneva; the case of the Russian peasant who beats the horse in the eyes, and then the cases of the children, culminating in the story of the child thrown to the savage dogs in front of his mother.

The General orders the child to be undressed; the child is stripped naked. He shivers numb with terror, not daring to cry. . . . "Make him run" commands the General. "Run, run!" shout the dog-boys. The boy runs. "At him!" yells the General, and he sets the whole pack of hounds on the child. The hounds catch him and tear him to pieces before his mother's eyes.

One sentence completes the story, and it is superbly ironic in its bathos: "I believe the General was afterwards declared incapable of administering his estates." How, in view of such things, can you believe in Providence?

Dostoevsky knew perfectly well that in his own terms Ivan could not be answered. The furnace of doubt through which Dostoevsky said he had passed before he was able to arrive at his faith, consisted of at least two flames: the devastating knowledge he had of the criminal and depraved tendencies to be found at the bottom of the human soul and of which he gives us in *The Brothers* three superb examples, Fyodor, Rakitin, and Smerdyakov; and the knowledge he has that injustice is inherent in the structure of human living and cannot be dislodged from it. These two flames, as I may continue to call them, cannot be smothered with social reforms or mechanical improvements. This is the hope of the[64] rationalistic liberal, a hope that springs from his shallow grasp of human nature, and which, when it is not a mere pretense, as it is with Miusov, is a diabolical lie, as it is with Rakitin. In "The Grand Inquisitor" he finally brought to full expression the implication of the conflict between God and freedom on the one hand and the atheistic effort to bring heaven to earth by dispensing with God on the other. The point of the conflict cannot be stated abstractly without vulgarizing it, but since the long marginal commentary which would be required to do it justice is not possible here we must risk a brief statement. The conflict is between The Grand Inquisitor and Father Zossima. The alternatives are clear and exhaustive, since compromises are unstable and futile for they reproduce the undesirable features of both terms and none of the virtues of either. The villain of Ivan's poem is Jesus, who rejected the prizes offered him by The Great Spirit, Satan, and wittingly loaded man with a burden he cannot carry, freedom. It is not freedom that man wants, but miracle, mystery, and authority. He "is tormented by no greater anxiety than to find someone quickly to whom he can hand over that gift of freedom with which the ill-fated creature is born." The Roman Catholic Church has managed to correct the harm that Jesus attempted to do, and socialism but carries on from where Rome leaves off. In order to give man happiness it has been necessary for the Church to take the sword of Caesar and in taking it of course it rejected Jesus and chose Satan. For this reason Dostoevsky believes that socialism and Catholicism are identical as to ends: both seek to relieve man of the burden of freedom. But happiness without God is a delusion that leads men to devour one another or leads a strong man to gain power over his fellows for their own good, and gives them happiness at the price of keeping them from realizing their full humanity.

The alternative then to the ideal of The Grand Inquisitor is to accept God, freedom, and immortality. But this alternative has somehow to dispose of Ivan's dossier. To give man freedom is not only to open to him the door of eternal salvation, it is also to open the other door, whose threshold hope cannot cross. You cannot have Heaven without Hell; Heaven entails the General and his dogs. It is a terrible choice and no one knew more clearly than[65] Dostoevsky how terrible it was: happiness without freedom, or freedom *and* hell. Ivan's dossier cannot be exorcised into thin air. What is the answer? It is found in Father Zossima, and that means in our acceptance of our condition as creatures. This calls for love at the heart of human existence; but not the abstract and self-deceived love of your rationalistic liberal, your Miusov, but the personal love of Father Zossima. The answer resolves the conflict because it reveals that hell is life without love. And it also reveals that Ivan's dossier is possible only through a lie. For Ivan forgets that he is a creature, that he therefore has no right to challenge God, nor to demand that God answer his question in a manner satisfactory to him or he will refuse to accept His world and "return His ticket." This is, of course, to fall back on the inscrutable designs of the Deity which Spinoza called the refuge of ignorance. But Dostoevsky is not frightened by this retort, since he is faced clearly with an either/or: either God and love or the world which the Rakitins, the Miusovs, and the Smerdyakovs would create, the world of the Grand Inquisitor. It will be retorted that what I have said makes no sense, for freedom rejects mystery and it is mystery Dostoevsky invokes when he invokes God. The answer is simple: what the Grand Inquisitor wants is mystification, superstition, and that is totally different from the mystery entailed by belief in a God of love.

It should not be overlooked, besides, that what Alyosha calls Ivan's rebellion is the challenge launched against God by a man who claims to be concerned with human tears:

I took the case of children only to make my case clearer. Of the other tears of humanity with which the earth is soaked from the crust to its center, I will say nothing.

But it is simply not true that Ivan loves man as he says he does. If he did, he would follow in the steps of Father Zossima. That, and that only, is the way of true love. The man who loves his fellows has neither time nor energy for rebellion. He realizes that he himself is guilty, for even if his own hands are not stained with blood, he is responsible for the blood shed by his fellows. And instinct with love and active about the misery of others he no longer hugs with bravado his little dossier against God. But this[66] Ivan was not capable of doing at this point in the novel. He first had to be an accomplice in the murder of his father, had to be brought by his complement, Smerdyakov, to see his complicity, and had to peer into the depths of his soul in the form of the devil, before there could be any hope that he might be reborn. As the novel closes we are left with the clear indication that that hope is a possibility. But we are also left with the insight that so long as a man remains in the world that possibility cannot be fully realized. Ultimately Dostoevsky's vision of secular life is supremely tragic.

4

The psychological and the metaphysical make up the concrete reality of Dostoevsky's human world. But the structure of that world and the values it embodies have only been referred to in passing, and the reader is entitled to ask what the critic takes them to be. Unfortunately a complete answer would require a study at least as long as the present; in the last few pages of this essay only a hasty sketch can be attempted.

By way of introduction let us note that Dostoevsky's great novels mirror comprehensively the bourgeois world of the Nineteenth Century, which is to say, a world in the first stages of an illness, which we today have the melancholy opportunity of seeing in a more advanced phase. Dostoevsky had a ground for optimism on which we cannot fall back: his faith that Zossima's "Russia" marked the direction toward which civilization would turn. But Rakitin and the other "Bernards" whom Dostoevsky dreaded have won, and the process by which man will destroy himself is already well under way. Thus the utopia of the

Grand Inquisitor turns out to be a relatively pleasant morning dream as compared with the brave new world which our twentieth-century Bernards and Rakitins have begun to build. We are not going back to Zossima's "Russia," but to the world of Marx and Dewey. Shigalyov was a poet whose prophecy fell too short. Dostoevsky feared Fourrier and Claude Bernard; we face the realities of Dewey and Marx.

What Dostoevsky achieves is a definition of the destiny of Western Man: he defines the alternatives and the corresponding values[67] of each. Against the background of nineteenth-century humanity move the heroes of his books. In his inclusive world there is only one specimen lacking, the militant industrial proletariat, and the reason is that he did not have models of this type in his industrially backward native land. Saints, murderers, debauchees, intellectuals mad with pride, virginal whores and depraved ladies are the heroes. The mediocre, who lack the energy to become heroes, are pathetic rather than tragic, self-deceived rather than hypocritical, and unhappy, although ignorant of the malaise from which they suffer. Out of this mass emerge two groups of men who are in opposition: the saintly on the one side and those I have called "liberals" and the sensualists on the other. Zossima is Dostoevsky's outstanding religious character, but Dostoevsky "studies" the religious type as objectively as he studies the other, and unsparingly exhibits the pathological perversions to which it can lead. This group is not exclusively made up of monks or priests, but includes also self-deceived "ladies of little faith" and "peasant women who have faith." Alyosha, who is called the hero of the book, belongs to this group of course, but his portrait is not fully enough developed for us to be able to say whether in the two volumes that were never written, his role was to mediate between the world of Zossima and the secular world. Is it possible to live according to the teachings of Zossima outside the monastery? Could a Karamazov do it? Perhaps Alyosha can, although Prince Myshkin could not. We shall never know.

Between sensualists and liberals there is a formal identity of ends, since the sensualist uses his body as instrument of pleasure and the intellectual his mind. As between these two types of men it may be hard to choose; but Dostoevsky seems to reveal in a man like Rakitin a greater depth of villainy than in Fyodor, since he is the source of far-spreading corruption, while the power of evil of a man like Fyodor Karamazov is limited to himself and those he uses for his pleasure. The sensualist is consumed with self-hatred and shame, and his end is to destroy himself, but the intellectual, consumed with pride, seeks either to challenge God or to become God, and succeeds in wreaking havoc among men. Above the adult world is the world of the children, whom Dostoevsky could depict with inward fidelity, without sentimentality or[68] condescension. Most of his children are lovable but some, like Kolya, have already begun to be corrupted, and some are full blown little demons: Lise knows clearly that she loves evil and wants to destroy herself.

From Dostoevsky's novels, as I have insisted, one can neither abstract an ethical imperative nor a systematic philosophy capable of doing justice to the dramatic tensions to be found in life as he grasped it. A Marxist or a Deweyan will find that the picture of Zossima expresses the failure of nerve which he thinks characterizes our society. But there is no question that the picture painted by Dostoevsky, for all its dramatic irony, reveals a vision of the world in which the answer to Ivan is found in the love of Zossima. In other words, Dostoevsky views human destiny from the standpoint of an anti-rationalism which is more radical than that of Kierkegaard or Schopenhauer or Nietzsche. His rejection of "reason,"—"the stone wall constituted of the laws of nature, of the deductions of learning, and of the science of mathematics,"—is clearly stated very early in his *Notes from the Underground*. But the full implications of "reason," and of his rejection of it, awaited the explorations which are to be found in his subsequent work, and particularly in the four major novels. It is his anti-rationalism which is the "source and head" of all his insights and attitudes, theological, psychological and political, and which therefore furnishes the ground on which he is often disposed of as a reactionary. That he should be dismissed in this way is intelligible; what is difficult to understand is how any serious reader can accept his psychological insights and simply ignore the matrix whence they rise and the theoretical and practical implications to which they lead. At a time when the conflict between "life" and "reason"—the reason of the stone wall—was not yet resolved, Dostoevsky, with full awareness of what he was doing, threw his lot on the side of life and against the stone wall. Old Karamazov is a depraved buffoon, shameless and corrupt; but there is a tremendous energy in him and love of life—the energy of the Karamazovs—and there is passion; there is something elemental in his sinfulness which flows whence all life, whether good or evil, flows, and which therefore draws our admiration since it is true, as Lise says, that in our secret hearts we all love evil. By contrast Rakitin is a thoroughly[69] depraved and contemptible reptile with nothing to his favor. Thus the meaning of human destiny which Dostoevsky reveals is not difficult to formulate: a life not built on love is not human, and a world without God is a world in which a triumphant cannibal frees the mass from the burden of their freedom in exchange for happiness. What Dostoevsky could not admit to himself is that the Bernards in the not too long run will win. One may sympathize with the writer of the *Notes from the Underground* when he says, "I am not going to accept that wall merely because I have to run up against it, and have no means to knock it down." But one should not forget that the tragic alternative is ineluctable: either accept it or smash your head against it.[70]

Ivan and Rebellion against God

ALBERT CAMUS

If the romantic rebel extols evil and the individual, this does not mean that he sides with mankind, but merely with himself. Dandyism, of whatever kind, is always dandyism in relation to God. The individual, in so far as he is a created being, can oppose himself only to the Creator. He has need of God, with whom he carries on a kind of a gloomy flirtation. Armand Hoog[1] rightly says that, despite its Nietzschean atmosphere, God is not yet dead even in romantic literature. Damnation, so clamorously demanded, is only a clever trick played on God. But with Dostoevsky the description of rebellion goes a step farther. Ivan Karamazov sides with mankind and stresses human innocence. He affirms that the death sentence which hangs over them is unjust. Far from making a plea for evil, his first impulse, at least, is to plead for justice, which he ranks above the divinity. Thus he does not absolutely deny the existence of God. He refutes Him in the name of a moral value. The romantic rebel's ambition was to talk to God as one equal to another. Evil was the answer to evil, pride the answer to cruelty. Vigny's ideal, for example, is to answer silence with silence. Obviously, the point is to raise oneself to the level of God, which already is blasphemy. But there is no thought of disputing the power or position of the deity. The blasphemy is reverent, since every blasphemy is, ultimately, a participation in holiness.

With Ivan, however, the tone changes. God, in His turn, is put on trial. If evil is essential to divine creation, then creation is unacceptable. Ivan will no longer have recourse to this mysterious God, but to a higher principle[55]—namely, justice. He launches the essential undertaking of rebellion, which is that of replacing the reign of grace by

Reprinted by permission of the publisher from "The Rejection of Salvation," in *The Rebel* by Albert Camus, trans. by Anthony Bower. Copyright © 1956 by Alfred A. Knopf, Inc.

[1] *Les Petits Romantiques.*

the reign of justice. He simultaneously begins the attack on Christianity. The romantic rebels broke with God Himself, on the principle of hatred. Ivan explicitly rejects the mystery and, consequently, God, on the principle of love. Only love can make us consent to the injustice done to Martha, to the exploitation of workers, and, finally, to the death of innocent children.

"If the suffering of children," says Ivan, "serves to complete the sum of suffering necessary for the acquisition of truth, I affirm from now onward that truth is not worth such a price." Ivan rejects the basic interdependence, introduced by Christianity, between suffering and truth. Ivan's most profound utterance, the one which opens the deepest chasms beneath the rebel's feet, is his *even if:* "I would persist in my indignation even if I were wrong." Which means that even if God existed, even if the mystery cloaked a truth, even if the starets Zossima were right, Ivan would not admit that truth should be paid for by evil, suffering, and the death of innocents. Ivan incarnates the refusal of salvation. Faith leads to immortal life. But faith presumes the acceptance of the mystery and of evil, and resignation to injustice. The man who is prevented by the suffering of children from accepting faith will certainly not accept eternal life. Under these conditions, even if eternal life existed, Ivan would refuse it. He rejects this bargain. He would accept grace only unconditionally, and that is why he makes his own conditions. Rebellion wants all or nothing. "All the knowledge in the world is not worth a child's tears." Ivan does not say that there is no truth. He says that if truth does exist, it can only be unacceptable. Why? Because it is unjust. The struggle between truth and justice is begun here for the first time; and it will never end. Ivan, by nature a solitary and therefore a moralist, will satisfy himself with a kind of metaphysical Don Quixotism. But a few decades more and an immense political conspiracy will attempt to prove that justice is truth.

In addition, Ivan is the incarnation of the refusal to be the only one saved. He throws in his lot with the damned and, for their sake, rejects eternity. If he had[56] faith, he could, in fact, be saved, but others would be damned and suffering would continue. There is no possible salvation for the man who feels real compassion. Ivan will continue to put God in the wrong by doubly rejecting faith as he would reject injustice and privilege. One step more and from *All or Nothing* we arrive at *Everyone or No One.*

This extreme determination, and the attitude that it implies, would have sufficed for the romantics. But Ivan,[2] even though he also gives way to dandyism, really lives his problems, torn between the negative and the affirmative. From this moment onward, he accepts the consequences. If he rejects immortality, what remains for him? Life in its

---

[2] It is worth noting that Ivan is, in a certain way, Dostoevsky, who is more at ease in this role than in the role of Alyosha.

most elementary form. When the meaning of life has been suppressed, there still remains life. "I live," says Ivan, "in spite of logic." And again: "If I no longer had any faith in life, if I doubted a woman I loved, or the universal order of things, if I were persuaded, on the contrary, that everything was only an infernal and accursed chaos—even then I would want to live." Ivan will live, then, and will love as well "without knowing why." But to live is also to act. To act in the name of what? If there is no immortality, then there is neither reward nor punishment. "I believe that there is no virtue without immortality." And also: "I only know that suffering exists, that no one is guilty, that everything is connected, that everything passes away and equals out." But if there is no virtue, there is no law: "Everything is permitted."

With this "everything is permitted" the history of contemporary nihilism really begins. The romantic rebellion did not go so far. It limited itself to saying, in short, that everything was not permitted, but that, through insolence, it allowed itself to do what was forbidden. With the Karamazovs, on the contrary, the logic of indignation turned rebellion against itself and confronted it with a desperate contradiction. The essential difference is that the romantics allowed themselves moments of complacence, while Ivan compelled himself to do evil so as to be coherent. He would not allow himself to be good. Nihilism is not only despair and negation but, above all, the[57] desire to despair and to negate. The same man who so violently took the part of innocence, who trembled at the suffering of a child, who wanted to see "with his own eyes" the lamb lie down with the lion, the victim embrace his murderer, from the moment that he rejects divine coherence and tries to discover his own rule of life, recognizes the legitimacy of murder. Ivan rebels against a murderous God; but from the moment that he begins to rationalize his rebellion, he deduces the law of murder. If all is permitted, he can kill his father or at least allow him to be killed. Long reflection on the condition of mankind as people sentenced to death only leads to the justification of crime. Ivan simultaneously hates the death penalty (describing an execution, he says furiously: "His head fell, in the name of divine grace") and condones crime, in principle. Every indulgence is allowed the murderer, none is allowed the executioner. This contradiction, which Sade swallowed with ease, chokes Ivan Karamazov.

He pretends to reason, in fact, as though immortality did not exist, while he only goes so far as to say that he would refuse it even if it did exist. In order to protest against evil and death, he deliberately chooses to say that virtue exists no more than does immortality and to allow his father to be killed. He consciously accepts his dilemma; to be virtuous and illogical, or logical and criminal. His prototype, the devil, is right when he whispers: "You are going to commit a virtuous act and yet you do not believe in virtue; that is what angers and torments you." The question that Ivan finally poses, the question that constitutes the real progress achieved by Dostoevsky in the history of rebellion, is the only one in which we are interested here: can one live and stand one's ground in a state of rebellion?

Ivan allows us to guess his answer: one can live in a state of rebellion only by pursuing it to the bitter end. What is the bitter end of metaphysical rebellion? Metaphysical revolution. The master of the world, after his legitimacy has been contested, must be overthrown. Man must occupy his place. "As God and immortality do not exist, the new man is permitted to become God." But what does becoming God mean? It means, in fact, recognizing that everything is permitted and refusing to[58] recognize any other law but one's own. Without it being necessary to develop the intervening arguments, we can see that to become God is to accept crime (a favorite idea of Dostoevsky's intellectuals). Ivan's personal problem is, then, to know if he will be faithful to his logic and if, on the grounds of an indignant protest against innocent suffering, he will accept the murder of his father with the indifference of a man-god. We know his solution: Ivan allows his father to be killed. Too profound to be satisfied with appearances, too sensitive to perform the deed himself, he is content to allow it to be done. But he goes mad. The man who could not understand how one could love one's neighbor cannot understand either how one can kill him. Caught between unjustifiable virtue and unacceptable crime, consumed with pity and incapable of love, a recluse deprived of the benefits of cynicism, this man of supreme intelligence is killed by contradiction. "My mind is of this world," he said; "what good is it to try to understand what is not of this world?" But he lived only for what is not of this world, and his proud search for the absolute is precisely what removed him from the world of which he loved no part.

The fact that Ivan was defeated does not obviate the fact that once the problem is posed, the consequence must follow: rebellion is henceforth on the march toward action. This has already been demonstrated by Dostoevsky, with prophetic intensity, in his legend of the Grand Inquisitor. Ivan, finally, does not distinguish the creator from his creation. "It is not God whom I reject," he says, "it is creation." In other words, it is God the father, indistinguishable from what He has created.[3] His plot to usurp the throne, therefore, remains completely moral. He does not want to reform anything in creation. But creation being what it is, he claims the right to free himself morally and to free all the rest of mankind with him. On the other hand, from the moment when the spirit of rebellion, having accepted the concept of "everything is permitted" and[59] "everyone or no one," aims at reconstruct-

---

[3] Ivan allows his father to be killed and thus chooses a direct attack against nature and procreation. Moreover, this particular father is infamous. The repugnant figure of old Karamazov is continually coming between Ivan and the God of Alyosha.

ing creation in order to assert the sovereignty and divinity of man, and from the moment when metaphysical rebellion extends itself from ethics to politics, a new undertaking, of incalculable import, begins, which also springs, we must note, from the same nihilism. Dostoevsky, the prophet of the new religion, had foreseen and announced it: "If Alyosha had come to the conclusion that neither God nor immorality existed, he would immediately have become an atheist and a socialist. For socialism is not only a question of the working classes; it is above all, in its contemporary incarnation, a question of atheism, a question of the tower of Babel, which is constructed without God's help, not to reach to the heavens, but to bring the heavens down to earth."[4]

After that, Alyosha can, in fact, treat Ivan with compassion as a "real simpleton." The latter only made an attempt at self-control and failed. Others will appear, with more serious intentions, who, on the basis of the same despairing nihilism, will insist on ruling the world. These are the Grand Inquisitors who imprison Christ and come to tell Him that His method is not correct, that universal happiness cannot be achieved by the immediate freedom of choosing between good and evil, but by the domination and unification of the world. The first step is to conquer and rule. The kingdom of heaven will, in fact, appear on earth, but it will be ruled over by men—a mere handful to begin with, who will be the Caesars, because they were the first to understand— and later, with time, by all men. The unity of all creation will be achieved by every possible means, since everything is permitted. The Grand Inquisitor is old and tired, for the knowledge he possesses is bitter. He knows that men are lazy rather than cowardly and that they prefer peace and death to the liberty of discerning between good and evil. He has pity, a cold pity, for the silent prisoner whom history endlessly deceives. He urges him to speak, to recognize his misdeeds, and, in one sense, to approve the actions of the Inquisitors and of the Caesars. But the prisoner does not speak. The enterprise will continue, therefore, without him; he will be killed.[60] Legitimacy will come at the end of time, when the kingdom of men is assured. "The affair has only just begun, it is far from being terminated, and the world has many other things to suffer, but we shall achieve our aim, we shall be Caesar, and then we shall begin to think about universal happiness."

By then the prisoner has been executed; the Grand Inquisitors reign alone, listening to "the profound spirit, the spirit of destruction and death." The Grand Inquisitors proudly refuse freedom and the bread of heaven and offer the bread of this earth without freedom. "Come down from the cross and we will believe in you," their police agents are already crying on Golgotha. But He did not come down and, even, at the most tortured moment of His agony, He protested to

---

[4] These questions (God and immortality) are the same questions that socialism poses, but seen from another angle.

God at having been forsaken. There are, thus, no longer any proofs, but faith and the mystery that the rebels reject and at which the Grand Inquisitors scoff. Everything is permitted and centuries of crime are prepared in that cataclysmic moment. From Paul to Stalin, the popes who have chosen Caesar have prepared the way for Caesars who quickly learn to despise popes. The unity of the world, which was not achieved with God, will henceforth be attempted in defiance of God.

But we have not yet reached that point. For the moment, Ivan offers us only the tortured face of the rebel plunged in the abyss, incapable of action, torn between the idea of his own innocence and the desire to kill. He hates the death penalty because it is the image of the human condition, and, at the same time, he is drawn to crime. Because he has taken the side of mankind, solitude is his lot. With him the rebellion of reason culminates in madness.[61]

The Grand Inquisitor

D. H. LAWRENCE

It is a strange experience, to examine one's reaction to a book over a period of years. I remember when I first read *The Brothers Karamazov*, in 1913, how fascinated yet unconvinced it left me. And I remember Middleton Murry saying to me: "Of course the whole clue to Dostoevsky is in that Grand Inquisitor story." And I remember saying: "Why? It seems to me just rubbish."

And it was true. The story seemed to me just a piece of showing off: a display of cynical-satanical pose which was simply irritating. The cynical-satanical pose always irritated me, and I could see nothing else in that black-a-vised Grand Inquisitor talking at Jesus at such length. I just felt it was all pose; he didn't really mean what he said; he was just showing off in blasphemy.

Since then I have read *The Brothers Karamazov* twice, and each time found it more depressing because, alas, more drearily true to life.

From *Selected Literary Criticism* (1961), ed. Anthony Beal. Copyright 1936 by Frieda Lawrence; 1964 by the Estate of Frieda Lawrence Ravagli. Reprinted by permission of The Viking Press, Inc. Originally published as the preface to *The Grand Inquisitor*, trans. S. S. Koteliansky, London, 1930.

At first it had been lurid romance. Now I read *The Grand Inquisitor* once more, and my heart sinks right through my shoes. I still see a trifle of cynical-satanical showing off. But under that I hear the final and unanswerable criticism of Christ. And it is a deadly, devastating summing up, unanswerable because borne out by the long experience of humanity. It is reality versus illusion, and the illusion was Jesus', while time itself retorts with the reality.

If there is any question: Who is the Grand Inquisitor?—then surely we must say it is Ivan himself. And Ivan is the thinking mind of the human being in rebellion, thinking the whole thing out to the bitter end. As such he is, of course, identical with the Russian revolutionary of the thinking type. He is also, of course, Dostoevsky himself, in his thoughtful, as apart from[233] his passional and inspirational self. Dostoevsky half hated Ivan. Yet, after all, Ivan is the greatest of the three brothers, pivotal. The passionate Dmitry and the inspired Alyosha are, at last, only offsets to Ivan.

And we cannot doubt that the Inquisitor speaks Dostoevsky's own final opinion about Jesus. The opinion is, baldly, this: Jesus, you are inadequate. Men must correct you. And Jesus in the end gives the kiss of acquiescence to the Inquisitor, as Alyosha does to Ivan. The two inspired ones recognise the inadequacy of their inspiration: the thoughtful one has to accept the responsibility of a complete adjustment.

We may agree with Dostoevsky or not, but we have to admit that his criticism of Jesus is the final criticism, based on the experience of two thousand years (he says fifteen hundred) and on a profound insight into the nature of mankind. Man can but be true to his own nature. No inspiration whatsoever will ever get him permanently beyond his limits.

And what are the limits? It is Dostoevsky's first profound question. What are the limits to the nature, not of Man in the abstract, but of men, mere men, everyday men?

The limits are, says the Grand Inquisitor, three. Mankind in the bulk can never be "free," because man on the whole makes three grand demands on life, and cannot endure unless these demands are satisfied.

1. He demands bread, and not merely as foodstuff, but as a miracle, given from the hand of God.
2. He demands mystery, the sense of the miraculous in life.
3. He demands somebody to bow down to, and somebody before whom all men shall bow down.

These three demands, for miracle, mystery and authority, prevent men from being "free." They are man's "weakness." Only a few men, the elect, are capable of abstaining from the absolute demand for bread, for miracle, mystery, and authority. These are the strong, and they must be as gods, to be able to be Christians fulfilling all the Christ-demand. The rest, the millions and millions of men throughout time, they are as babes or children or geese, they are too weak, "impotent, vicious, worthless and rebellious" even to be able to share out the earthly bread, if it is left to them.

This, then, is the Grand Inquisitor's summing up of the[234] nature of mankind. The inadequacy of Jesus lies in the fact that Christianity is too difficult for men, the vast mass of men. It could only be realized by the few "saints" or heroes. For the rest, man is like a horse harnessed to a load he cannot possibly pull. "Hadst Thou respected him less, Thou wouldst have demanded less of him, and that would be nearer to love, for his burden would be lighter."

Christianity, then, is the ideal, but it is impossible. It is impossible because it makes demands greater than the nature of man can bear. And therefore, to get a livable, working scheme, some of the elect, such as the Grand Inquisitor himself, have turned round to "him," that other great Spirit, Satan, and have established Church and State on "him." For the Grand Inquisitor finds that to be able to live at all, mankind must be loved more tolerantly and more contemptuously than Jesus loved it, loved, for all that, more truly, since it is loved for itself, for what it is, and not for what it ought to be. Jesus loved mankind for what it ought to be, free and limitless. The Grand Inquisitor loves it for what it is, with all its limitations. And he contends his is the kinder love. And yet he says it is Satan. And Satan, he says at the beginning, means annihilation, and not-being.

As always in Dostoevsky, the amazing perspicacity is mixed with ugly perversity. Nothing is pure. His wild love for Jesus is mixed with perverse and poisonous hate of Jesus: his moral hostility to the devil is mixed with secret worship of the devil. Dostoevsky is always perverse, always impure, always an evil thinker and a marvellous seer.

Is it true that mankind demands, and will always demand, mir-acle, mystery, and authority? Surely it is true. To-day, man gets his sense of the miraculous from science and machinery, radio, aeroplanes, vast ships, zeppelins, poison gas, artificial silk: these things nourish man's sense of the miraculous as magic did in the past. But now, man is master of the mystery, there are no occult powers. The same with mystery: medicine, biological experiment, strange feats of the psychic people, spiritualists, Christian scientists—it is all mystery. And as for authority, Russia destroyed the Tsar to have Lenin and the present mechanical despotism, Italy has the rationalised despotism of Musso-lini, and England is longing for a despot.[235]

Dostoevsky's diagnosis of human nature is simple and unanswer-able. We have to submit, and agree that men are like that. Even over the question of sharing the bread, we have to agree that man is too weak, or vicious, or something, to be able to do it. He has to hand the common bread over to some absolute authority, Tsar or Lenin, to be shared out. And yet the mass of men are *incapable* of looking on bread as a mere means of sustenance, by which man sustains himself for the purpose of true living, true life being the "heavenly bread." It seems a strange thing that men, the mass of men, cannot understand that *life* is the great reality, that true living fills us with vivid life, "the heavenly bread," and earthly bread merely supports this. No, men cannot understand, never have understood that simple fact. They cannot see the distinction between bread, or property, money, and vivid life. They think that property and money are the same thing as vivid life. Only the few, the potential heroes or the "elect," can see the simple distinction. The mass *cannot* see it, and will never see it.

Dostoevsky was perhaps the first to realise this devastating truth, which Christ had not seen. A truth it is, none the less, and once recognised it will change the course of history. All that remains is for the elect to take charge of the bread—the property, the money—and then give it back to the masses as if it were really the gift of life. In this way, mankind might live happily, as the Inquisitor suggests. Otherwise, with the masses making the terrible mad mistake that money is life, and that therefore no one shall control the money, men shall be "free" to get what they can, we are brought to a condition of competitive insanity and ultimate suicide.

So far, well and good, Dostoevsky's diagnosis stands. But is it then to betray Christ and turn over to Satan if the elect should at last realise that instead of refusing Satan's three offers, the heroic Christian must now accept them? Jesus refused the three offers out of pride and fear: he wanted to be greater than these, and "above" them. But we now realise, no man, not even Jesus, is really "above" miracle, mystery, and authority. The one thing that Jesus is truly above, is the confusion between money and life. Money is not life, says Jesus, therefore you can ignore it and leave it to the devil.

Money is not life, it is true. But ignoring money and leaving[236] it to the devil means handing over the great mass of men to the devil, for the mass of men *cannot* distinguish between money and life. It is hard to believe: certainly Jesus didn't believe it: and yet, as Dostoevsky and the Inquisitor point out, it is so.

Well, and what then? Must we therefore go over to the devil? After all, the whole of Christianity is not contained in the rejection of the three temptations. The essence of Christianity is a love of mankind. If a love of mankind entails accepting the bitter limitation of the mass of men, their inability to distinguish between money and life, then accept the limitation, and have done with it. Then take over from the devil the money (or bread), the miracle, and the sword of Caesar, and, for the love of mankind, give back to men the bread, with its wonder, and give them the miracle, the marvellous, and give them, in a hierarchy, someone, some men, in higher and higher degrees, to bow down to. Let them bow down, let them bow down *en masse,* for the mass, who do not understand the difference between money and life, should always bow down to the elect, who do.

And is that serving the devil? It is certainly not serving the spirit of annihilation and not-being. It is serving the great wholeness of mankind, and in that respect, it is Christianity. Anyhow, it is the service of Almighty God, who made men what they are, limited and unlimited.

Where Dostoevsky is perverse is in his making the old, old, wise governor of men a Grand Inquisitor. The recognition of the weakness of man has been a common trait in all great, wise rulers of people, from the Pharaohs and Darius through the great patient Popes of the early Church right down to the present day. They have known the weakness of men, and felt a certain tenderness. This is the spirit of all great government. But it was not the spirit of the Spanish Inquisition. The Spanish Inquisition in 1500 was a newfangled thing, peculiar to Spain, with her curious death-lust and her bullying, and, strictly, a Spanish-political instrument, not Catholic at all, but rabidly national. The Spanish Inquisition actually was diabolic. It could not have produced a Grand Inquisitor who put Dostoevsky's sad questions to Jesus. And the man who put those sad questions to Jesus could not possibly have been a Spanish Inquisitor. He could not possibly have burnt a[237] hundred people in an *auto-da-fé.* He would have been too wise and far-seeing.

So that, in this respect, Dostoevsky showed his epileptic and slightly criminal perversity. The man who feels a certain tenderness for mankind in its weakness or limitation is not therefore diabolic. The man who realises that Jesus asked too much of the mass of men, in asking them to choose between earthly and heavenly bread, and to judge between good and evil, is not therefore satanic. Think how difficult it is to know the difference between good and evil! Why, sometimes it is evil to be good. And how is the ordinary man to understand that? He can't. The extraordinary men have to understand it for him. And is that going over to the devil? Or think of the difficulty in choosing between the earthly and heavenly bread. Lenin, surely a pure soul, rose to great power simply to give men—what? The earthly bread. And what was the result? Not only did they lose the heavenly bread, but even the earthly bread disappeared out of wheat-producing Russia. It is most strange. And all the socialists and the generous thinkers of to-day, what are they striving for? The same: to share out more evenly the earthly bread. Even *they,* who are practising Christianity *par excellence,* cannot properly choose between the heavenly and earthly bread. For the poor, they choose the earthly bread, and once more the heavenly bread is lost: and once more, as soon as it is really chosen, the earthly bread begins to disappear. It is a great mystery. But to-day, the most passionate believers in Christ believe that all you have to do is to struggle to give earthly bread (good houses, good sanitation, etc.) to the poor, and that is in itself the heavenly bread. But it isn't. Especially for the poor, it isn't. It is for them the loss of heavenly bread. And the poor are the vast majority. Poor things, how everybody hates them to-day! For benevolence is a form of hate.

What then is the heavenly bread? Every generation must answer for itself. But the heavenly bread is life, is living. Whatever makes life vivid and delightful is the heavenly bread. And the earthly bread must come as a by-product of the heavenly bread. The vast mass will never understand this. Yet it is the essential truth of Christianity, and of life itself. The few will understand. Let them take the responsibility.[238]

Again, the Inquisitor says that it is a weakness in men, that they must have miracle, mystery and authority. But is it? Are they not bound up in our emotions, always and for ever, these three demands of miracle, mystery, and authority? If Jesus cast aside miracle in the Temptation, still there is miracle again in the Gospels. And if Jesus refused the earthly bread, still he said: "In my Father's house are many mansions." And for authority: "Why call ye me Lord, Lord, and do not the things which I say?"

The thing Jesus was trying to do was to supplant physical emotion by moral emotion. So that earthly bread becomes, in a sense, immoral, as it is to many refined people to-day. The Inquisitor sees that this is the mistake. The earthly bread must in itself be the miracle, and be bound up with the miracle.

And here, surely, he is right. Since man began to think and to feel vividly, seed-time and harvest have been the two great sacred periods of miracle, rebirth, and rejoicing. Easter and harvest-home are festivals of the earthly bread, and they are festivals which go to the roots of the soul. For it is the earthly bread as a miracle, a yearly miracle. All the old religions saw it: the Catholic still sees it, by the Mediterranean. And this is not weakness. This is *truth*. The rapture of the Easter kiss, in old Russia, is intimately bound up with the springing of the seed and the first footstep of the new earthly bread. It is the rapture of the Easter kiss which makes the bread worth eating. It is the absence of the Easter kiss which makes the Bolshevist bread barren, dead. They eat dead bread, now.

The earthly bread is leavened with the heavenly bread. The heavenly bread is life, is contact, and is consciousness. In sowing the seed man has his contact with earth, with sun and rain: and he *must not* break the contact. In the awareness of the springing of the corn he has his ever-renewed consciousness of miracle, wonder, and mystery: the wonder of creation, procreation, and re-creation, following the mystery of death and the cold grave. It is the grief of Holy Week and the delight of Easter Sunday. And man must not, must not lose this supreme state of consciousness out of himself, or he has lost the best part of him. Again, the reaping and the harvest are another contact, with earth and sun, a rich touch of the cosmos, a living stream of activity, and then the contact with harvesters,[239] and the joy of

harvest-home. All this is life, life, it is the heavenly bread which we eat
in the course of getting the earthly bread. Work is, or should be, our
heavenly bread of activity, contact and consciousness. All work that is
not this, is anathema. True, the work is hard; there is the sweat of the
brow. But what of it? In decent proportion, this is life. The sweat of
the brow is the heavenly butter.

I think the older Egyptians understood this, in the course of their
long and marvellous history. I think that probably, for thousands of
years, the masses of the Egyptians were happy, in the hierarchy of the
State.

Miracle and mystery run together, they merge. Then there is the
third thing, authority. The word is bad: a policeman has authority, and
no one bows down to him. The Inquisitor means: "that which men
bow down to." Well, they bowed down to Caesar, and they bowed
down to Jesus. They will bow down, first, as the Inquisitor saw, to the
one who has the power to control the bread.

The bread, the earthly bread, while it is being reaped and grown,
it is life. But once it is harvested and stored, it becomes a commodity, it
becomes riches. And then it becomes a danger. For men think, if they
only possessed the hoard, they need not work; which means, really,
they need not live. And that is the real blasphemy. For while we live
we must live, we must not wither or rot inert.

So that ultimately men bow down to the man, or group of men,
who can and dare take over the hoard, the store of bread, the riches, to
distribute it among the people again. The lords, the givers of bread.
How profound Dostoevsky is when he says that the people will forget
that it is their own bread which is being given back to them. While
they keep their own bread, it is not much better than stone to them—
inert possessions. But given back to them from the great Giver, it is
divine once more, it has the quality of miracle to make it taste well in
the mouth and in the belly.

Men bow down to the lord of bread, first and foremost. For, by
knowing the difference between earthly and heavenly bread, he is
able calmly to distribute the earthly bread, and to give it, for
the commonalty, the heavenly taste which they can never give it.
That is why, in a democracy, the earthly bread loses its taste,[240]
the salt loses its savour, and there is no one to bow down to.

It is not man's weakness that he needs someone to bow down to. It
is his nature, and his strength, for it puts him into touch with far, far
greater life than if he stood alone. All life bows to the sun. But the sun
is very far away to the common man. It needs someone to bring it to
him. It needs a lord: what the Christians call one of the elect, to bring
the sun to the common man, and put the sun in his heart. The sight of
a true lord, a noble, a nature-hero puts the sun into the heart of the
ordinary man, who is no hero, and therefore cannot know the sun
direct.

This is one of the real mysteries. As the Inquisitor says, the mystery of the elect is one of the inexplicable mysteries of Christianity, just as the lord, the natural lord among men, is one of the inexplicable mysteries of humanity throughout time. We must accept the mystery, that's all.

But to do so is not diabolic.

And Ivan need not have been so tragic and satanic. He had made a discovery about men, which was due to be made. It was the rediscovery of a fact which was known universally almost till the end of the eighteenth century, when the illusion of the perfectibility of men, of all men, took hold of the imagination of the civilized nations. It was an illusion. And Ivan has to make a restatement of the old truth, that most men *cannot* choose between good and evil, because it is so extremely difficult to know which is which, especially in crucial cases: and that most men *cannot* see the difference between life-values and money-values: they can only see money-values; even nice simple people who *live* by the life-values, kind and natural, yet can only estimate value in terms of money. So let the specially gifted few make the decision between good and evil, and establish the life-values against the money-values. And let the many accept the decision, with gratitude, and bow down to the few, in the hierarchy. What is there diabolical or satanic in that? Jesus kisses the Inquisitor: Thank you, you are right, wise old man! Alyosha kisses Ivan: Thank you, brother, you are right, you take a burden off me! So why should Dostoevsky drag in Inquisitors and *autos-da-fé*, and Ivan wind up so morbidly suicidal? Let them be glad they've found the truth again.[241]

The Sources and Significance of "The Legend of the Grand Inquisitor"

PHILIP RAHV

I

Until recently Dostoevsky's Western interpreters were open to the reproach of making far too little of his Legend of the Grand Inquisitor. The same, however, can hardly be said of his Russian critics, who

Reprinted from *The Myth and the Powerhouse* by Philip Rahv, by permission of Farrar, Straus, & Giroux, Inc. Copyright 1954 by Philip Rahv.

repeatedly stressed its significance long before the onset of totalitarianism in our time brought on the widespread recognition, if not of the Legend's actual content and meaning, then surely of its close relevance to modern historical experience.

The late Nicolas Berdyaev, writing from a philosophical standpoint, maintained that in the Legend Dostoevsky reached the summit of his creation; and some five decades ago V. V. Rozanov, whose insight into Dostoevsky is[144] unsurpassed among Russian commentators, declared it to be of exceptional profundity as a revelation of the structure of human destiny—"terrifying unbelief and the deepest and most ecstatic faith are inconceivably mingled in it." There is some evidence, too, that its author himself thought of it in such terms. In 1902 one witness (V. F. Putzikovitch) published an account of a conversation he had had with the novelist in the summer of 1879, while *The Brothers Karamazov* was still running serially in the *Russky Vestnik,* in which he speaks of the chapter on the Grand Inquisitor as the "culminating point" of his creative career; and when questioned as to his reasons for interpolating a devised legend of sixteenth-century Spain into a narrative of contemporary Russia, his reply was that its theme had haunted him since early youth and for fear that he might not live to complete another major work he had resolved to try his hand at it without delay and incorporate it in the novel he was then engaged in writing.

One need not agree with Berdayev that the Legend of the Grand Inquisitor represents the summit of Dostoevsky's creation in order to make out that as an excursus on the theme of man's historical fate, its terror, despair and absurdity, it is nearly without equal in world literature. It enriches the ideological content of the novel in which it is embedded, enabling us to understand more fully the far-ranging implications of Ivan Karamazov's "rebellion," but it is even more meaningful in terms of Dostoevsky's development as a whole; and the figure of the Grand Inquisitor is dramatically compelling enough to stay permanently in our minds as a symbolic character-image of the dialectic of power. Moreover, the Legend lends itself to analysis, quite apart from its local narrative setting, as a unique essay in[145] the philosophy of history. Deceptively easy on the surface, it is at bottom one of the most difficult texts in the Dostoevskyean canon. By the same token, however, it is also one of the most rewarding. And the difficulty is not in its dramatic form but in the complexity of the ideas, their immense suggestiveness and scope, and the dissonances of belief and emotional discords that sound in them.

But the dramatic form is indispensable to Dostoevsky. That he would have been capable of making substantially the same statement without recourse to the dramatized consciousness of a fictional character is extremely doubtful. For the truth is that this most daring of novelists is apt to decline abruptly to lower levels of performance whenever he puts himself in the position of addressing the reader directly—a stance that rarely suits him, as is shown by the inferior quality of most of the articles included in his *Diary of a Writer*. Now a disjunction of this sort would scarcely surprise us in a novelist deficient in intellectual force and stamina. In Dostoevsky's case, however, he felt disjunction between the qualities of his direct discourse and those emerging through the sustained imaginative projection of his fiction is due, I think, to the fact that when writing in the first person—out in the open so to speak—he at once loses the advantages of complicity. For it is complicity above all which is the secret of his creative triumph over the propagandist in himself. It arises in the process of his identification as novelist with his characters, but it is necessary to distinguish between its genesis and the larger uses to which he puts it. It saves him from the one-sidedness, the fanaticism of commitment, and the casuistry to which as an embattled reactionary ideologue he was all too prone. There is an ambiguity of feeling and attitude in him, a[146] tension between sympathies and antipathies, finding its release in this complicity. He fully depends on it in the creation of his characters; and the few from whom he withholds it are reduced to stereotypes, as, for example, Grushenka's Polish suitor and the student-radical Rakitin in *The Brothers Karamazov*. Creatures of their author's political malice, they fall below the level of the world into which he injects them.

Ivan, on the other hand, it has frequently been observed, is the figure in the novel to whom as author he most readily gives himself in the process of identification.[1] This must be taken into account in examining the Legend recounted by Ivan to his brother Alyosha in the course of that prolonged dialogue which is perhaps the most audacious and masterful in the whole of Dostoevsky. Ivan calls the Legend "a poem in prose" that he had not written down but simply made up, as he says, and he tells it to Alyosha in order to support, in a manner at once dramatic and metaphysically provocative, his denial not so much of God as of His creation. The denial consists of a relentless scrutiny of man in general, and particularly Christian man, in the light of what he has made of history and history has made of him.

In his assault on God and the traditional faith Ivan proceeds in a way that transcends the rationalistic argumentation of the old-time atheists. For him it can no longer be[147] a question of attempting to disprove God's existence logically. Ivan is not one to permit his intellectual faculties to linger in the modes of the past. He has made

[1] My impression is that the identification is more on the intellectual plane than on that of intimate subjectivity. But of course in Dostoevsky ideas are never divorced from feeling; in his critical statements he was wont to link them by inventing such new-fangled terms as "idea-forces" and "idea-feelings." In her memoirs Aimée Dostoevsky recalls the family tradition that her father, in looking back to his youth, "portrayed himself in the person of Ivan."

the essentially modern leap from the static framework of analytic thinking to thinking in terms of the historical process. But his leap is made in the typical Russian fashion of that epoch. That is to say, it lands him not in the somewhat placid "historicism" then prevailing in the consciousness of the West but in the eschatological frame of mind common to the Russian intelligentsia of the latter part of the past century. For whatever their outlook, whether revolutionary or not, inclined to nihilism or given to apocalyptic visions, in the main those people tended to see history as verging toward the ultimate and bringing forth a final solution compounded either of pure good or pure evil. "The orientation toward the end," as Berdyaev calls it, mastered the most sensitive spirits among them, some predicting the approach of anti-Christ and others fervently awaiting the imminent erection of the City of Man; and in the intensity of their longing for an incontrovertible decision they transform the historical realm into the realm of prophecy and revelation. This is the mood that Ivan's "rebellion" exemplifies to perfection.

His version of atheism is all the more forceful in that it allows for God's existence, if need be, but not for the justifications of His world as revealed progressively *in* and *through* history. Ivan proclaims that no restitution is possible: that the ultimate harmony or reconciliation in the fullness of time could never expiate the suffering of even a single innocent child, let alone efface the innumerable horrors of injustice which humanity has endured through the ages. Hence he refuses God's creation ("returns his entrance[148] ticket") thus proclaiming the right of indifference to the issue of His existence.

Nor does Ivan dispute the ideality and supreme goodness of Christian teaching. On the contrary, it is this very ideality and goodness that he turns into the motive of his dissent from it when he depicts the Grand Inquisitor upbraiding Christ for thinking much too highly of man in endeavoring to augment his freedom of choice between good and evil instead of heeding the counsel of the wise and dread spirit of the wilderness to strip man of his freedom so that he might at long last live in peace and brutish happiness. God, confronted by the radical proofs of the meanness of His world, the senseless suffering prevailing in it and man's congenital inability to enter the promised spiritual kingdom, is disposed of through His works.[2]

But if Ivan does not believe in God, neither does he believe in man. It is true that he loves man—there is no one else left to love and

---

[2] Dostoevsky appears to have been inordinately proud of Ivan's subversive intelligence. "Ivan is deep," he wrote in his private notebook; "he is not one of your present-day atheists whose unbelief demonstrates no more than the narrowness of their point of view and the obtuseness of their small minds." And again: "Those thickheads never dreamt of so powerful a negation of God as that embodied in the Inquisitor and in the preceding chapter, to which the entire novel serves as an answer. . . . Even in Europe there have never been atheistical expressions of such power."

perhaps there has never actually been anyone else. Yet how can he believe in man's freedom in the face of the appalling testimony of history proving his incapacity to achieve it? And in what way does Ivan envisage the future? If we take the Grand Inquisitor as his *persona*, then he thinks that just as historical Christianity has failed man, so socialism—the Tower of Babel of the coming centuries—will fail him and afterwards the[149] authoritarian theocrats will resume command. And the fault, from first to last, is in man himself because he is an "impotent rebel," a slave even if rebellious by nature. Implicit here is the idea of freedom as the consummation of rebellion and of happiness as the total renunciation of it. The choice is between freedom and happiness. But so long as man is unable to carry his rebellion through to the end, or alternatively, renounce it once and for all, he will attain neither goal. Ivan torments himself with the question of what is to be done with man if you at once love and despise him. The ideology of the Grand Inquisitor, which repudiates freedom for the sake of happiness, is the means he devises for forcing a solution. Yet it also is a means of exposing it. The very manner in which Ivan develops this ideology expresses his loathing of it even as he despairingly accepts it.

This is but another way of saying that in the last analysis he is not really possessed by it, that his mind moves freely in and out of it. The Legend as a whole, in its interplay of drama and ideology, is to be taken, I think, as an experiment, one of those experiments in frightfulness with which modern literature has the deepest affinity. Dostoevsky stands at two removes from the Inquisitor, and Ivan at one remove; and this placing, or aesthetic "distancing," reflects precisely the degree of commitment we are entitled to assume. Therefore to identify Ivan wholly with the Inquisitor, as so many commentators have done, is an error, though a lesser one than that of wholly identifying Dostoevsky with him. The fact is that the Legend has not one but two protagonists, Jesus and the Inquisitor, and that Ivan makes no real choice between them. Jesus is freedom and transcendent truth, whereas the Inquisitor typifies the implacable logic of historical reality; but so stark a[150] confrontation in itself demonstrates that Ivan's dilemma is absolute. After all, he has no God to whom he can appeal for a guaranty of his choice; Jesus is his hero but not his God. Ivan, like his creator, is split through and through, torn between love and contempt, pride and submission, reason and faith, teleology and the extremest pessimism. Inherently a stranger in the world of action, he is capable, however, of apprehending his thought with such urgency and fearlessness that it comes almost to resemble an action. And in his rage of love he invokes with prophetic violence a totalitarian elite whose rule is justified by humanity's refusal of Christ's tragic gift of freedom.

The scene of Ivan's "poem in prose" is Seville at the time of the Inquisition. On a day when nearly a hundred heretics had been burnt *ad majorem Dei gloriam* by the cardinal, the Grand Inquisitor, in a splendid *auto da fé*, Christ reappears in His human shape, as He appeared fifteen centuries earlier. The people, recognizing their Savior, welcome Him with cries of love and faith, but at that moment the cardinal—"an old man, almost ninety, tall and erect, with a withered face and sunken eyes, in which there is still a gleam of light"—orders the guards to seize and lead Him away to the dungeon of the Holy Inquisition. At night the door of the cell is suddenly opened and the aged cardinal comes in alone to confront his prisoner. On the morrow, he announces, he will condemn and burn Him at the stake as the worst of heretics: "And the very people who have today kissed Thy feet, tomorrow at the faintest sign from me will rush to heap up the embers of Thy fire." Throughout the long scene that follows Christ is speech-less. Only the Inquisitor speaks, and his speech is an[151] astonish-ingly coherent and complete apology for the total power of man over man. It has grandeur, penetration and enormous audacity—thus would the Inquisitor's counterparts in real life speak if they had candor and were capable of making independent forays into the philosophy of history. The phenomenon of power has always been surrounded by taboos. Power is in some sense the deepest of mysteries. hence taboo, for whatever is behind it is at once holy and unclean. But the Inquisi-tor breaks all taboos. It was the recommendation of Edmund Burke, that enemy of extremism and of theory, that a "sacred veil" should ever be drawn "over the beginnings of all governments." Now if by "begin-nings" we understand the motive-force or inner principle of govern-ment, then the Inquisitor is bent on rending asunder the veil that shrouds it and letting us in on its secret. Not that he is not himself a firm believer in the beneficent uses of Burke's "politic, well-wrought veil." He is that above all, but in the séance with his speechless prisoner he is for once intent on putting all things plainly.

What he puts most plainly to his prisoner is the enormity of the error of rejecting coercion and domination for the sake of man's free love. The three powers with which Satan had tempted Him in the wilderness are miracle, mystery and authority, the sole means of vanquishing the conscience of men forever and holding it captive for their own good. The churchly hierarchy has found it necessary to correct that error and to found its work on those powers. Never has anything truer been said than what was revealed by the wise and dread spirit of the wilderness in the three questions later recorded in the Gospels as "the temptation." For in those questions "the whole subsequent history of mankind is, as it were, brought together into[152] one whole and foretold, and in them are united all the unsolved historical contradictions of human nature. . . ."

Man, hungering both for "earthly bread" and "common worship," and on no account wanting the one without the other, will gladly exchange his freedom for the promise that his double hunger will be appeased. He longs "to find someone quickly to whom he can hand over the gift of freedom with which the ill-fated creature was born"; and he prefers to worship the one who feeds him, the one performing the miracle rejected by Jesus, the miracle of turning stones into bread. Yet man is so constituted that he seeks to worship only that which he believes to be established beyond dispute:

> For those pitiful creatures are concerned not only to find what one or the other can worship, but to find something that all would believe in and worship; what is essential is that all may be *together* in it. This craving for *community* of worship is the chief misery of every man individually and of all humanity from the beginning of time. For the sake of common worship they have slain each other with the sword. They have set up gods and challenged one another, "Put away your gods and come and worship ours, or we will kill you and your gods!" And so it will be to the end of the world, even when gods disappear from the earth; they will fall down before idols just the same.

Jesus' hope that man would cling to God and not crave miracles is futile. Man seeks not so much God as the miraculous, and when deprived of it he creates "new miracles of his own for himself, and will worship deeds of sorcery and witchcraft, though he might be a hundred times over a rebel, heretic and infidel." The Inquisitor foretells that[153] the downfall of the Church will come about exactly through such a deed of sorcery and witchcraft when men, declaring that there is no crime and no sin but only hunger, will erect the terrible Tower of Babel. But after a thousand years of suffering, of the confusion of free thought and of science ending in "cannibalism," the people will seek out the priestly elite hidden in their catacombs: "They will find us and cry to us, 'Feed us, for those who have promised the fire from heaven haven't given it!' And then we shall finish building their tower. . . . And we alone shall feed them in Thy name, declaring falsely that it is in Thy name. . . . And we shall sit upon the beast and raise the cup, and on it will be written, 'Mystery.'"

The Inquisitor sneers at the nihilists and socialists even while appropriating what he conceives to be their principal idea: materialism and technics, the miracle of turning stones into bread. In other words, ecclesiastical totalitarianism comes to terms with the socialist cause by absorbing it. Only then begins the reign of the universal state—"an harmonious antheap"—assuring peace for all. Its principle of organization is power. Jesus repudiated power, but not the theocrats of Rome, who have taken up the sword of Caesar, proclaiming themselves the lords of the earth. "We shall triumph and we shall be Caesars," the Inquisitor cries, "and then we shall plan the universal happiness of mankind." All will be happy except the members of the ruling caste, since it is they alone who are not absolved from the knowledge of good and evil. They keep that knowledge strictly to themselves, just as they keep the secret of their atheism. The millions whom they rule submit meekly to their commands and die peacefully believing in the rewards of heaven and eternity, as they have been[154] told to believe, though of course beyond the grave nothing whatever awaits them.

The only answer the Inquisitor receives from his prisoner is a kiss on his withered lips. The old man shudders and, opening the door of the cell, exclaims: "Go, and come no more . . . come not at all, never, never!"

II

The Legend of the Grand Inquisitor did not of a sudden spring full-grown from Dostoevsky's imagination. For its sources, and that peculiar combination in it of elements seldom found in close association, we must look to his intellectual development and political and literary biography.

What is first to be accounted for is the strange amalgam of socialism and Catholicism. The critique of socialism is no more than insinuated in the Legend. Its specifications of time and place are such that socialism can come into it only through oblique references and allusions of an allegoric nature. Thus in the Inquisitor's gloss on the Gospel story of "the temptation" the motif of "stones turned into bread" is brought in again and again so as to convert it into the formula for socialism. The linkage of socialism with the Roman Church, though it may strike western readers as fantastic, is integral to Dostoevsky's thought.

The connection he saw between these two apparently hostile forces actually dates back to the period of the 1840's, when in his youth he belonged to the Petrashevsky circle of intellectual conspirators. Even then, while reading such ideologues as Fourier, Saint-Simon, Proudhon, and Pierre Lerroux, he was still holding fast to the image of Christ and searching for a way of reconciling it with the[155] socialist creed;[3] and he was doubtless influenced by the example of Lamennais, the Catholic priest and social philosopher, the apostle to the poor as he was called, who stood for a kind of theocratic democracy and preached the ideals of the French Revolution. His writings were well known to the members of the Petrashevsky circle, and so were such works as V. Menier's *Jésus Christ devant les conseils de guerre* and Cabet's *Le vrai christianisme suivant Jésus Christ*. Now after Dostoevsky's return from penal servitude in Siberia, as he gradually shed his radical views, he began interpreting the connection he had once seen between the Catholic Church and the socialist movement in a different sense, positing the authoritarian principle as the root idea of both. To be sure,

---

[3] In this he differed markedly from his fellow conspirators. Petrashevsky, for instance, once referred to Christ in a private letter as "that notorious demagogue who ended his career somewhat unfortunately."

the animus against Rome is partly explained by the anti-western turn of his thought and his growing inclination to identify Christianity exclusively with the Russian people and their national Church. In the main, however, it was the authoritarian idea of the "compulsory organization of human happiness" that was the essential link in his conception of socialism and Catholicism as two aspects of the same heretical self-will driving toward the obliteration of human dignity and freedom of conscience. In *The Diary of a Writer* as in his private notebooks he predicted time and again that the Catholics, deserting the "earthly potentates" with whom they had been allied in the past, would inevitably join forces with the socialists. At other times he varied the prediction (and this is the variant given in the Legend) by saying that socialism would fail and that[156] thereafter the Catholic hierarchy would adopt the socialist dogma of "earthly bread" and by uniting it with its own dogma of "common worship" forge an ideological instrument for the conquest of the universal power it had always striven for. And if we go further back into Dostoevsky's fiction we learn that in *The Idiot* (1868) he was already experimenting with the notions that more than ten years later found their definitive form in the Legend. Thus Myshkin, in a ranting monologue, denounces Catholicism as an unchristian religion that preaching a "distorted Christ" is "even worse than atheism itself." "The Pope," he cries, "seized the earth . . . and grasped the sword. . . . How could atheism fail to come from them?" And socialism also comes "from despair in opposition to Catholicism on the moral side, to replace the lost moral power of religion . . . and to save humanity not by Christ but by violence. . . ."

The critique of socialism in the Legend has its source, too, in a crucial experience of Dostoevsky's youth. This was his relationship with Belinsky, the great radical critic and one of the most dominant and fascinating figures in Russian cultural history, who intervened decisively in Dostoevsky's early career by his laudatory appraisal of his first novel, *Poor Folk*. It can be shown that a key passage in the Inquisitor's speech is a direct transposition of arguments to which Belinsky had recourse in the passionate debates of that early period. Many years later, in a reminiscence entitled "Old People" (*The Diary of a Writer, 1873*), the intrinsic significance of which exceeds any interest we may have in it from the standpoint of provenience in the narrow sense, Dostoevsky summed up what was at stake for him in those debates by recollecting certain scenes involving[157] Belinsky that had long haunted his mind; and the piece as a whole, with its marvelously vivid portrait of the radical critic, suggests, as no purely conceptual formulation could ever do, the agitation of soul and the importunity and immediacy with which those people grasped ideas, striving with might and main not so much to master them for their own sake as to extract from them at all costs a meaning or a truth that would dispel the darkness in which men live and redeem their suffering. "Old People" is in fact a little masterpiece that, in its recovery of the past, recalls us to the very origins of Dostoevsky's complex of ideas. It discloses, if not the personal, then at least the intellectual conditions under which he formed some of his powerful obsessions, as, for instance, the obsession with the personality of Christ to which he at all times yielded even at the expense of Christianity itself.

"Dost Thou know that ages will pass, and humanity will proclaim by the lips of their sages that there is no crime, and therefore no sin; there is only hunger. 'Feed men, and then ask of them virtue!' that's what they'll write on their banner, which they will raise against Thee." Thus begins the passage in the Legend directly echoing Belinsky's thought. It is by no means the only passage of its kind, as the account given in "Old People" sufficiently makes clear.[4]

Belinsky was not primarily a reflective person. He was above all an enthusiast, always and throughout his life. My first novel, *Poor Folk,* delighted him . . . but then, from the first days of our acquaintance, he threw himself with the most simple-hearted haste into the task of converting me to his creed. . . . I found him to be a passionate socialist, but it was his atheism rather that he at once began urging upon me. There is much that is noteworthy in that, for it reveals his astonishing intuition and extraordinary ability to sound an idea to its very depth. Some two years ago the International began one of its manifestoes with the significant declaration: "We are first of all a society of atheists," that is to say, it began with the essence of the matter. Likewise Belinsky. Valuing above all reason, science, and realism, he nevertheless understood better than anyone else that by themselves reason, science, and realism could produce an antheap but not the social "harmony" in which a human being would be able to dispose of his life properly. He knew that the moral principle is at the root of everything. As for the new moral principle of socialism . . . he believed in it fervently and without reflection; in this respect there was nothing but enthusiasm in his approach. But as a socialist, knowing as he did that the revolution must positively begin with atheism, it was his duty first of all to depose Christianity—the religion from which emerged the moral principles of the society he negated. And he radically negated the family, property, the moral responsibility of the individual. (I might add that, like Herzen, he was himself a good husband and a good father.) No doubt he understood that in denying the moral responsibility of man he was depriving him of his freedom; yet at the same time he believed with his whole being that socialism not only does not wipe out the freedom of the individual but, on the contrary, that it actually raises it to unheard-of grandeur, establishing it on adamantine foundations.

All that remained then, was the glowing personality of Christ, with which it was most difficult to cope. As a socialist Belinsky was in duty bound

---

[4] The translation is by the present writer. I have found the English version of *The Diary of a Writer,* brought out in this country in 1949, to be virtually unusable, inept in point of style and frequently far from accurate in rendering the plain meaning of the text.

to subvert the teaching of Christ, terming it a mendacious and ignorant idolatry of[159] man, condemned by contemporary science and the principles of political economy. However, there still remained the luminous image of the Son of God, His ethical inaccessibility, His wondrous and miraculous beauty. Belinsky, in his constant, unquenchable enthusiasm, would not be stopped even by this insuperable barrier, as Renan was stopped, who, in his book *Vie de Jésus,* full of unbelief, none the less declared that Christ is the ideal of human beauty, an inaccessible type which humanity can never be expected to bring forth again.

"Do you know?" Belinsky screamed at me one evening (he was always screaming as he got excited). "Do you know that it is not ethical to heap sins upon man and to put him under all sorts of obligations, when society is so badly organized that man cannot help doing evil, since he is economically led to wickedness (*ekonomichesky priveden k zlodeistvu*). It is inept and cruel to demand of man that which he cannot fulfill according to the laws of his nature, even if he wished to do so."

That evening we were not alone. A friend of Belinsky's was present, a person whom he greatly esteemed and listened to with attention.

"It hurts me to look at him," Belinsky suddenly interrupted his vehement discourse, pointing toward me. "Every time I mention Christ his face changes so, falling to pieces as if he were about to cry. Yes, believe me, simple-hearted man that you are," and here again he threw himself at me, "believe me that that Christ of yours, had he been born in our time, would be the most ordinary, inconsequential person; he would have to efface himself in the presence of contemporary science and leaders of humanity."

"Well, not quite," Belinsky's friend intervened. (I remember that we were sitting down while Belinsky was racing up and down the room.) "Well, no. If Christ were to appear now he would surely join the movement and become its head. . . ."

"Yes, that's it," Belinsky agreed with surprising alacrity. "He would follow the socialists and certainly join them."[160]

"Feed men, and then ask of them virtue!" is the Inquisitor's blunt way of stating Belinsky's protest against the demands made on abused and hungry men in the name of the Christian ethic.[5] Dostoevsky, ignoring with typical guile the concrete political meaning of this protest, which lay in the struggle against arbitrary power and oppressive institutions, transposed the issue to the philosophical plane and applied himself to disclosing the implications of unfreedom and refusal of moral responsibility in his antagonist's position. He continued his quarrel with Belinsky through the years; but the particular formulation of "stones turned into bread" he first hit upon in the May 1876 issue of *The Diary of a Writer,* where he analyzed the case of a young girl by the name of Pisareva who had committed suicide and whose letter taking leave of her friends had been printed in the newspapers.

[5] This is of course a recurrent theme of all radical literature, e.g., Bertolt Brecht's famous line in the *Dreigroschen Oper: Erst kommt das Fressen, dann kommt die Moral.*

Pisareva, the daughter of formerly well-to-do landowners, came to Petersburg, as Dostoevsky put it in his article, "to pay her respects to progress and become a midwife . . . but not finding enough significance in earthly medicine and undergoing moral fatigue took her life." He seized upon a part of her letter containing very precise instructions as to the disposal of her petty savings to preach a sermon on the materialistic learnings of the younger generation. "The importance attached to money is perhaps the last echo of the chief prejudice of her life, that of 'stones turned into bread.' In short, here we come upon the leading conviction that if all were economically secure all would be happy and if there were no poor people there would be no crime.[161] There is no such thing as crime. It is a morbid state, induced by poverty and unfortunate circumstances, etc., etc. This comprises the small, conventional, terribly characteristic and ultimate catechism with which they enter life . . . a catechism which they substitute for the living life, for bonds with the soil, faith in the truth, everything, everything." Thereupon the musician V. V. Alexyev wrote to Dostoevsky to inquire about his quotation from the Gospels, the phrase "stones turned into bread." To this query from a reader he replied at length, explaining the import of "bread and stones" in terms of the social pathos of the age and outlining in some detail the main ideological theme of the Legend, which he did not actually write till three years later, in 1879.

The letter to Alexyev contains the ideas of the Legend but no hint of its plot. And of this plot of Christ's return to earth and His encounter with the Inquisitor it should be said that it is not quite so original as it appears at first sight, far less so in fact than the ideological content of the Legend. The return of Christ is a theme touched upon in one way or another by not a few writers whose work Dostoevsky knew well, among them Voltaire, Goethe, Schiller, Jean-Paul Richter, Balzac, Hugo, and Vigny. Here we can only indicate two possible sources that are of particular interest and that Russian scholars have remarked upon. The first is Jean-Paul's fantastic story "A Dream," in which an atheist gives an account of finding himself in a cemetery at midnight and overhearing a colloquy between Jesus and the dead. The dead ask Him whether God exists and He replies that He had sought God in vain and that everywhere He had come upon nothing but emptiness. Then children rise from their graves and ask: "Jesus, are we[162] really without a father?" "Yes," is the answer, "we are all orphans." The second source is Victor Hugo's poem *Le Christ au Vatican*, an anticlerical pamphlet published in Geneva in 1864. (Dostoevsky, an assiduous reader of Hugo, wrote a preface to the Russian translation of *Notre Dame de Paris*.) In this poem Christ, fearing that men had forgotten his message, resolves to return to earth in His human shape. (*Dépouillons, il le faut, ma divine nature/Prenons l'habit modeste et l'humaine figure/ que j'avais en Judée. . . .*)

He appears in Rome but is denied access to the Pope. In a conversation with some officials of the Vatican, among them a cardinal, he learns that the popes have long ago assumed the role of Caesar and that *La sainteté a d'autres choses à faire/Que de penser au Christ, au ciel, au breviaire.* Christ's retort to this startling news is rendered in the last stanza of the poem:

Le cardinal parlait encore
Que Jésus Christ comme sur le Thabor
S'etait transfiguré. Dans son regard austère
S'allumaient les éclairs de la sainte colère
Qui l'anima lorsque jadis
Il chassa les vendeurs loin du sacré parvis.

Hugo's Christ responds angrily to the cardinal's tale of betrayal, and this must have struck Dostoevsky as an egregious error on the part of the French poet, a symptom no doubt of the pride and self-will ruling the West. In his own version Christ kisses the cardinal and departs quietly—a meek exit entirely in keeping with Dostoevsky's conception of Russian Christianity.[163]

III

But if Dostoevsky's Christ is so very Russian in his meekness, his Inquisitor is no less Russian in his cruelty. Though appearing in the role of a Catholic hierarch, he is in fact quite as Byzantine as he is Roman, if not more so. However considerable the part he has played in the history of the West, in Russian history he gained even greater ascendancy. From Ivan the Terrible to Stalin he has always known how to apply cruelty, violence and deception, as well as how to make use of doctrine and dogma, in order to subjugate the people, depriving them of all rights but one—the right to practice the Christian virtue of meekness; and to this day that virtue is still widely practiced in Russia, though to call it a Christian virtue has now been forbidden. Why call it meekness when there are other words for it, such as obedience and discipline?

The historian Kliuchevsky once summed up Russian history in a single sentence: "The state thrives while the people grow sickly." It is this brutalizing national experience which makes for the compelling force of the Legend and is by far the deeper explanation of it. Whatever Dostoevsky's manifest intention, actually it is one of the most revolutionary and devastating critiques of power and authority ever produced. What it comes to in the end is a total rejection of Caesar's realm, a rejection of power in all its forms, in its actuality as in its rationalizations; and it exposes above all the fatal effect of power on such ideals and aspirations of humanity as are embodied in the original Christian teaching. Clearly, then, the Legend cuts under Dostoevsky's persistent efforts to present Eastern Orthodoxy as a viable alternative to the Orthodoxy of the[164] West; the czars, autocrats of Church and State alike, were after all quite as grand as any Roman Pontiff in their inquisitorial absolutism. Hence it can be said, on this ground and other grounds too, that the implications of the Legend belie the "official" national-religious thesis of the novel as a whole.

For implicit in the Legend is another thesis altogether, that of Russian Christian anarchism. And apart from the Legend there are many intimations of this latent thesis in the novel. It almost emerges to the surface in chapter 5 of Book II, where Ivan, beginning with an exposition of the ideas in his article on the ecclesiastical courts, ends up by advocating the dissolution of all "earthly states" and their absorption into a Church that has in truth abjured "every purpose incongruous with its aims as a Church." To this sketch of a religious Utopia Father Zossima assents, if anything going even further than Ivan, while Father Paissy cries: "So be it, so be it!" One must know how to read the Aesopian language of this singular dialogue, with its undertones, political hints and ideological anecdotes cunningly introduced at strategic moments and then deliberately cut short before their full intent is disclosed. One such anecdote, for example, is related by the liberal Miusov whose very liberalism serves here as a screen behind which the author can have his say without too obviously compromising himself. Miusov tells of meeting a Frenchman in Paris, an influential personage in the Government, who confides in him that "we are not particularly afraid of all those socialists, anarchists, infidels and revolutionists. . . . But there are a few peculiar men among them who believe in God and are Christians, but at the same time are socialists. These are the people we are most afraid of. . . . The[165] socialist who is a Christian is more to be dreaded than a socialist who is an atheist." In the given context this comes through as virtually a confession on Dostoevsky's part. The crypto-anarchist or socialist element in the novel was not noticed, to be sure, by Dostoevsky's reactionary mentors, such as Pobedonostsev for instance,[6] who lauded him for showing up the disrupters of the imperial authority without suspecting that he himself—or was it his double?—was inextricably involved with them. Merezhkovsky was essentially right, I think, in the claim he once made that the author of *The Brothers Karamazov*, though fearful of speaking out, was at bottom a religious revolutionist.

The Russian intelligentsia of the nineteenth century was deeply

---

[6] Pobedonostsev, at that time Procurator of the Holy Synod and tutor of the Crown Prince, was an out-and-out reactionary authoritarian bearing in his role and personality a rather strong family-likeness to the Grand Inquisitor: so much so in fact that some Russian critics (e.g., Georgi Chulkov in *Kak rabotal Dostoevski*) have speculated on the possibility of Dostoevsky actually having had him in mind as a model even while enjoying his patronage and writing him letters of fulsome flattery.

antagonistic to State and Empire. It produced all sorts of libertarian ideas, secular and religious, which, while related to Western influences, at the same time reflect the elemental hatred of authority prevailing among the peasant masses, a hatred sometimes taking the form of blind anarchic revolt but more often that of meek submission; yet the submission has something about it so flagrant, a perfection of abjectness as it were, which is in itself a kind of challenge and provocation. It goes without saying that Dostoevsky was thoroughly infected with such feelings, and that their ambivalence suited his psychological make-up. And, in speaking of this anarchism, what is meant by it is nothing like a theoretically worked-out doctrine, as that of Bakunin or Kropotkin; he was hardly[166] able to distinguish between anarchism and socialism. The one emphatic distinction he did make was between believing and unbelieving rebels; and if he was an opponent of the socialists it was, on the conscious level at any rate, because of their atheism, which he struggled to suppress in himself, and the totalitarian potential he discerned in their designs. Inevitably his religious anarchism brings to mind the anarchism of Tolstoy, and in this respect it is instructive to compare the two novelists. Dostoevsky's anarchism is fully as Utopian as that of Tolstoy but with these important differences: it is latent rather than manifest in his work and it is mystical rather than rational in conception; its political aims are ill-defined and ambiguous; intrinsically it is more the expression of an apocalyptic mood than of a radical will to revolution as a practical enterprise. The notion of a "free theocracy" expounded by Ivan is a contradiction in terms—a system of government by priests is scarcely the medium in which freedom might be expected to flourish. But if it is a contradiction, it is exactly of the type, holding in balance his conflicting impulses toward rebellion and submission, to which Dostoevsky was always irresistibly drawn.

In the late 1870's, the period of the composition of *The Brothers Karamazov*, his exasperation grew as he watched the continuing attraction of Russian youth to subversive doctrines. He felt the need to provide some kind of alternative to those godless doctrines, and one surmises that that was the motive for his advancing, even if tentatively, the idea of the regeneration of society through the rise of a "free theocracy." This idea, however, is so vaguely related to the real forces at work in Russian society, so Utopian in essence, as to suggest its makeshift character as a hastily mounted countermove, from the position of[167] religious radicalism, to the atheistical radicalism of his opponents among the intellectuals. On a deeper level, and without abandoning in any way his faith in the Russian Christ, he yet reacted to the signs of disintegration all around him by becoming more and more skeptical of man's capacity for salvation and the meaningfulness of his history. Thus he came to fear that the weakness of men would eventually bring on a successful attempt to organize their happiness by compulsion. This theme was not new to him. He had dealt with it before, in *Notes from Underground* and in *The Possessed*.

It is interesting to compare his earlier and later handling of this theme of "the compulsory organization of human happiness." Let us begin, then, by putting the Grand Inquisitor into relation with another and quite as famous protagonist of Dostoevsky's, the hero-narrator of *Notes from Underground*. It is for the content of their thought that they are worth comparing, and not primarily as novelistic creations. The aged cardinal of Seville, lacking the dimension of subjectivity so conspicuous in the underground man, is not a character in the proper sense of the term but simply the personification of a *Weltanschauung*— that of Ivan Karamazov in its most heretical and negative aspects. The undergroundling, on the other hand, is very far from being merely the embodiment of an idea. Still, in linking him with the Inquisitor, our concern is not with the undergroundling's prostrate personality, with his nausea of consciousness and enjoyment of his own degradation, but rather with the theory of human nature he propounds, a theory in which the bold affirmation of freedom is combined with the equally bold negation of "reason, progress and enlightenment."[168]

What this theory has in common with that of the Inquisitor is that both are centered on the question of freedom. Where they differ is in their answers to this question, the undergroundling's answer being as positive as the Inquisitor's is negative. Hence the contrast between the two theories gives us the measure of the growth and change of Dostoevsky's thought between the early 1860's, when he wrote *Notes from Underground*, and the period of his last and greatest novel. The earlier work is written from the perspective of the isolated and perversely recalcitrant individual, who, in his "moral obliquity," will never consent to join the "universal and happy antheap" projected by the ideologues of rational self-interest and progress toward an harmonious society. Through the figure of this unconsoled and unconsolable individual Dostoevsky pointed to the chaos and irrationality of human nature, thus mocking the utilitarian formulas of the radicals and liberals. "Man everywhere and at all times . . . has preferred to act as he chose and not in the least as his reason and advantage dictated. . . . One's own unfettered choice, one's own caprice . . . is that very 'most advantageous advantage' . . . against which all systems and theories are shattered to atoms. . . . What man wants is simply *independent* choice, whatever that independence may cost and wherever it may lead." He readily admits that man "likes to make roads and to create," but this admission goes with the emphatic reminder that man also loves chaos and destruction. He is therefore convinced that the organization of a rational society—which, in his view, cannot but turn out to be a human antheap—will prove forever impossible.

Now this is a vision entirely at variance with that of the[169] Inquisitor, whose idea it is that "independent choice" is exactly what men fear most; that is the source both of his contempt for them and his paradoxical determination to strip them of the useless gift of free choice so as to convert them into the childishly happy and ignorant members of a totalitarian collective. He proclaims the failure of historical Christianity to illuminate and sanctify human existence, but this failure he imputes not to the Church but to the falsity of Christ's message in the light of the proven inadequacy of human nature. Consequently the Church can have no function but that of an instrument of power in the hands of an elite that has taken up the sword of Caesar. Since man is feebler and baser than Christ believed him to be, it was senseless to bring him the gift of freedom. The weak soul is unable to benefit from such heady gifts. The Inquisitor is not a psychologist pure and simple, like the undergroundling. In his thought psychological insights are supported by historical facts. Another difference is that the primary object of his polemic is what he takes to be the illusion of human freedom, whereas the undergroundling makes reason the target of his devaluating analysis.

When it came to writing *The Brothers Karamazov* Dostoevsky had wholly surmounted the standpoint of defiant and obdurate individualism exhibited in *Notes from Underground*. He then thought that the Palace of Crystal (at that time his prime symbol of socialism, superseded later by the Tower of Babel, a more cheerless symbol) would never be built because men were too independent to permit its construction. This type of individualism, however, with its stress on the unfettered human will and the inexhaustible intransigence of self-pride, is not really[170] consonant with the religious valuation of life. It is, in fact, a secular type of individualism which can be turned quite as effectively against Christian philosophies as against the philosophy of social progress; the recalcitrant individual may after all refuse to choose Christ in the same "irrational" way as he refuses to submit to the dictates of reason and self-interest. "Moral obliquity" provides as insecure a foundation for the Kingdom of God as for the Kingdom of Man. It is only in later years, as his religious consciousness became fully engaged in his creative effort, that Dostoevsky developed a new idea of freedom, based not on "moral obliquity" but on Christian love and the unviolated conscience.

Also, it is important to note that so far as socialism is concerned it is mainly the conception of it dramatized in *The Possessed* which is epitomized in the Legend, and that, in a sense, the figure of the Inquisitor also derives from that novel, being an elaborated and historically enriched variant of the sketchy figure of Shigalyov. It will be remembered that Shigalyov, an eccentric ideologue, comes to the conclusion that unlimited freedom can be attained only through unlimited despotism, or, rather, that the extremes of freedom and despotism are in reality identical. Accordingly he proposes, as no less than "a final solution of the social question," that mankind be divided into

two unequal parts, one-tenth enjoying "absolute liberty and un-
bounded power over the other nine-tenths. The others have given up
all individuality and become, so to speak, a herd, and, through
boundless submission, will by a series of regenerations achieve pri-
meval innocence, something like the Garden of Eden. They'll have to
work, however." The society envisaged by the Inquisitor is plainly a
later[171] edition of Shigalyov's herd, and the latter's elite is even
further reduced in numbers by the Inquisitor: "There will be thousands of millions of happy babes, and a hundred thousand sufferers
who have taken upon themselves the curse of the knowledge of good
and evil." The reign of the "sufferers" will be cruel, of course, for they
believe that their cruelty will guarantee the happiness of the rest of
mankind. Moreover, as Albert Camus has remarked, they excuse their
cruelty by claiming, like the Satan of the Romantics, that it will be
hard for them to bear.

Yet there is no denying that even this mordant reading of the
historical past and future did not deter Dostoevsky from asserting his
belief that freedom of choice in the knowledge of good and evil is the
essence of man's humanity and the essence of Christ's teaching. The
kind of faith or obedience that is bought with bread is evil, and so is
any constraint on man's conscience, in whatever form, even if the
constraint is exercised for ostensibly good ends. Freedom is not to be
confounded with goodness or happiness. Goodness festers if bred by
constraint, and happiness turns into brutish contentment. Only when
freely chosen do they acquire a human content. This is precisely what
makes Dostoevsky a novelist of tragic freedom, his perception that
genuine freedom, being open to the choice between good and evil, is
unthinkable without suffering. That is the price of freedom, and he
who refuses to pay it can only dream of freedom without experiencing
it, without substantiating it within the actual process of living. It is a
conception which on one side of it is close to existentialist thought. For
Dostoevsky, as for the existentialists, it is above all through the
experience of choice and decision, resolutely entered upon, that the
individual comes to[172] self-realization. But this grasp and possession
of one's own being, which is the human creature's truest rapture, is at
the same time inescapably associated with anxiety and suffering, and
for this reason men are continually driven to shirk meaningful choices.
However, the difference between some of the latter-day existentialists
and Dostoevsky is that for him the act of choosing is wholly a moral if
not always a religious act while for them it is an act unconditionally
open to existence in all its sheerness and totality, not limited to any
single sphere, ethical or otherwise.

Now in the Legend Dostoevsky so represents the truth of history—that is, the truth not of what ought to be but of what is and has
been—that we see it as patently belonging to the Inquisitor, not to
Christ. Dostoevsky none the less takes his stand with Christ. This
should not surprise us; if we consider his biography in its temporal

depth, so to speak, we find that he committed himself very early to this clinging to Christ in the face of all the malignant realities of history and man's nature. More than twenty-five years before composing the Legend he wrote in a letter from his place of exile in Siberia that if it were proven to him that Christ is "outside the truth, and if the truth really did exclude Christ, I should prefer to stay with Christ and not with the truth."

This paradoxical attitude is not to be taken as mere sentiment. It has its consequences. In the context of the Legend it means that if Dostoevsky rejects the wisdom of the Inquisitor, it is solely in the terms of the desperate paradox of his faith in Christ. Otherwise he apparently neither doubts nor denies that malign wisdom. What is to be observed, too, is that he thus indirectly fulfills his ideological aim of excluding any middle ground between[173] Christ and the Grand Inquisitor. And the starkness and ultimatism of the choice he offers, which has the effect of shrinking our sense of historical possibilities and reducing our resourcefulness in the face of extremes, reminds us of other great thinkers of the nineteenth century, like Kierkegaard and Marx, who likewise made war, though from other standpoints, on that century's liberal humanism—Kierkegaard with his either-or formula that is spiritually quite as terroristic as that of the Russian novelist, and Marx with his inexorable idea that if humanity fails to choose socialism it will inevitably fall back into barbarism.[174]

A Psychological View of Alyosha's Reaction to Father Zossima's Death

MARK KANZER

Dostoevsky's *The Brothers Karamazov* was used by Freud himself as a paradigm of the parricidal drives involved in the Oedipus complex. In the present study, an effort will be made to illuminate further this universal tendency as it is manifested in the Russian novel, particularly with respect to the formation of religious phantasies as defenses against such impulses.

Reprinted from "The Vision of Father Zossima from *The Brothers Karamazov*" by Mark Kanzer, in *American Image*, VIII (December 1951). By permission of Wayne State University Press. Copyright © 1951 by Wayne State University Press.

Actually, Dostoevsky's tale describes two fathers: the sensual and despicable Fyodor Karamazov, the actual parent, and the monk, Zossima, who is the spiritual father of the youth Alyosha. The murder of Fyodor by his presumptive offspring, Smerdyakov, becomes the occasion for the author's thesis that all men harbor parricidal wishes and therefore share, in a measure, the burden of guilt for such a crime. Alyosha alone escapes responsibility since he has already turned to religion and has therefore cleansed himself of such inclinations.

The details of the process by which it is accomplished are indicated in the book, yet will not be apparent in their full significance without the application of psychoanalytic insight. A review of the voluminous literary and psychological commentaries on this famous novel also fails to disclose evidence that the obvious relationship between the deaths of Father Zossima and old Karamazov has been recognized. Actually, these two men meet their ends on successive nights, and the recital of events that occur between the two tragedies contains the key to their inherent psychological relationship and to Alyosha's escape from sharing the responsibility for parricide with his brothers.[329]

The first death, the passing of the monk, unlooses a series of remarkable reactions in the "good son," Alyosha. Father Zossima's repute as a man of God had commanded such awe during his lifetime that his demise was confidently expected by his followers to be the signal for earth-shaking omens and miracles; instead, a prosaic and, under the circumstances, even scandalous turn of events took place— the earthly remains of the venerated saint underwent speedy and offensive decomposition. His recently devoted followers were shocked and dismayed. Even the loyal and deeply intelligent Alyosha seemed to experience an intense revulsion; leaving the monastery without the accustomed permission, he became prey to impulses such as one would scarcely have believed to exist within him.

With obvious symbolism, the passing of Father Zossima is placed on the eve of Lent, and the rebellious spirit that has seized possession of the youthful Karamazov inclines him first toward breaking the fast, then to the consumption of intoxicating drinks, and finally, as the repressed tendencies emerge with ever greater daring, to a visit to the same woman, Grushenka, whose charms had already brought his father and his brother into murderous rivalry. It is this encounter between Alyosha and Grushenka which contains the psychological pivot of the novel; in this turning point of the action is concealed the secret of the incestuous aspect of the Oedipal problem which the author passes over with symbolism in contrast to the frankness, though not full motivation, with which he treats the parricidal aspect.

Here the master of psychology is forced to resort to artifice in order to prevent the natural consummation of the meeting between this passionate pair; for at this moment a former lover of Grushenka is introduced to the scene and Alyosha is permitted to escape with unscathed virginity. The incest barrier is more than hinted at in the oaths exchanged between Alyosha and Grushenka to care for each other as brother and sister; the almost psychoanalytic procedure with which *The Brothers Karamazov* uncovers the deeper[330] motives of men finds here an impenetrable resistance.

The pendulum whose inner laws have been revealed by the swing from Father Zossima to the mother-sister figure Grushenka has thus reached the limit of its arc. The returning sweep helps us to understand more clearly the function of the monk in the mental economy of the sexually frustrated young man. Whereas Alyosha's reactions after the death of his esteemed master demonstrated with unmistakable force and clarity the tensions held in check by this veneration, the aftermath of the decisive interview with Grushenka shows how his piety provided not only a repressive agent but also an outlet for his banished libidinal impulses as well. Retracing literally—and symbolically—his footsteps to the monastery, he arrived once more before the bier of his spiritual father. He had oscillated between love and death, the poles of existence; and as one barrier had circumscribed his orbit in the direction of the woman, so another—his own life—interposed itself between him and the man.

The resources of the unconscious now broke through this new frustration. In a trance, Alyosha sank to the ground before the corpse and joined him, in a dream, beyond the gateway of death. He beheld himself in Heaven, and Christ was before him celebrating once more the first of his miracles, the conversion of water into wine for the wedding guests at Cana. In the vision, the virgin Mary moved among the assembled people, and in a few words Dostoevsky let us see that in Alyosha's mind she is identified with Grushenka—i.e., she is the mother figure, forever unattainable. Jesus sits apart, apparently preoccupied with his own thoughts, but on his mother's insistence takes note of the situation and uses his miraculous powers to provide simple folk with the wine which they require for their happiness.

Then, in the dream, Zossima himself arises from his coffin and in a similar joyful gesture, urges Alyosha to join in the festivities. At the touch of his hand and the sound of his voice, the feelings of tension within the young man dissolve and, in a rapturous mood, he awakens. Back in the[331] cell with the corpse of the monk, the impulses of the dream persist. Stepping out into the night, Alyosha throws himself on the earth, weeping, and kisses the ground ecstatically over and over again. Then something from outside himself seems to take possession of him and when he arises, it is with a resolution and certainty about himself that he is to carry with him for the rest of his life. It was also at this hour—perhaps at this very moment, although the author does not make it clear—that Alyosha's real father was being murdered through the joint will of his other sons.

This typical religious conversion scene may now be viewed in its proper psychological perspective. Alyosha, unable to attain the love he craves from Grushenka, finds a substitute in the kindliness of Jesus and Zossima. If they can not be the chief participants at the wedding feast, they can find joy and a place for themselves by ministering to others. Alyosha, at the bier of the monk, is confronted with the materialization of his death wishes against his own father; the true miracle which occurred on this occasion was the transformation of the hatred into love. The passing of Zossima served as signal for the eruption of repressed erotic drives which had been held in check by the component of fear present in the awe for his saint; even his physical departure from the scene, however, could not remove the inhibitions against the break-through of the incest barrier, and the reactivated libido could find no other course than to return to the ambivalently regarded religious figure and strengthen the "good father" component in the mixed character which he represented to the youth.

It is not difficult to see here that Dostoevsky is intuitively presenting us with the same problems that have always constituted the underlying sense of puberty rites for young men; and in particular, his narrative shows an amazing resemblance to and even supplements and gives a deeper meaning to the concepts used by Freud in his delineation of the totem feast. The impulses released in Alyosha by the passing of Zossima are overwhelmingly oral; there is a craving[332] for food, then for drink, and, in the ensuing quest for the mother figure, doubtless a revival of early memories of the breast. Christ and Zossima re-exert their claim to libidinal attachments by the dispensal of wine, as though to say that food may be obtained from the body of the father as well as of the mother; the nature of the "water" and the "wine" become apparent in this context.

Within this framework, certain aspects of the odor of the monk's corpse gain a new meaning. The disgust aroused is familiar to analysts as a defense against the desire for oral incorporation; in this light, the unspecified excitement with which the followers were filled must be interpreted in relation to the unconscious cannibalistic phantasies which follow upon the death of the father and play such an important part in shaping the mourning process that ensues.

These oral drives are also used regressively as substitutes for sexual activities of a genital nature; and, in the culminating drama of Alyosha's conversion—as he lies on the ground, clutching and kissing the earth in ecstasy while an outer force takes possession of him, we find bisexual gratification which is interesting to relate to Lewin's concept of mania as a reconciliation with the superego at the breast of the mother. It is apparent, too, that in Freud's outline of the psychological events attendant upon the totem feast, which was put forward at a time before he had recognized the negative Oedipus complex, he did not consider the important fact that the father figure in these rites also serves as a screen for components derived from the image of the mother.

Dostoevsky's unconscious insight into these problems was, of course, derived from personal experience. His own father had been murdered while he was still a youth much like Alyosha and apparently he spent much of the rest of his life attempting to work through the sense of guilt inspired in him by the extent to which this violent act served to fulfill his own wishes. His conflicts over the father-son relationship were particularly intense at the time of writing[333] *The Brothers Karamazov* because of the recent death of his own little son whose name, as might be expected, was Alyosha. The author was apparently acutely possessed at the moment by the sense of identity between father and son, and on the murdered elder Karamazov he bestowed his own name, Fyodor. There is a striking and curious analogy here to the processes which appear to have inspired Shakespeare to compose Hamlet after the death both of his father and of his son Hamnet. Presumably guilt emanating from the counter-Oedipal as well as Oedipal tendencies was involved. Father Zossima himself was drawn from the real personality of Father Amvrosi, a monk whose words of comfort to the bereaved writer moved him to the extent of choosing the monastery of this good man for his burial.

Freud has called attention to the role assigned by the novelist to the epileptic Smerdyakov as the murderer of old Karamazov; the psychological meaning of the writer's own illness both as an expression of uncontrollable forces within himself and as punishment for them becomes fear. There is assuredly some correlation, too, between the writer's creative urges and the convulsive seizures, which increased notably during periods of literary creativity.

Furthermore, we find little difficulty in recognizing, in Alyosha's swoon, his falling to the ground, his writhing and his ecstasy, phenomena of epilepsy; his ambivalent religiosity, suppressed criminal impulses and hallucinatory experiences represent familiar psychic concomitants. Out of such intense travail was born anew the "good son," counterpart to the "good father"; purged in this process were the parricidal impulses which came to fulfillment at the same moment through the hands of the epileptic Smerdyakov. More specifically— since Alyosha's vision was also Dostoevsky's and conveyed the solution derived by his own unconscious—we may say that the novelist applied to himself the message of Cana and learned to transform the waters of his bitter experiences into the literary wine that was to be set before the multitudes. In the identification with Jesus, he carried[334] to a climax the psychic processes underlying the composition of "The Brothers Karamazov."[335]

Myth and Symbol in *The Brothers Karamazov*

RALPH MATLAW

A larger unit of Dostoevsky's technique is the myth and the mythical construct. Myth is an immediate intuition of reality, and it is primarily ritualistic or religious in character, but it may, like Ivan's Legend, be purely literary. We must distinguish between the reality apprehended and the poetic function the myth may have. Many of the myths in the book are simple in nature and occur in single scenes. Like literary references, however, they eventually coalesce into mythic constructs, so that realization may arise through a succession of related episodes.

The central myth, of course, concerns regeneration, whether expressed in religious terms or considered as psychological rehabilitation. It is stated in several forms in the two chapters "Women of Faith" and "A Lady of Little Faith" during Father Zossima's ministrations to physical and mental illnesses, and affects in turn the leading characters in the narrative. Grushenka is the first to undergo a transformation, occasioned by Alyosha's presence and having a reciprocal effect on him. The scene takes place under the most propitious circumstances: Alyosha's temporary loss of faith has led him to Grushenka, but in place of a temptress he finds a creature mollified by the imminent reunion with her first seducer, the man who can make complete amends to her. Grushenka in any case is a profound believer, and her reaction to the news of Zossima's death need not depend on immediate circumstances. By her consideration for Alyosha's feelings and her respect for Zossima's position, she restores belief to Alyosha. And he, in turn, verbalizes his estimate of her goodness and moral stature. At this point we are given the folk legend of[20] "the little onion," mythologically representing the charitable act that leads to redemption, but

From *Technique in* The Brothers Karamazov, Part II (1957). Reprinted by permission of the publisher, Mouton and Co., The Hague.

simultaneously emphasizing that it is the spirit of the act, rather than the gift itself, that leads to the desirable theological conclusion. The same myth is echoed in the trial, but represents simply human recognition of kindness, when Dr. Herzenstube estimates Mitya's character solely on Mitya's remembering the gift of a pound of nuts. The turning point in Mitya's career, the beginning of his regeneration, occurs during his dream of "the babe" in Book IX. His dream intensifies the feeling involved in the myths of onions and nuts into an overwhelming compassion for suffering humanity. Alyosha's spiritual resurrection naturally assumes an explicitly religious statement of the same myth, Cana of Galilee. Ivan performs a similar deed when he rescues a peasant in the snow and himself comments that he would not have done so had he not decided to confess his guilt during the trial (contrition). Negative involvement in this mythic construct relates to Fyodor Pavlovich, whose vacillations between a sensual perversion of love and a certain anxiety about the nether regions of a possible after-life are terminated by his murder; to Smerdyakov, whose inability to accept either Ivan's moral anarchy or orthodox religion leads to his suicide; and Rakitin, whose identity with Judas is obvious in promising to convey Alyosha to Grushenka for twenty-five rubles.[1]

Another level of myth appears in connection with parricide, the pivot of the plot. It is impossible to account satisfactorily for Smerdyakov's act if only psychological or material motivations are considered. The procuror and Fetyukovich each has a different "character analysis" of Smerdyakov, but neither completely accounts for the murder. Similarly Mitya and Ivan have their views, the first dismissing (with some uncertainty) the possibility of Smerdyakov as murderer, the second, after different doubts, finally being confronted with irrefutable proofs of his guilt. But in Smerdyakov's confession to Ivan extenuations appear.[21] Circumstances were extremely favorable and the idea had only occurred to Smerdyakov after Grigory was struck down. That is, in part chance guides the action. It may further be added that other motivations are possible: Smerdyakov's bastardry, the taunting by Fyodor Pavlovich, the desire to please Ivan, the possibility of financial gain. Whatever else may be involved in parricide, and echoed in Ivan's shattering remark at the trial "Who does not desire his father's death?" can only be adumbrated, hinted in a novel, not stated or solved. Smerdyakov's role in the murder, then, can never be justified on purely rational grounds. But another literary level is possible:

But isn't the criminal rape and impregnation of the idiot Liza by Fyodor Karamazov a simple and sculpturesque motif, worthy of the most antique art, a frieze interrupted and taken up again, where Vengeance and

---

[1] The concept of charity, or love, is stated in innumerable ways in the book, most pithily and memorably in part ix of the life of Zossima: "Hell . . . is suffering for the inability to love."

Expiation unfold; and then the mysterious, unexplained animal movement
of the mother, an instrument of the vengeance of destiny without knowing
it, motivated perhaps by something of resentment mixed with physical
gratitude for her violator, going off to give birth at the home of Fyodor
Karamazov. This is the first act—mysterious, grand, august, like the creation
of the Woman in the sculptures of Orvieto. The second act, echoing the
first, takes place more than twenty years later: the murder of Fyodor
Karamazov, the disgrace on the Karamazov family by the son of the idiot,
Smerdyakov, followed by an act as mysteriously sculpturesque and unexplained as the obscure and natural beauty of giving birth in the garden of
Fyodor Karamazov—his crime accomplished, Smerdyakov hanging himself.[2]

Cultural anthropologists provide a less imaginative but more specific
interpretation. Particularly in earlier and more primitive myths, parricide is an integral and vital stage in the development of the mythic
figure, and under various guises is intimately connected with the
concepts of maturity, fertility and rebirth. While tapping the profound
primitive significance of parricide, Dostoevsky treats it in *The Brothers
Karamazov* primarily in psychological and ethical terms. Thus the
murder involves not only the actual culprit, but all the brothers, Ivan
who provides the theory, Dmitry who creates the opportunity in the
turmoil during the sexual rivalry of[22] father and son, and Alyosha,
who foresees a crime but remains passive. Beyond the immediate
family, the myth involves Fetyukovich, "An Adulterer of Thought," the
townspeople who desire to see Mitya convicted and, by extension, all
of Russia and humanity, since the trial becomes a *cause célèbre*,
evincing interest throughout the land.

Another method of creating a literary myth consists of dramatizing
ideas (without specific mythological statements) and repeating or
varying these ideas, in applying them to various personages. A significant example exists in the problem of immortality or the after-life. In
addition to such discussions as were here treated under other headings,
Dostoevsky treats the problem as one of resurrection. Thus in the
mother's description of her son Aleksey her very reminiscence recap-
tures the image of her son and reintroduces him into the actual world.
A more sophisticated approach, that of Khokhlakova, presents the
possibility of an after-world as a constant source of torment and a
deterrent to belief. Among the clerics Miusov again raises the question,
as the fundamental tenet of Ivan's system (and hence one of the causes
of the murder), that man need have no moral compunctions if he
believes neither in God nor in the after-life. A "return" from the other
world is implied in the life-long memory Alyosha retains of his mother
and even receives verbal, though vague, mention from Mitya's "I don't

   [2] Marcel Proust, *La Prisonnière* (Paris, 1947), II, 222–3. Translated by the
Editor.

know whether my mother prayed to God . . . at that moment." The secret of Ivan's ethics is disclosed by the Inquisitor when he denies the possibility of an after-life. After-life is a fundamental article of belief in Ferapont, the devil crusher, and is derided specifically by Ivan's devil, who calls Ferapont's ilk "spiritualist." In a slightly different sense, there is a resurrection in Kolya after his escapade with the train. But the most dramatic implementation of the concept occurs in that extraordinary final chapter of the epilogue, the summation, resolution and promised amelioration in the future of the deepest conflicts presented in the book, when the influence of Ilyusha from beyond the grave becomes an ethical imperative.

This theme and others like it could be traced in still greater[23] detail. However, another equally important device must first be noted, that of the symbol. It is frequently difficult to determine whether something is only symbolic or whether it assumes a still larger mythic meaning, particularly since Dostoevsky's symbolic procedure depends upon large symbolic scenes as much as on the specific, limited symbol. There are scenes and even symbols, usually echoed elsewhere in the book, that achieve almost mythic stature. Moreover, they are analogous to the interrelation between myth and rational statement in combining real (natural) phenomena with a metaphysical ambiguity that is solvable only in terms of the whole structure. In general, the first scene is long, stated in considerable detail, while the second is at times only a passing remark. Our first example concerns the corruption of Zossima's body.

Natural conditions point toward the fact that rapid decomposition is unavoidable and is hastened by the expectation of a miracle. The day is described as clear, the season is late summer, consequently the temperature is high. Zossima's partisans await the odor of sanctity and therefore keep the window shut; they refuse to place flowers in the room, in order to notice at once the slightest smell. There is a constant throng around the bier, composed of those paying their last homage and the merely curious (whatever their motives they all breathe and thereby raise the room temperature). The aged elder had been moribund for some time. In other words, chemically and biologically it would be rather sanguine to expect anything other than the actual result. Under different conditions Zossima's sparse frame might indeed have been helpful in slowing the process of decomposition, but the point here is that such miracles are not to be predicted, expected and abetted by human volition. When man predicts a miracle, which theologically he cannot do, he may also hinder the miracle physically. The matter might have rested here except that error continues in both camps. Those of "little faith" accept the smell as God's judgment on[24] Zossima's perversion of his office and those who still believe in him anticipate another miracle as the justification of their trust. This new sign, however, entails another argument, on the merits or correctness of innovations introduced at Mt. Athos, and both factions again lose sight of the real issue.[3]

Much later, another set of circumstances precedes Ilyusha's funeral. Although the boy has been ill, his body is young. The season is winter, and while his body lies inside, Snegiryov's room is badly heated. There are fewer visitors; Katerina Ivanovna sends flowers. Thus while a certain ambiguity exists in the physical conditions, the absence of odors is quite logical. Dostoevsky reintroduces the metaphysical note: "Strangely, there was hardly any smell from the body." Zossima's decomposition is presented in eleven pages and its repercussions extend to the end of the book; Ilyusha's is treated in a paragraph. The comment on the boy's odor reports a fact which may be variously interpreted, but Dostoevsky clearly wishes something to be made of it. It is certainly not for the reader to judge whether a miracle has taken place, or to adduce proper biblical texts on the innocence and purity of children, or to postulate ethical or religious redemption through love and suffering, despite the fact that all are suggested. They are suggested not in the particular scene, but in the larger complex of the book, where the ramifications of suffering, redemption, corruption and love occur.

Another example of scenic echo is seen in Kolya Krasotkin's mirroring Ivan's thought and behavior. The impingence of reason on belief, or, in Dostoevsky's formulation, the corrupting effect of Roman Catholicism, western socialism and utopian theories, shakes Ivan's belief. Disbelief assumes many forms, ranging from the tortured doubts of Ivan, through the complacent Rakitin and shallow Fetyukovich, to the precocious but inexperienced Kolya. It is a widespread phenomenon, propagated less easily by the involved compositions of Ivan than by the superficial, "popularized" views of Rakitin. Each has his follower, Ivan in Smerdyakov, Rakitin in Kolya, who is receptive to a proselytizer of liberal views.[25] The central fact of disbelief finds expression in deeds attuned to the respective characters. Mitya and others note, and Smerdyakov ultimately acts, on Ivan's rational hypothesis "all is permitted if there is no God." The problem of Ivan's guilt is enormously complex and provides the subject for much of the book. Yet the same problem appears in its simplest form in the strangling of the goose, where the issue is perfectly clear, the guilt and moral consequences (if any) obvious. Like Ivan, Kolya states a scheme; the peasant, putting the scheme into operation, pulls the horse, thereby killing the goose. The episode also points ahead to the trial, for the amused judge condemns the peasant (the instrument) to

---

[3] This is the second time the monastery at Mt. Athos is maligned in the *Brothers.* Fyodor Pavlovich attributes specific sexual connotations to the absence of female animals and fowl from that monastery.

pay, while he dismisses Kolya (the instigator) with a warning to stop projecting such schemes.

Disbelief may also stem from psychological causes, but here again Kolya resembles Ivan. The chapters devoted to Kolya's background and his behavior among his schoolmates graphically illustrate that he tries to stifle all demonstrative, "emotional" behavior, to seem aloof and indifferent. The same psychological mechanism, developed and petrified, produces Ivan's incapacity for love. Each has had an over demonstrative mother or female relative; each suffers from the absence of a father. But Kolya is still sufficiently young to permit Alyosha's consideration and good nature to provide a remedy that Ivan would only be able to attain after a grave crisis.

One of the most fascinating repetitions of symbolic scenes involves making important metaphysical or moral statements by means of a distasteful object. During the preliminary investigation Mitya is forced to undress. That moment presents the nadir of his life:

'Well, if it's necessary . . . I . . .' Mitya mumbled and, sitting down on the bed, started to take off his stockings. He was unbearably disturbed. Everyone was dressed while he was undressed and, strangely, when undressed he himself somehow felt that he was guilty before them, and most important, almost agreed himself that really he suddenly became inferior to all of them, and that they now had a perfect right to despise him. 'When all are undressed one isn't ashamed, but when you're the only one who's undressed while the rest look at you—it's disgraceful!' flashed through his mind again and again. 'It's just like a dream, sometimes I've dreamed of being disgraced like this.' But it was absolutely[26] torture for him to take off his socks. They were awfully dirty, and his underwear too, and now everyone saw it. And most important, he himself disliked his feet, for some reason all his life found his big toes on both feet monstrous, particularly one coarse, flat, somehow ingrown nail on the right foot, and now they would all see it. Through unbearable shame he suddenly became even more coarse, and this time intentionally. He ripped off his shirt himself.

'Wouldn't you like to search anyplace else, if you're not ashamed?'

This scene is a prime example of the sublime rendered in terms of the distasteful. Like King Lear's casting off his garments on the heath, Mitya is reduced to the essential man. The guilt he feels has little or no basis in real, material terms, but is delineated with incredible finesse psychologically and mythically. Mitya is completely isolated. His degradation, his misery is exacerbated by the knowledge that his physical deformity, his hygienic indifference will be taken as a sign of moral degeneracy. Nothing could be further from the truth, for symbolically Mitya reasserts his dignity and stature in his frantic personal shame and his contempt for the "material proofs" sought by the investigators.

This fleeting scene is echoed in Ivan's third meeting with Smerdyakov. Smerdyakov has hidden the money in a long white stocking. While he slowly searches for it and then pulls it out, Ivan is overcome with an incredible feeling of horror. Ivan's reaction must be noted by the reader, but cannot equal the reader's, for it is based on Ivan's dawning realization of his guilt, his physical repugnance to Smerdyakov, who is sick, sallow, in an over-heated room where the swarming of innumerable cockroaches provides an audible background. In part, however, the reader shares Ivan's horror, for this scene exactly reverses Mitya's. Now the stocking is not filthy but white (purity), yet it conceals the wages of crime and exposes a moral void. Unlike Mitya, Smerdyakov remains dressed, but his world is collapsing, too. The dandy who spent all his money on pomades and clothes is now encased in a dirty dressing[27] gown. Dostoevsky enlarges the symbolic meaning: when Marya Kondratyevna brings in lemonade, Smerdyakov starts to cover the banknotes with his handkerchief, but since it is dirty he prefers to cover them with a book, the *Holy Saying of Saint Isaac*. This book, previously noted as Grigory's property, has been abandoned by Smerdyakov after, presumably, an unsuccessful attempt to find a meaningful moral scheme. The symbolic juxtaposition of book and banknotes in preference to handkerchief and banknotes, not only startlingly underlines Smerdyakov's complete indifference to everything, but states the corollary to Mitya's scene: laudable or innocuous external trappings are no guarantee of inner value, no more than dirt and deformity signal inner corruption.[4]

An explicitly stated concept may be dramatically illustrated by objects which become symbolic. I take the ethical center of the book to lie in Mitya's conclusion in the first part of his confession:

Beauty is a terrible and dreadful thing! Terrible because it cannot be and must not be defined, since God only set us puzzles. Here the extremes meet, here all contradictions coexist. I am very uneducated, brother, but I've thought a lot about it. There are terribly many secrets. Too many puzzles oppress man on earth. Solve them as best you can and keep your head above the water. Beauty! I cannot even endure the idea that a man of lofty heart and great intellect begins with the ideal of the Madonna and finishes with that of Sodom. And even more terrible, a man with the ideal of Sodom in his heart doesn't renounce the ideal of the Madonna either, his heart is aflame with it, truly, truly aflame as in his young, innocent days. No, man is broad, too broad even, I'd have him narrower. The devil only knows what it all means. What the mind considers shameful, the heart takes as outright beauty. Is there beauty in Sodom? Believe me that for the overwhelming majority of people it lies just there. Did you know that secret or not? It's dreadful that beauty is not only a terrible but also a secret thing. Here the devil struggles with God and man's heart is the battlefield.

The possibilities of good and evil constantly coexist in Mitya. He may kill his father, he may not. He may reform, or he may wind up in a slum. At one point they exist in physical objects side by side: as

---

[4] Similarly, Fyodor Pavlovich's envelope achieves a symbolic meaning completely out of proportion to its thematic value.

Khokhlakova sends Mitya off to the gold mines, she[28] hangs a medallion of St. Varvara around his neck. The reader of course remembers the other object around Mitya's neck.

Such symbolism pervades the *Brothers Karamazov*, as it does other works. In his notes to the novel there is an indication that this is a conscious method. A *nota bene* for the meeting in Book VII between Alyosha and Grushenka admonishes *"Don't forget*—candles," clearly a symbolic counterpart to the spiritual illumination Grushenka under-goes. Symbols like these can be conveniently grouped. Although physical details are comparatively few in Dostoevsky's works, a description may contain a symbolic detail. Thus Fyodor Pavlovich's fleshy, oblong Adam's-apple, the fleshy bags under his eyes accentuate his propensity for physical debauchery. Ivan's sagging right shoulder, Alyosha's downcast eyes and Mitya's gesture toward his heart also emphasize characteristic traits. Perhaps the most striking descriptive detail con-cerns Fetyukovich: as he rises to speak "he constantly bent his back in a peculiar way, particularly at the beginning of the speech, not quite bowing, but as if he were rushing or flying toward his listeners, bending, as it were, just with half of his long back, as though a spring had been placed in the middle of that long, thin back which would enable him to bend almost at a right angle." The mechanical device and bending at unnatural angles perfectly symbolize Fetyukovich's mind.

In addition to those object-symbols previously mentioned, note should be taken of the rock in the epilogue (and the stone casting among the schoolboys), the "dozen" schoolboys who come to Ilyusha's funeral, the envelope Fyodor Pavlovich prepares for Grushenka, the pestle Mitya picks up, the pillow Mitya finds under his head when he wakes from his dream about "the babe"—symbolic proof that his feelings are shared by someone among those surrounding him.[5]

Another group of symbols, derived from animal life, usually involves religious connotations. Zossima's brother begs forgiveness[29] for having sinned from the birds he hears outside the window. Ilyusha asks that bread be put on his grave to attract birds, so that he may not be lonely. Alyosha further indicates the function of the little band in calling them "blue doves." The same myth is inverted when Father Ferapont claims to be visited not by the Holy Ghost in the form of a dove, but by the Holy Spirit in the form of a swallow, goldfinch or blue-bonnet. Smerdyakov's only reaction to religion is to the ritual in it: as a boy he solemnly hangs cats and buries them with ceremony. A vital part of the section on the boys is concerned with the metamorphosis of the dog Zuchka ("little beetle") into Perezvon ("bell peal"). On a lower scale in the animal world, but much more important in the novel,

---

[5] The point is made more explicitly later, when Kalganov is the only person who will shake Mitya's hand. But the Samaritan remains anonymous.

are some forty references to spiders, insects, bugs, cockroaches and reptiles.[6] All the Karamazovs are sooner or later called insects or bugs, with much of the connotation of Mitya's "insect lust." Ivan, Mitya, Fyodor Pavlovich, Katerina Ivanovna and Grushenka are affiliated with something reptilian, as a peculiarly loathsome form of human depravity. Mitya's and Fyodor Pavlovich's sexual perversions and Ferapont's religious vagaries are heralded by the spider image. Fyodor Pavlovich's threat to crush Mitya like a beetle, and Smerdyakov's fears of being similarly treated, find their culmination in Smerdyakov's cockroach infested room. The incessant rustle is an audible reminder that the insect imagery, the symbol of human corruption, now constantly accompanies the parricide.

Even colors, though by no means all of them, form a symbolic scheme, in an interplay of red, black and white. A plethora of red colors appears during and after Mitya's vigil under Fyodor Pavlovich's window, and is clearly designed to emphasize blood spilling. The dominating color of the book, however, metaphorically and literally, is black. When it is not merely descriptive, as in Grushenka's dress (though there is something funereal about her reunion with the Pole), it is associated with the elemental force (or black "humor") of the Karamazovs, a corruption of earth's life giving force. Both elements are present in the name: Karamazov[30] is derived from a Turkish root (*kará*) meaning black, and a Russian one (*maz'*) signifying tar or grease. To emphasize the blackness, Dostoevsky purposely distorts the name in the mouth of Snegiryov's wife, when she substitutes Russian for Turkish and refers to Alyosha as Chernomazov. Probably the two most important uses of the color occur during Mitya's dream of the black, charred earth, and in the chapter title "In the Dark" while Mitya is in his own Gethsemane. Black's symbolic counterpart appears most strikingly during Ilyusha's funeral, when the snow is not only a harbinger of winter but of spiritual purification as well, and in Ivan's rescue of the peasant.

Other names, too, form a kind of symbolic shorthand, while remaining perfectly common cognomens. They are sometimes revealed at critical junctures, as during the trial: Grushenka's—Svetlova (light, bright) or Katerina Ivanovna's—Verkhoventsa (upper, supreme—*i.e.*, proud). Dmitry's name is derived from Demeter (earth), Khokhlakova's, like the person, a risible appellation, Fetyukovich (blockhead), Snegiryov (bullfinch, also snow), Rakitin, who is supple like a willow, Smerdyakov (stink), Dr. Hertzenstube. Place names are significant— Chermashnya works into the symbolism of red; Mokroe, comparable to the wetting of the earth with tears; and, most important, the town of the action, Skotoprigonevsky (stockyard), aptly characterizes the in-

---

[6] I have traced these through Dostoevsky's work in "Recurrent Imagery in Dostoevskij," *Harvard Slavic Studies*, III (1956), pp. 203–227.

habitants, but is not disclosed until the full symbolic meaning can be felt.

More traditional symbolism of the four elements, particularly earth and fire, is naturally widespread in the novel. I shall merely note here their main occurrences and functions. The earth as regenerative substance appears first in the epigraph from St. John the Evangelist (later quoted again by Zossima and in a different form by the devil and is most extensively applied to Mitya: his name, his lengthy exposition of the earth's blessings in the Schiller quotations, the scorched barren earth in his dream at[31] Mokroe, expiation through hard labor underground in Siberia, his project to till the soil in America, his ardent desire to return to Russian soil; even, in comic relief, Khokhlakova's advice to extract gold from the mines. This flighty commercial venture has a double echo in Smerdyakov's returning the money he picks off the ground to Fyodor Pavlovich and Snegiryov's trampling money into the ground. Mitya is also the recipient of the symbolic bow to the ground, from Katerina Ivanovna and Zossima. It is Zossima and Alyosha who are most specifically involved in this symbol, so much so that the earth almost discloses its symbolic function: Zossima in his many pronouncements and in his remarkable death (embracing and kissing the earth) and Alyosha whose faith is restored when he repeats his mentor's prostrations. We must also note, and pass over quickly, references to Russian soil and the Russian troika in the trial speeches.

The images of fire in *The Brothers Karamazov* operate primarily as symbols for spiritual ardor and, strikingly, frequently misdirected or excessive ardor. Thus Mitya is physically and symbolically in the dark while he waits in his father's yard, but his is the "Confession of an Ardent Heart." When he is illuminated by (artificial) lights he is at his impulsive worst: he rushes in to beat up Fyodor Pavlovich, he receives Katerina Ivanovna, he hails the lights at Mokroe before his final fling. Grushenka uses the image in concealing her presence before departing to the officer: "Draw the curtains . . . otherwise he'll fly directly into the fire." Similarly, Ivan's Legend is permeated with burning and fire; Smerdyakov's indifference occurs in an over-heated room; artificially induced heat by use of liquor or wine leads to excesses in Mitya, Fyodor Pavlovich and even Grigory, while Lyagavy and Mitya almost die of asphyxiation by smoke waiting for the former to sober up. On the other hand, all the moments of regeneration involve not fire but cold: Mitya's dream of the cold babe, Ivan's rescuing the peasant from freezing, Alyosha's prostration onto the earth on a cold, clear night, the schoolboys during the winter funeral. Dostoevsky almost directly states his meaning. When Katerina[32] Ivanovna comes to Mitya for the money Mitya reports "I looked at her then for three or four seconds with terrible hatred, that very hatred that only hair separates from love, from the maddest love! I went up to the window, placed my head against the frozen window-pane, and I remember that my head started to burn from that ice as if it were fire." At the farthest extreme from Ivan's *auto da fé*, his devil recounts his sufferings from the excessive cold between planets.

Water in the novel is conspicuous by its absence. Ditches intersect the town, but fresh water is only available outside the town. When water is mentioned, it becomes significant: dew, redeeming tears, snow. It appears in each of the regeneration scenes: Ivan's snow, Alyosha's dew, Mitya's vision of the babe's frozen clothes.[7]

There are unquestionably other symbols in *The Brothers Karamazov*,[8] but those I have traced here indicate sufficiently clearly that the minutiae of the novel are as carefully controlled by Dostoevsky as the thematic and structural lines. Moreover, they illustrate the amazing unity achieved by subordinating every detail to the complex richness presented in the book, yet endowing those details with vitality and meaning that reach far beyond their immediate function. Larger aspects of technique, of balance and imaginative economy must next be examined.[33]

The Brothers Karamazov: Idea and Technique

EDWARD WASIOLEK

After the preliminary exposition *The Brothers Karamazov* begins with one of Dostoevsky's great scenes. Ostensibly a gathering in the Elder's cell to settle the grievance between Dmitry and Fyodor, the scene captures in image and dramatic gesture the polarities and

From "*The Brothers Karamazov*," in *Dostoevsky: the Major Fiction* (1964). Reprinted by permission of the publisher, the M. I. T. Press.

7 It is very difficult to find specific symbolism in the last element, air. A distinction could be made between those events taking place in the open, which are, on the whole, propitious, and those taking place or germinating indoors, which are frequently harmful. Such schematizing, however, is inconclusive.

8 Other possibilities include enclosed places, usually having something cavernous about them; doors and events taking place beyond them; money; dreams and the chiaroscuro alternation between dreams and waking. There are also a large number of topical references which are not symbolic, as those dealing with non-

dialectical oppositions of the novel. It is a magnificent introduction
to the entire novel. Near the end of the scene, Dmitry Karamazov
springs at his father and cries out in agonized rage, "Why does a man
such as he live?" As Fyodor raises the cry of "father-killer," and the cell
fills with commotion and disorder, the Elder rises from his seat, and
supported by Alyosha, shakily walks up to Dmitry, where he falls to
the ground and asks for forgiveness. The scene ends, and the novel
begins with the hand of the child raised against the father. But only
raised. For his cry of hate is muted into silence, and his gesture of
violence is stayed by the long bow of expiation by the Elder. Like a
camera click, the oppositions that Dostoevsky will dramatize in the
novel are caught and stilled in the gestures of the father, son, and
Elder: child against father; humility against hate; monastery against
the world; expiation against threat. Only[149] the novel itself will
resolve the oppositions. When the scene ends, we do not know whether
the son will destroy the father, or whether the act of humility will
destroy the hate for him.

What is at stake is important: the right of the child to raise his
hand against his father is for Dostoevsky the right of man to raise his
hand against God. Later, Ivan will base his rebellion against God on
the rights of children against the fathers who mistreat them, and by
analogy the rights of men against the God who has mistreated them;
the defense attorney at Dmitry's trial will argue that a child has the
right to demand that a father prove his love, and that a child has
the right to look upon a bad father as an enemy; and Dmitry will feel
the stirrings of a new man within him when he accepts the suffering of
children in his dream of the burnt-out huts. Finally, Alyosha will see in
children the first signs of corruption and the first impulses of faith.
Children are the moral touchstone of the novel.

In the same opening scene Ivan gives us the law by which a child
is set against his father, and the law by which man humbles himself
before man. *The law, in short, that propels Dmitry's spring and the law
by which the Elder bows before the murderer are both given by Ivan.*
The oppositions that are caught in the gestures of Dmitry and the
Elder are both carried in the breast of Ivan. The external drama is
Ivan's internal drama. In the ecclesiastical article Ivan had written, he
maintains that the church cannot logically come to terms with the state
and occupy a clearly defined but limited place in the state, as his
ecclesiastical opponent had argued. According to him, the church must,
to fulfill its true purpose, contain the whole state. The logic is impecca-
ble, for the church, as the true representative of God, can no more give
power to a temporal authority than God can. But while seemingly
insisting on a theocracy of the most absolute kind, Ivan is also saying,

---

Euclidian minds.—Dostoevsky would be acquainted with Lobachevsky, but he is
never mentioned by name, probably for the same reason Grushenka's officer is not—
both are Poles.

as Miusov gleefully and quickly points out, that there is no natural law to compel man to love his fellow man. According to Ivan, if men[150] have loved others, it is only because they have believed in immortality; and if you were to destroy the idea of immortality, you would destroy virtue and the love of others. If there is no immortality, all is permitted —and not only permitted, but enjoined. Every "right"-thinking and honest man will be obligated to express his self-interest, even to the point of crime. Miusov, who has been miffed by the attention Ivan's ecclesiastical article has provoked, gives the group this résumé so as to expose what he believes are contradictory views as well as Ivan's insincerity. The Elder Zossima knows that Ivan's views are not contradictory. He looks into Ivan's eyes and says, "If you so believe, you are blessed or most unhappy." With this statement, the Elder has drawn the logical consequences from Ivan's views. He sees that Ivan has logically drawn conclusions from two different premises, the most important and the most irreconcilable in Dostoevsky's whole work. If God exists, then what Ivan has written in his article about the church follows; if God and the attendant idea of immortality do not exist, then indeed there is only the law of self-interest, and man is obliged—if he is to live without deception—to express this law even to the point of crime. There is no contradiction in Ivan's views, but there is dreadful indecision, and this, too, the Elder sees. As the novel begins, the reader waits to see not only whether Dmitry's leap will reach his father or whether it will be stayed by the law of Zossima, but also whether Ivan, who carries both laws in his breast, will choose one or the other. *What is objectified in Dmitry against his father and in Zossima against both is internalized in Ivan against Ivan.*

Dmitry and Katerina

In the confession of an ardent heart, Dmitry tells Alyosha—he is our ears—what Katya means to him. But he tells only what he knows, and she means more to him than he knows. The relations between them bristle with paradoxes.[151] A high-minded, well-educated, rich girl insists on an engagement with an impoverished, dissolute army officer. When Dmitry basely repays her generosity by stealing her money and spending it on a wild orgy with another girl, Katerina rises nobly to forgiveness. Throughout the novel she stands ready to bear everything for his sake: vice, theft, unfaithfulness, insult, and even marriage to Grushenka. Despite all this, Dmitry not only is incorrigibly ungrateful but unaccountably sees her love and sacrifice as oppressive burdens. Katerina's "goodness" drives him to murder. The incriminating letter he writes Katya threatening his father's life makes this clear. In that letter he states that only by paying her back the money he had stolen from her could he preserve his honor, and if he could not get the money any other way, he would kill his father to get it. If the Elder's bow stays Dmitry's hand against his father, Katya's had originally moved it and continues to move it throughout the novel. The first meeting with Katerina begins with a bow, as low and as long as the Elder's bow of expiation. It is characteristic of Dostoevsky that he uses the same gesture for opposite meanings, as if to emphasize that the act remains without significance until we ourselves choose the significance.

On the simplest level it would appear that Katerina is sacrificing herself out of gratitude for Dmitry's noble gesture in saving her father and sparing her. This is the way that Alyosha understands her motives and her relations with Dmitry. As he goes to see Katya at her request early in the novel, he tells himself: "The girl's aims were of the noblest, he knew that. She was trying to save his brother Dmitry simply through generosity (*velikodushie*), though he had already behaved badly to her." And this is the way he understands it in his conversation with Dmitry, when his brother tells him about his first meeting with Katya: he assures Dmitry that Katerina loves him, and not Ivan. When Dmitry tells him about the 3,000 rubles that he had stolen from Katerina, Alyosha says:[152]

"Katerina Ivanovna will understand it all," Alyosha said solemnly. "She'll understand how great this trouble is and will forgive. She has a lofty mind, and no one could be more unhappy than you. She'll see that for herself."

Yet even while Alyosha is convinced that Katerina's motives are lofty, pure, and sincere, he has moments of uneasiness. From the very beginning, something about her troubles him. On his way to his first meeting with her, even while paying justice to her fine qualities, "a shiver began to run down his back as soon as he drew near her house." When he sees her, he sees pride, self-confidence, and strong will in her face. Her black burning eyes are set beautifully in a thin, pale, almost yellow face, and he sees why Dmitry could easily fall in love with her. But he also sees unclearly something that makes it unlikely for Dmitry to love her for a long time. He tells his brother: "Perhaps you will always love her, but perhaps you will not always be happy with her." But he no sooner says this than he feels ashamed of himself. Later, when he goes to her with Dmitry's farewell message, he feels that his first impression must have been wrong. As she comes out to meet him, he sees in her face only simplicity, goodness, and sincerity.

Again and again Alyosha tries to take her as she sees herself, but each time he is stopped by a feeling he cannot understand. He swings from facing up to his doubt about Katerina's motives to feeling ashamed of having that doubt. Alyosha is our ears and our eyes, and the difficulty he has in understanding Katerina is our difficulty. And the difficulty is great. Engaged to Dmitry, Katerina regards him as a repugnant monster; determined to save him, she plots his ruin; frantic to keep him faithful, she provokes his betrayal of her. It is she who almost saves him at the trial, and it is she who most irrevocably ruins him legally by the letter she produces in which he had uttered threats against his father's life. Throughout her relations with Dmitry, her fitful character sweeps her from love to hate,[153] generosity to spite, arrogance to submissiveness. She is all contradiction, flailing each action with its opposite. There is something in her relations with Dmitry that she cannot forgive, something that drives her to pursue him with an unrelenting, self-punishing love. She herself best expresses it in Mrs. Khokhlakova's drawing room before Ivan and Alyosha, when after a night of shame and rage at Grushenka's insult, she triumphantly announces that she will bear that too out of love for Dmitry:

"I've already decided, even if he marries that—creature" (she began solemnly), "whom I never, never can forgive, *even then I will not abandon him.* Henceforward I will never, never abandon him!" she cried, breaking into a sort of pale, hysterical ecstasy. "Not that I would run after him continually, get in his way and worry him. Oh, no! I will go away to another town—where you like—but I will watch over him all my life—I will watch over him all my life unceasingly. When he becomes unhappy with that woman, and that is bound to happen quite soon, let him come to me and he will find a friend, a sister. . . . Only a sister, of course, and so forever; but he will learn at least that that sister is really his sister, who loves him and has sacrificed all her life to him. I will gain my point. I will insist on his knowing me and confiding entirely in me, without reserve," she cried, in a sort of frenzy. "I will be a god to whom he can pray—and that, at least, he owes me for his treachery and for what I suffered yesterday through him. And let him see that all my life I will be true to him and the promise I gave him, in spite of his being untrue and betraying me."

It is this something that Alyosha finally understands as he listens to Katerina's final decision, even though he had been firmly convinced up to the previous night that she loved Dmitry: "Alyosha had till the evening before implicitly believed that Katerina Ivanovna had a steadfast and passionate love for Dmitry; but he had only believed it till the evening before." When he had awakened that morning—after dreaming of Grushenka all night—the word *nadryv* is on his lips. It is this word that startles him [154] when it is used by Mrs. Khokhlakova about Katerina's love for Dmitry, and which—while listening to Katerina—sparks his illumination. For as he excitedly expresses it to the startled Katerina, her love for Dmitry is a love from *nadryv,* that is, a self-punishing love, delighting in its self-hurt, needing the hurt, and only masquerading as love. Ivan proves a further illumination: "Believe me, Katerina Ivanovna, you love only him. And the more he insults you, the more you love him—that's your 'laceration.' You love him just as he is; you love him for insulting you. If he reformed, you'd give him up at once and cease to love him. But you need him so as to contemplate continually your heroic fidelity and to reproach him for infidelity. And it all comes from your pride."

Alyosha and Ivan tell us what Katerina's love is, but they do not tell us why it is so. We can begin to understand why by going back—as indeed Katerina and Dmitry keep going back—to that first fateful meeting. The scene had ended with Dmitry's heroic and successful struggle to overcome the noxious Karamazov insect of passion within him. The tragic relations between them have their seeds in that success, or rather in the gesture that accompanies the "triumph" of Dmitry: Dmitry's long bow of respect, and Katerina's low bow of respectful gratitude. They know it, and the fateful bow is insisted upon by both of them in their conversations.

Katerina Ivanovna is convinced that Dmitry hates her, and he hates her because he had compelled her to bow to him. She explains the reason for "his hatred" for her in this way:

Oh, he has despised me horribly, he has always despised me, and do you know, he has despised me from the very moment that I bowed down to him for that money. I saw that. I felt it at once at the time, but for a long time I wouldn't believe it. How often have I read in his eyes. "You came of yourself, though." [155]

Forgetting that it was she, not Dmitry, who had insisted on marriage, Katerina adds: "He was always convinced that I should be trembling with shame all my life before him, because I went to him then, and that he had a right to despise me forever for it, and so to be superior to me—that's why he wanted to marry me." Despite his contempt and monstrous ingratitude, "I tried to conquer him by my love, a love that knew no bounds. I even tried to forgive his faithlessness; but he understood nothing, nothing! How could he understand indeed? He is a monster!"

But the truth is that the hate and contempt that she ascribes to Dmitry is the hate and contempt she herself feels for him. This is, I think, clear to the reader who can pierce the rather transparent attempt to hide her own hate by giving the hate and all base qualities to Dmitry and all noble qualities to herself. In the notebooks to *The Brothers Karamazov* Dostoevsky makes the hatred she feels explicit. He writes of her in the first sketch of the scene: "Oh, he laughed at me because of that long, low bow. I hated him." It is his bow, out of respect to her, that hurts. For with the bow Dmitry changes from one who abases and humiliates to one who respects and forgives. And she hates the long low bow she must return, for it acknowledges his triumph over her.

We can now understand Katerina's paradoxical and contradictory motives, for once we perceive the subtle deceptions she has drawn over her feelings, perhaps without knowing it, we can see that her motives and actions have followed consistently from what the bowing scene meant to her. Katerina wishes only to hurt because her meeting with Dmitry is compounded of nothing but hurt. She is humiliated in having to appeal for help to the repugnant sensualist, and she is humiliated in having to receive the respectful bow from him. The heroic sacrifice of Dmitry in overcoming the noxious Karamazov insect within him by his deep bow of respect is not an act of sacrifice executed in selflessness and taken in gratitude, but an act of[156] sacrifice given and taken as a subtle and exquisite insult. It is sacrifice used as insult; and ravishment, by comparison, would have been kind. After Dmitry's respectful bow, Katerina carries away in her heart the intolerable burden of an act of sacrifice and the desire to repay it with an equally intolerable act of sacrifice. Is it any wonder, then, that she is obsessed, from this point on, with only one idea: to save Dmitry, to sacrifice herself wholly and fully, to repay the burning insult of sacrifice with the burning insult of sacrifice. The oscillations between arrogance and submissiveness, love and hate, and unselfishness and spitefulness are not the struggle of a proud nature between its good intentions and, as has been usually suggested, the selfish impulses of its spirit. The love no less than the hate, and the submissiveness no less than the arrogance, are needed to bring to her feet a Dmitry ruined and ashamed before all, but contrite and nobly forgiven by her. As a consequence, she courts his betrayal, provokes his humiliations of her, works for his shame, and plots her own injury. The more sunken Dmitry is, the stronger her spirit is in lifting him; the deeper the injury to herself, the more lofty her forgiveness; and the more lofty her forgiveness, the sweeter her repayment of the insult of Dmitry's respectful bow.

Dmitry understands this. He understands why she gives him the 3,000 rubles when she knows that he will use it to carry Grushenka away. He knows that she gives him the money to destroy his honor and to provoke his humiliations of her. And he understands that she wants to be dishonored, so that her forgiveness will be all the nobler. How else is one to explain his agonized cry, "Katya, why have you destroyed me!" when at the trial he hears with dismay her generous account of their first meeting. As Katerina tells Alyosha, she is ready to bear all for his sake. Referring to the 3,000 rubles Dmitry had "stolen" from her, Katerina says: "Let him be ashamed of himself, let him be ashamed of other people's knowing, but not of my[157] knowing. He can tell God everything without shame. Why is it he still does not understand how much I am ready to bear for his sake? . . . I want to save him forever."

What Katerina cannot bear is the possibility of a Dmitry who does not want to be forgiven. This is why, for instance, she becomes hysterical when Alyosha, after a meeting with Dmitry in the garden adjoining the Karamazov house, comes to convey to her Dmitry's "good-bye." Katerina is startled by the word "good-bye" and insists that Alyosha must have made a mistake in giving her the message. In the face of Alyosha's assurances that there has been no mistake, since Dmitry has asked him three times not to forget it, Katerina flushes and insists that Dmitry must not have said it deliberately but in a moment of reckless indecision. "He's merely in despair, and I can still save him," she infers exultantly.

It is at this point in the narration that translations blur this intention to trace back the drama of insult and repayment to Dmitry's respectful bow. The word "good-bye" (Magarshack has "good-bye" and Garnett "give his compliments") is in Russian the verb *klanyat'sya*, that is, "good-bye" by bowing. The Russian word expresses at once the sense of parting and recalls Katerina the insulting respectful bow of the first meeting, when the same verb was used in a different aspect. The blurring in translation of Dostoevsky's intention is unfortunate since a phrase like "to bow out" would have caught, as does the Russian, both the sense of parting and a reminder of the fateful bow. Is it any wonder, then, that Katerina clings almost hysterically to the possibility of some mistake in Alyosha's message, which doubles the intolerable insult by recalling the first sacrifice and severing the possibility of repayment.

Dmitry, as the dissolute officer who struggled against the Karamazov sensuality within him, seemed unconscious of the enormity of the insult he had offered the proud girl, although in the ecstasy of self-satisfaction after she[158] leaves, when he almost stabs himself with his sword, Dostoevsky hints that Dmitry has shared in the intention to insult. The Dmitry who reminds Katerina that she is rich and he but a poor rake, when she writes her letter of declaration of love for him, is also conscious of Katerina's motives. At times his awareness comes out sharply, though involuntarily, as when he retorts to Alyosha's assurance that Katerina loves him, and not Ivan: "She loves her virtue, and not me." He is always sorry for statements of this kind, ashamed of his base nature that erupts in criticism of Katerina, when morally he considers himself infinitely below her. Yet, despite his conscious intentions, he insists again and again in reminding her of the bow. In his last incriminating letter to her, he returns once again to the bow: "Farewell, I bow down to the ground before you, for I've been a scoundrel to you. Forgive me! No, better not forgive me, you'll be happier, and so shall I! Better Siberia than your love." Better murder and prison than such love! Such love and sacrifice, and the bow that symbolizes them, are not purifying and uplifting but abasing and persecuting. They are not Zossima's love, nor is Katerina's bow Zossima's bow. Zossima's bow stays the hand of the murderer; Katerina's raises it. What is wrong with such a love?

Katerina loves Dmitry from *nadryv*, and in this word Dostoevsky catches the vortex of her emotions and motives; with this word he points to one of his most penetrating insights into human motives. Dostoevsky devotes all of Book Four of Part Two to examples of *nadryv*, pointing to something that Ferapont, Captain Snegiryov, Katerina, and little Ilyusha have in common. Magarshack has ineptly translated the word as "heartache," Garnett less ineptly as "laceration."

It is impossible to think of a translation more misleading than Magarshack's. It is romantic and trivial in connotation, and wholly inappropriate to what sears Katerina's breast. Garnett's translation is not much more[159] helpful, but it is not the positive hindrance Magarshack's translation is.

The word comes from the verb *nadryvat'*, which means—apart from its literal meaning of tearing things apart, like paper—"to strain or hurt oneself by lifting something beyond one's strength." To this must be added Dostoevsky's special use of the word to mean a *purposeful* hurting of oneself, and to this, an explanation of the purpose. *Nadryv* is for Dostoevsky a purposeful and pleasurable self-hurt. Father Ferapont's ascetic deprivations are a self-denial from *nadryv*. He "hurts" himself, so that he can hurt the other monks; he needs the "indulgent" monks (which his exercises in asceticism create) as much as Katerina needs a fallen Dmitry. Father Ferapont's ascetic deprivations are weapons of humiliation of others and exaltation of self. Captain Snegiryov's *nadryv* is more pathetic and less violent than Father Ferapont's, but it shares some of the same quality. He deliberately hurts himself—when he stamps on the money Alyosha offers him and which he needs so desperately—because of the beautiful and noble image he has of himself at that moment.

Nadryv is for Dostoevsky a primal psychological fact. It is the impulse in the hearts of men that separates one man from another, the impulse we all have to make the world over into the image of our wills. Katerina *loves* from *nadryv*; Father Ferapont *fasts* from *nadryv*; Captain Snegiryov *loves honor* from *nadryv*. Dostoevsky shows this basic psychological characteristic working to corrupt what seem to be good motives. From the Underground Man on, one of the premises of Dostoevsky's mature dialectic has been that the Will will subvert the best and highest motives to its own purposes. *Nadryv* is Dostoevsky's mature pointing to the psychological impulse that works to corrupt everything to its own purposes.

Ivan has his *nadryv* also, for his hurt is his bruised sense of justice. He raises *nadryv* to a level of universal revolt against God.[160]

Ivan

In the opening scene the Elder Zossima had looked into Ivan's eyes sympathetically and had seen the great choice Ivan had to make between the two irreconcilable principles he had defined. But Ivan refuses to make the choice; he attempts to reconcile the irreconcilable. And this is his great deception: his attempt to elevate the law of self-interest to the law of disinterestedness. If there is no immortality, then according to his own words, "all is permitted." Ivan believes that there is no immortality, but he wants to believe that only the good and the noble will be permitted.

Ivan's revolt against God is deep and powerful and *unanswerable*. The roots go deeper than reason; the antagonist is more powerful.[1] Ivan's revolt is based on the belly, on the sensibilities, on personal revulsion toward historical reality. Ivan knows that reason is a whore that will serve any purpose, that it can be used to prove God's existence as well as disprove it. Reason can justify the list of horrors that have been visited upon man; he knows this and dismisses it. Ivan knows only that suffering exists and that he wants the suffering avenged. After recounting his scrapbook of Russian atrocities against children, he dismisses what are conventional *rational* justifications:

"With my pitiful, earthly, Euclidian understanding, all I know is that there is suffering and that there are none guilty; that cause follows effect, simply and directly; that everything flows and finds its level—but that's only Euclidian nonsense, I know that, and I can't consent to live by it! What comfort is it to me that there are none guilty and that cause follows effect simply and directly, and that I know it—I must have justice, or I will destroy myself. And not justice in some remote infinite time and space, but here on earth, and that I could see myself."

Even if Ivan is wrong (what kind of rationalist is that?), he will remain with the sufferers and demand that they be[161] avenged. "I would rather remain with my unavenged suffering and unsatisfied indignation, *even if I were wrong.*" If reason shows that there is no one to avenge, or that somewhere, someday, all will be explained, he will not be satisfied, but will stand by the facts and his own "irrational" feelings. It is fact, not reasoning, he wants. He tells Alyosha: "I want to stick to the facts. I made up my mind long ago not to understand. If I try to understand anything, I shall be false to the facts and I have determined to stick to the facts." And the facts are: Turks sticking babies with their bayonets; an enlightened father and mother tormenting their five-year-old daughter with excrement and locking her up in a privy all night because had wet her bed; philanthropic Christians teaching Richard to bless God for the grace he has been taught to accept, as he goes to be beheaded for a crime society had forced him to commit; a General deprived of the administration of his estates because he had had a hound tear an eight-year-old boy to pieces for hurting the paw of one of his favorite dogs. Because of these facts, Ivan refuses to accept God's world, although he accepts God.

But he accepts God, so that he can dismiss him. God is a metaphysical concept; the world is a three-dimensional fact. And Ivan refuses to deal with anything but fact. He has a Euclidian mind, which can understand a Euclidian universe. But the idea of God is something

---

[1] A conventional view is the following: "Ivan is proud of his reason, and it is easier for him to give up God's world than to give up his reason. If the world is not justified by reason, he finds it impossible to accept." K. Mochul'sky, *Dostoevsky: zhizn' i tvorchestvo* (Paris, 1947) p. 505. Translated by the Editor.

beyond fact. To reject God would be to go beyond fact. He accepts God only in the sense that one accepts a hypothesis that cannot be proved. As Dostoevsky made abundantly clear in his letters, Ivan's acceptance of God is not a mitigation of his revolt, but simply a historic reality. To N. A. Liubimov, he wrote:

In the text which I have just sent out I express the basic convictions of one of the most important characters in the novel. These convictions are precisely what I consider to be the synthesis of contemporary Russian anarchism: the denial not of God but of the meaning of his creation. Socialism began with[162] the denial of the meaning of historical reality and ended in a program of destruction and anarchism. . . . My hero defends, in my opinion, an unanswerable position: the senselessness of the suffering of children and he deduces from that the absurdity of historical reality.[2]

And to K.P. Pobedonostsev, he said:

This book is the culmination of my novel and is called *Pro and Contra*. Its meaning is the following: blasphemy and its answer. The blasphemy is already finished and sent in; I'll send the answer in July. I took the blasphemy as I understood and felt it to be strongest, that is, as it exists in Russia today among (almost) all the higher classes, and particularly among the young. Our socialists today are not concerned with scientific and philosophic arguments against the existence of God (as were the whole last century and the first half of this century); these have been given up. Rather, they are interested in denying as strongly as possible the creation of God, his world, and his meaning. Only in these questions does contemporary civilization find meaning. In this way I flatter myself with the hope that even in such an abstract theme I have not betrayed realism.[3]

It simply doesn't matter whether God exists or not. Ivan accepts God's existence as you would accept the hypothesis of the universe supported by fishes. His acceptance implies its irrelevance, for the existence of God is an unreal question for the Euclidian mind. What is real, and what does matter is the world we live in, and that world is unacceptable because it is racked with senseless suffering. Ivan does not want rational justification, or Christian forgiveness. He wants justice, not justice at the last clanging of the world's gates, but justice here and now; such justice is the condition he poses for accepting God's world. But whose justice? Surely not the world's, for it is the world's justice that has condoned the birching of the eight-year-old, the tragedy of Richard's life, the terrors of the five-year-old in the privy; it is the world that has punished the General by taking away the administration of his estates from him.

---

[2] Letter to N. A. Liubimov, an editor of *The Russian Messenger,* dated May 10, 1879, to be found in Volume IV of Dostoevsky's untranslated letters, Moscow, 1959.

[3] Letter to K. P. Pobedonostsev, dated May 19, 1879, in Volume IV of the untranslated letters.

Whose justice? The answer can only be—Ivan's justice.[163] And the dream of that justice is the dream of a world remade in the image of him. This dream is the legend of the Grand Inquisitor.

The Grand Inquisitor

D. H. Lawrence first read "The Legend of the Grand Inquisitor" in 1913 at John Middleton Murry's recommendation. "The whole clue to Dostoevsky is in that Grand Inquisitor story," said John Middleton Murry. After finishing the piece, Lawrence asked Murry, "Why? It seems to me just rubbish." He found it to be an irritating "cynical-satanical" pose. But later he found it to be more true and more depressing with every reading. True and depressing because the Grand Inquisitor was right and Christ was wrong. His later interpretaton is representative of a large body of critical opinion that sees the Grand Inquisitor as the victor of the duel with Christ:

Since then I have read *The Brothers Karamazov* twice, and each time found it more depressing because, alas, more drearily true to life. At first it had been lurid romance. Now, I read *The Grand Inquisitor* once more and my heart sinks right through my shoes. I still see a trifle of cynical-satanical showing off, but under that I hear the final unanswerable criticism of Christ. And it is a deadly-devastating summing up, because borne out by long experience of humanity. It is reality versus illusion, and the illusion was Jesus, while time itself retorts with reality.

And:

And we cannot doubt that the Inquisitor speaks Dostoevsky's own final opinion about Jesus. The opinion is, badly, this: Jesus, you are inadequate, men must correct you. And Jesus in the end gives the kiss of acquiescence to the Inquisitor, as Alyosha does to Ivan.

Lawrence takes his stand with the Grand Inquisitor and, thus, with the spirit of darkness and destruction. He takes[164] his stand reluctantly (note the "more drearily true"), for he would like man different. He is perceptive enough to recognize that in taking his stand with the Grand Inquisitor, he accepts man as weak, slavish, and self-deceptive; that he gives up immortality, true freedom, and salvation. But he takes his stand because these are the facts and the rest is illusion. Even more, Lawrence tries, as those who have chosen the truth of the Grand Inquisitor have characteristically tried to do, to bring Dostoevsky over to his side.

We know that Lawrence's interpretation is not what Dostoevsky intended, at least consciously, but it is interesting that the truth of the Grand Inquisitor should have been chosen—and attributed to Dostoevsky—by so many distinguished critics and by critics of different philosophical background and culture. Leo Shestov's whole book *Dostoevsky i Nietzsche* is dedicated to proving that Dostoevsky was really on the side of his godless heroes, and Rozanov is similarly convinced that Dostoevsky was on the side of the Grand Inquisitor. In the *Legend of the Grand Inquisitor* Rozanov says:

When Dostoevsky died, he did not carry the secret of his soul to the grave with him. Before his death, he left us, as if by some instinct revealing his soul, an astonishing scene by which we can see that the words of Alyosha to Ivan "And you are with him" can be definitely applied to the author himself, who so clearly is on his side.[4]

The revolt of so many distinguished readers against Dostoevsky's conscious intention is, whatever else, a testimony to the force and persuasiveness with which Dostoevsky was able to state the other case.

Before the Grand Inquisitor is through talking, the Christ of all the people is the Christ of the chosen few; the Christ who had come to suffer for man has come only to make him suffer; and the Christ of compassion and love is the Christ of indifference and unconcern. The word "revolt"[165] for the Grand Inquisitor's stand is not strong enough; Guardini's "aggression" is better, but it is even more than that. It is *despoilment*, for what Christ had stood for, now the Grand Inquisitor stands for. It is not Christ who loves all the people, who suffers for them and sacrifices not only his life but perhaps his eternal life for them. It is the Grand Inquisitor. This reversal is clearly implied in the final text, and in the notebooks to *The Brothers Karamazov* Dostoevsky made the contrast explicit. There the Grand Inquisitor tells Christ: "We are more humane than thou. We love the earth." And, "I love humanity more than thee." The Grand Inquisitor does not merely oppose his truth to Christ's truth, but he is the truth Christ had failed to erect. He is light and truth; Christ is darkness and falsehood. In the notebooks, the Grand Inquisitor goes so far as to identify Christ with the forces of hell and evil: "I have only this to say to you: you have been disgorged from hell; you are a heretic."

The Grand Inquisitor's argument is not based on idle rhetoric or cheap tricks. Nor is it contradictory as some have claimed. Logic is on his side, not Christ's, although the truth of each is finally subject to more than logic. Lawrence, Shestov, Guardini, Rozanov, and many other distinguished critics have taken the side of the Grand Inquisitor against Christ because his argument is powerful and indeed unanswerable. And they do this despite the fact that Dostoevsky made the case he wanted to make for Christ. There is no weakness in Christ's argument, and there is no weakness in the Grand Inquisitor's argument. Mochul'sky's argument that the Grand Inquisitor is wrong because he argues from love of mankind, yet portrays mankind as weak and slavish is clearly a *non sequitur*. One can love what is weak

---

[4] V. V. Rozanov, *Dostoevsky's Legend of the Grand Inquisitor*. This is the translated title of the untranslated work, first published in 1890. Quoted material from pp. 167–168 of 1906 edition.

and slavish, and perhaps love more deeply. Those who try to help out
Dostoevsky by showing that the Grand Inquisitor's argument is self-
contradictory do not understand the Grand Inquisitor, and they do not
understand Dostoevsky. Dostoevsky made the only case he[166] could
for Christ, and the truth of Christ he presents does not demolish the
Grand Inquisitor's truth any more than the Grand Inquisitor's truth
demolishes Christ's truth. We are concerned here with two ways of
understanding man's nature, and they are discontinuous; one cannot
stand in refutation by the other because there are no common assumptions. This will become clear by seeing and understanding the nature
of the Grand Inquisitor's truth, which is consistent and complete and
deep in its appeal.

Christ had bade men to follow his example, the essence of which
was contained in his rejection of Satan's three temptations in the
wilderness: (1) to turn stones to bread, (2) to prove his divinity by
performing a miracle, (3) to agree to the worship of earthly power. It
is curious, as an aside, that many important critics have failed to
understand what the three temptations are as Dostoevsky understands
them, even though a single careful reading will make this clear. For
some perverse reason—Magarshack and Rahv are examples—many
critics persist in seizing upon the words "miracle, mystery, and authority" as the three temptations, whereas for Dostoevsky these are clearly
the instruments of the second temptation only: man's eternal desire for
proof or certainty before giving his faith. The eternal instruments of
this deceptive proof are miracle, mystery, and authority. Rahv's understanding is representative: "The three powers with which Satan had
tempted Him in the wilderness are miracle, mystery, and authority, the
sole means of vanquishing the conscience of men forever and holding it
captive for their own good."

The three temptations are the three great limitations of a *free
faith*. Christ's example is of a faith freely given, standing without the
support of bread, miracles, or the need of collective earthly power.
Christ had bade men believe in him with the same faith. But Christ
had, according to the Grand Inquisitor, cruelly misunderstood the
nature of man, for fifteen centuries had proved that man by his very
nature was incapable of what Christ had asked. Men[167] had always
cried—and were crying in Dostoevsky's time—"feed us and then we
will be virtuous,"[5] and men had always asked not for the anxiety and
fear of choosing freely but for the certainty of miracles, mystery, and
authority, and they had always been afraid of being alone, craving
always the sheeplike comfort of worship with everyone else. Christ had
asked men to be alone and unafraid in the presence of things unseen,
supported only by the free movement of the heart, but men had always

---

[5] In a letter to V. A. Alekseev, June 7, 1876, Dostoevsky interpreted "stones
to bread" to mean the social problem of environment. See translation of this letter
on p. xv of this volume.

chosen material comfort, the certainty of proof, and the assurance of collective worship.

But man's nature was such that Christ's demands were beyond his strength, and Christ's demand of a free faith could only visit upon him pointless sufferings. Fifteen centuries had proved that only a handful of men were strong enough to follow Christ's example, and that the rest could never follow it. From this it follows—and the Grand Inquisitor makes this charge again and again—that Christ had acted as if he had not loved man, as if he had cared only for the few strong and free and not for the millions upon millions who had not been able to bear his terrible freedom. It also follows that Christ had either misunderstood man's nature or understood it and visited needless sufferings upon man. If the first, then he was not Christ; if the second, then he had been gratuitously cruel.

If the Grand Inquisitor were simply opposing man's slavery to Christ's freedom, man's sheeplike desire for the peace and comfort of body and conscience to Christ's dignity of suffering body and conscience; man's weakness to Christ's strength, then there could be little appeal in his argument against Christ. Even we of the twentieth century have not yet grown callous enough to prefer weakness to strength and slavery to freedom. No, the appeal of the Grand Inquisitor lies deeper, and those like Lawrence and Shestov, who have cast their lots with the Grand Inquisitor, have sensed this appeal. They too would prefer the strength and beauty and freedom of Christ, but with the[168] Grand Inquisitor they have seen that it is not a question of *what man would like to be* but *what he is and can be*. For them, all of history has shown man to be as the Grand Inquisitor has painted him, not as Christ had demanded him to be.

It is the failure to see the fundamental, sincere, and believable appeal of the Grand Inquisitor's argument—as I am convinced Dostoevsky saw it—that had led his supporters to argue in support of Christ on false premises. It is useless to argue on the grounds of which is the more attractive picture of man and to grant on that basis the truth to Christ. The Grand Inquisitor would be the first to grant that Christ's view of man is more attractive than his own, but he would correctly maintain that this does not establish the truth of Christ one bit. Mochul'sky, for instance, argues correctly that without Christ there is no essential manhood, humanity, or love. But he fails to see that this does not prove that there *are* such things as essential manhood, humanity, and love. The Grand Inquisitor is not wrong because he sees man as weak and slavish, or because he is contemptuous of man. Nor does he contradict himself when he speaks of working for man's happiness, while seeing him as weak and slavish. He loves man for what he is, not for what he is not, and he accepts the melancholy fact of man's weakness because it is a fact. The Grand Inquisitor is wrong only if his view of human nature is wrong, and neither logic nor the facts of history are against him. The testimony of things seen are overwhelmingly on his side. But Christ never based his truth on the testimony of things seen, but on the testimony of things unseen. The demand for proof is the second temptation, and what he offers men is the freedom and struggle to reject the demand for proof. What he offers them is the same as what he demands of them. He asks them to rise above their natures, to make over their natures in his image, and they can do that only as he had done it: in loneliness, terror, and anxiety. Men crave what he asks them to give up: the firm foundations of conduct that will assure them that they are [169] acting rightly; the assurance that they are right beforehand, so that they may be relieved of the terrors and anxiety of a free conscience, and so that they may have the comfort of knowing that others and, best of all, all others are doing the same thing. But Christ asks something different: though all men be against you, though history prove it impossible, choose what the heart whispers as possible, even though this choice will most certainly be in loneliness, anxiety, and despair, with no other guide than Christ. This choice—against logic, and history and the examples of others—is Christ's freedom. Why is it freedom? Because for Dostoevsky freedom is what is determined by nothing else. A free choice based on the condition of earthly comfort, on the assurance beforehand from miracle, mystery, and authority, or on the condition that your neighbor believes as you do, is not a free choice. A free faith for Dostoevsky is a faith without conditions; it is a faith that knows only the free movement of the heart.

Dostoevsky had never before offered himself and his readers a choice so stark, because he had never granted so much to his antagonists before. He had not granted so much in *Notes from the Underground*, where the bulls had been portrayed as callous, stupid, and slavishly attracted to the laws of nature; nor in *Crime and Punishment*, where he had been eager to prove Christ right and Raskolnikov wrong; and he had not granted so much in *The Possessed*, where the antagonists of freedom, the socialists, are cruelly crushed by satire, and the antagonists of Christ, Stavrogin and Kirilov, are led down the path to self-destruction. The Grand Inquisitor's monologue is an argument against Christ, and it is an argument against almost everything Dostoevsky had written up to this point. For the Grand Inquisitor grants Dostoevsky every premise he had worked so hard to establish, only to show that the nature of man Dostoevsky had defined supports not Christ but the imitation of Christ. Man is a rebel, as Dostoevsky had shown in *Notes from the Underground*, but he will tire[170] of his rebellion; he hungers for immortality, but he will accept and, indeed, can endure only the pretense of immortality; he hungers for freedom, but can suffer only the illusion of freedom; he will find neither peace nor equality in socialism, but he will accept socialism because it will give him a *false* peace and equality.

This is Dostoevsky's final statement against God. It is Dostoevsky confronting himself with the candor and courage to place everything he had built up into the balances again. It is his final confrontation with the testimony of things seen and with man's desolating weakness and infinite capacity for self-deception. Only the words he wrote from prison to a friend remain at the end to sustain him, as they had all his life, and to sustain his world: "If anyone proved to me that Christ was outside the truth, and it really was so that the truth was outside Christ, then I should prefer to remain with Christ than with truth."

Smerdyakov

Who is the Grand Inquisitor? He is, of course, first and foremost, Ivan. He is Ivan's hypothetical dream; he is Ivan remaking the world. In his conversation with Alyosha before narrating the poem, he says—as does the Grand Inquisitor—"The kind of love Christ had for people is a miracle that is not possible on earth." When Ivan finishes his catalogue of tales of suffering, he poses for Alyosha precisely the question of remaking God's world without suffering. And this is what the Grand Inquisitor does. Ivan, like the Grand Inquisitor, bases his revolt on the unjustified suffering in the world, a case made stronger by restricting his example to the suffering of children. Like the Grand Inquisitor, he bases his revolt on the evidence of his Euclidian mind, that is, on the testimony of things seen. Both Ivan and the Grand Inquisitor are identified with Satan in the notebooks, and both sum up and express in[171] its most complete form the various antagonists of God that had appeared in Dostoevsky's novels.

Is there an answer to Ivan and the Grand Inquisitor in *The Brothers Karamazov?* Formally, the answer is given in the chapters on the Elder Zossima, although these chapters have often been found wanting. But it is wrong to look only at these chapters for the answer. The full answer is in the words of the Elder Zossima, the character of Alyosha, in Dmitry's regeneration, in the rallying of the boys about Alyosha's truth, and, most powerfully of all, in the consequences of the Grand Inquisitor's views on Ivan. "The Legend of the Grand Inquisitor" is Ivan's dream of a world built on enlightened, virtuous self-interest; but Smerdyakov is the real embodiment of the world built on self-interest. The Grand Inquisitor is what Ivan would like; Smerdyakov is what he is forced to confront. Ivan is both the Grand Inquisitor and Smerdyakov. Ivan makes the poem of the Grand Inquisitor, and he *makes* Smerdyakov, for Smerdyakov's views are formed largely by the long conversations he has with Ivan.

As the dream of the hard, necessary, and tragic conflict against an unjust Christ fades and Ivan turns to go home, reality presses upon him. He is overwhelmed, for some unknown reason, by a vague, nasty feeling, the cause of which he cannot drive away or make clear. It becomes clear when he sees Smerdyakov languidly cooling himself on a bench outside the Karamazov property. At first sight, Ivan understands "that the lackey Smerdyakov lay in his soul and it was precisely he whom his soul could not bear." When he first addresses Smerdyakov, he wants to say: "Get away, miserable idiot. What have I to do with you? But to his astonishment, he asks: "Is my father still asleep, or has he waked?" From the first question, Dostoevsky makes clear what the relations between Ivan and Smerdyakov are and what they will be. It is Ivan who speaks first and he who waits for Smerdyakov's answers; it is Ivan who becomes irritated, excited, perturbed; Smerdyakov is calm[172] and assured. It is Ivan who is deferential; Smerdyakov is almost contemptuous. Ivan is alternately attracted and repelled: he hates the smirking, contemptible lackey, and yet he cannot tear himself away from him. He cannot, because Smerdyakov lies in his soul; it was Ivan who taught Smerdyakov how to see the world, and now it is Smerdyakov who teaches Ivan. Smerdyakov maintains a tone of "I'm only saying what both of us already understand," and he ends up speaking for Ivan: "If I were in your place I should simply throw it all up rather than stay on in such a position."

Reality confronts Ivan with Smerdyakov, and Smerdyakov confronts Ivan with Chermashnya. Ivan's moral problem concerns what appears to him to be a nonsensical and irrelevant decision to go to Chermashnya. But, though simple, the decision represents the moral choice Ivan has to make, and Chermashnya takes on symbolic overtones. The first syllable of the word, *Cher*, is the root of the Russian word "dark," and the practical reason why Fyodor is pressing Ivan to go to Chermashnya is to sell a wood. Chermashnya is a "dark wood." This dark wood points symbolically to the Karamazov corruption. If Ivan goes to Chermashnya and sells the wood for Fyodor, he will save his father 3,000 rubles, precisely the amount Fyodor is using to lure Grushenka to him, and precisely the amount that the desperate Dmitry needs to liberate himself from Katya and to take Grushenka away. Dmitry is convinced that the wood belongs to him, because it is part of the inheritance that Fyodor has stolen from him. The "dark wood" is a point of struggle between father and son, and it lies at the core of the decision Ivan must make: whether to accept his responsibility for his father or whether to turn his back on him. In "The Legend of the Grand Inquisitor" Ivan could reconcile the irreconcilable, but in real life, he must choose. He can prevent the murder, or he can let it happen, and no amount of subtlety can obscure this simple moral decision. The meaning of Smerdyakov's smirking, leering[173] suggestions is clear to the reader, if not to Ivan. Smerdyakov is telling Ivan that if he goes to Chermashnya it will be a signal for Smerdyakov to kill Fyodor.

After leaving Smerdyakov, Ivan is filled with vague feelings of hate, spite, and revenge. He cannot understand his motives. He wants

to go out, for some reason, and beat up Smerdyakov; he is filled with
hate and spite even against Alyosha; and he cannot sleep. He gets up
twice to listen to the restless movement of his father, imagines how he
must be peering into the dark and eagerly awaiting Grushenka, and his
curiosity fills him with self-revulsion. Later, he will remember it as the
vilest act of his life, because his imagination was already anticipating
his father's death, and in imagining it, wanting it. He will understand
that on that night he wanted his father's death, and in wanting it, he
was already his father's murderer.[6] The next morning, at his father's
prompting, he promises to stop off at Chermashnya on his way to
Moscow. At the relay station, however, he "morally" triumphs by
changing his mind and going straight to Moscow. The change has no
moral significance at all. It made no difference whether Ivan went to
Chermashnya or to Moscow; it only made a difference whether Ivan
stayed by his father's side.

Ivan comes back to Skotoprigonevsky five days after his father's
death, and a day after Fyodor is buried. Ivan did not give his address
to anyone, and it takes five days to find him. But distance and
ignorance does not modify the ugly truth in his heart; the vague
suspicion that tortured him remains with him, and on the first day of
his return he goes to see Smerdyakov. He sees him for the second time
two weeks later, and for the third and last time a little over a month
afterwards. Smerdyakov is like some epicenter of his moral being, from
which he cannot tear himself away and to which he must return. Ivan
wants to be convinced that Mitya is the murderer, and he is convinced
again and again, but each time the evidence—even though seemingly
irrefutable—does not satisfy him. Smerdyakov convinces[174] him on
the first interview that he could not possibly have been the murderer
and that there has been no "plot" between them and indeed no
preparation for the crime. If a clever man were planning a crime,
Smerdyakov tells Ivan, he would not leave such a clue as to tell another
of it beforehand. Ivan is so satisfied after this interview that he tells
Smerdyakov: "I don't suspect you at all, and even consider it ridiculous
to do so; on the contrary, I am grateful to you for having put me at
peace." But he is not set at peace; neither the official arraignment of
Dmitry, nor Smerdyakov's assurances, nor the document Katerina
shows him—after the second meeting with Smerdyakov—can quiet
him. In the third meeting with Smerdyakov, he learns what he dreads
knowing, but must know: that Smerdyakov has murdered Fyodor, that
he, Ivan, knew it would happen, wanted it to happen, and encouraged
Smerdyakov to do it. When Smerdyakov tells him that, the face of
Smerdyakov—physically wasted by sickness and his yellow eyes
sunken—appears to him to be that of a phantom. At that moment Ivan

---

[6] Ivan is referred to in *The Notebooks* as "the murderer." See translated
selections in this volume.

understands that the repulsive thing Smerdyakov represents is in himself, and the objective Smerdyakov is indeed unreal.

When he hears the ugly truth from Smerdyakov that he is the murderer, the ditty of a drunken peasant, "Vanka Has Gone off to St. Petersburg," rings through his mind. And it rings through his mind because the ditty reminds him of the hardness of his heart, where the impulse to murder had come and where it still lay. This is the refrain that a drunken peasant was singing when Ivan had picked his way through the snowstorm on his way to the third meeting with Smerdyakov. He had collided with the peasant, pushed him to the ground, and had indifferently left him to freeze to death. Ivan recognizes that he is the murderer of his father, because his heart is indifferent—as it was to the peasant—to the fate of his fellow man. On his way back, Ivan finds the peasant again and attempts to[175] make up for his hardness. He has made up his mind to confess the next day, and he spends almost an hour seeing to it that the peasant is well cared for. But it is his head that moves his actions, and not his heart. He is too satisfied with his deed and too conscious of the clarity of his mind. Ivan's heart first moves only after the Devil's last visit to him and after he learns of Smerdyakov's death. Alyosha comes to give him the news that Smerdyakov had hanged himself, and Ivan notices that Alyosha is cold. Feeling sympathy for him, he says, "Alyosha you are frozen, you've been out in the snow. Would you like some tea? Are you cold? If you want, I'll order some tea? *C'est à ne pas mettre un chien dehors.*"

Ivan dreamed of a world in which "all was permitted" and of a hero who, like the Grand Inquisitor, would by sacrifice and suffering build a better world. But the living embodiment of his dream is a knavish, cowardly, simpering cook who dreams, not of sacrificing himself for the happiness of all men, but of establishing a restaurant in Moscow, wearing lacquered boots, and, if possible, trading Russia, a nation of scoundrels, for a wiser nation, France. Ivan had deceived himself, but in his deception lay the seed of a better Ivan. The sign of the better Ivan is the suffering he undergoes before the ugly truth of his part in the murder.

As Smerdyakov stands behind the figure of the Grand Inquisitor, so too the sponging, shabby, low-thinking Devil who visits him in his room stands behind the august antagonist of Christ. There is even some evidence that Smerdyakov and the Devil are one; as Smerdyakov withdraws from life—he strikes Ivan as a phantom in his last talk with him—the Devil appears. The Devil appears for his third meeting with Ivan—the only one that is dramatized—at precisely the moment that Smerdyakov dies. Ivan tells us that his conversation with the Devil takes an hour—he can tell this by the wet towel he put to his brow to[176] dispel what he thinks is a hallucination—and Alyosha arrives to tell Ivan that Smerdyakov has hanged himself an hour before.

Father Zossima and Alyosha

To Ivan's law of "all is permitted," the Elder Zossima answers that "All are responsible for all." This may seem like pretty weak ammunition against the onslaught of the Grand Inquisitor, but the two arguments are incommensurate. What does the law of "all are responsible for all" mean? It means that every person has the obligation, or rather the constant and never ending opportunity, of changing the world and himself by accepting and suffering the outrages of the world. Our responsibility lies most in suffering the beast of self-will in ourselves; we confront this beast at every moment, and we can conquer it only by denying it wholly and unconditionally. The impulse to assert our wills expresses itself in endless variety, but most directly in the hurt we inflict on others. The impulse can also spring from, and corrupt, our good impulses: from the pity we give others, from our demands for justice, from love, reason, virtue, and even from our faith in God. For Zossima—and for Dostoevsky—there can only be one answer: a total acceptance of others, all others. There is only one right way to accept (the wrong ways are endless), and that is to humble oneself before all others; and there is only one way to humble oneself (the wrong ways are endless), and that is to see oneself as endlessly and hopelessly more sinful than all others. At the first impulse to see oneself as less sinful than anyone, the will and the self spring to birth, bringing with them separation, hardness, and the endless duels of Dostoevsky's world. *This is why the hardest thing—and the most beautiful—is not to forgive but to accept forgiveness.* To forgive is to imply that one has the right to forgive, but to accept forgiveness is to acknowledge one's need of forgiveness. The Elder even[177] goes so far as to say that one must humble oneself before all nature, asking forgiveness even of the birds. All nature is one unity, and the smallest act reverberates through all of it. This is a thought that will be repeated by Sartre and other existentialists much later: "Everything is like an ocean; everything flows and touches. You touch the universe in one place, and like a lyre, it trembles in another place." If one were able to humble oneself before all others, Dostoevsky seems to say, the world would be beautiful, because in denying oneself, one would be gaining all others. Although suffering is a key to Elder Zossima's and Dostoevsky's religious ideal, it is not an end. Again and again, in both his fictional and nonfictional writings, Dostoevsky insists on the *joy* of religious consummation.

The mysterious stranger whom Father Zossima guides to rebirth learns that "the love of humility is a terrifying strength," and it is a love that is bought by hard work and struggle. The struggle for that kind of love is embodied in Alyosha. Zossima is his spiritual father—the embodiment of the law "all are responsible for all"—and Fyodor is his natural father, the embodiment of the law "all is permitted." Alyosha's spiritual illumination, the dream of the miracle of Cana, occurs when his natural father is being murdered. Alyosha lives in two worlds, and his ceaseless trips between the Karamazov house and monastery point to this split. His heart is filled with anxious compassion for the fates of his brothers and his father; he also feels the Karamazov lust Dmitry speaks of, the rebellion Ivan feels (he tells Lise that perhaps he doesn't believe in God), but he is most seriously tempted by his love for the Elder. This man, in his eyes the most worthy of all men, suffers in the eyes of the world—and temporarily in his eyes—shame and disgrace.

Everyone had expected the Elder to receive at his death a special sign from heaven as a reward for his sanctity, and according to popular tradition the sign was to manifest itself in the nondecomposition of his body. When the body[178] not only decomposes and smells—but does so even more quickly than the body of an ordinary sinner—many gloat in the hardness of their hearts, but Alyosha despairs in the mildness of his heart. But the despair is as much wrong as is the cynicism and glee. Alyosha needs help to bring him out of a bruised, self-pitying love which refuses to accept what is not his to judge. This help comes from a sinner, Grushenka, who offers him her onion of compassion. What Grushenka touches is completed in the vision of the Cana of Galilee. After returning from Grushenka's, he returns to the coffin of his Elder, where, with the monotonous praying of Father Paissy filling the air, he falls asleep and has his vision. Dostoevsky has called this scene the most essential in Book Seven of Part Three and perhaps the most essential in the novel. As Alyosha prays, his heart becomes filled with sweetness, and the "self-pitying, aching, torturing pity he had felt that morning no longer afflicted his soul." The miracle he had wanted for his Elder is effected in his heart and symbolically in the dream he has of Christ's turning of the vessels of water into wine at the marriage of the Cana of Galilee. Here Christ creates a miracle for the joy of others, and not for himself, "not to show his own terrible power, but to visit gladness upon men." The miracle Alyosha experiences in his heart is the change from his own "hurt" feelings to the shared joy of others. The Elder, who has been humbled, takes the hand of Alyosha, who has rebelled against the humbling, and together they are wedded in Christ's joy, the joy of forgiveness by the acceptance of forgiveness. "All that is true is beautiful, and all that is beautiful is completely filled with forgiveness," Alyosha whispers to himself in understanding.

The Beast Pen

When Ivan makes his decision to leave his father's side for Chermashnya-Moscow, he leaves the way clear for the[179] murder to take place. Smerdyakov has his simulated fit; Grigory has his attack of lumbago; Marfa prepares her remedy, rubs him down, and together they drink what is left; Dmitry runs off in foolish quest of the 3,000 rubles he needs to save his honor and to stay his hand from murder; he tries to borrow it from Samsonov, Grushenka's keeper, where he is dismissed; then he goes to Mme. Khokhlakova's, where she advises him to seek his fortune in gold mining; and finally he goes to Chermashnya, where he makes a futile and frustrating trip to sell the dark wood. When Dmitry returns to town, he learns that Grushenka is not where she told him she would be—at Samsonov's—and he assumes that she has gone to Fyodor's. He grabs a pestle, and with murder in his heart leaps over the Karamazov fence. All his hate is centered on the repulsive old man who has stolen his inheritance, who has destroyed his self-respect before Katerina, and who is now (symbolically with the same 3,000 rubles) stealing the woman he is in love with. He is crazed with desire for Grushenka, with hate for his father, and he is oppressed by Katerina's sacrificial love.

When Dmitry leaps over the fence into the Karamazov garden, Dostoevsky brings to completion a symbolic pattern of detail that he has built up throughout the novel. It begins with the basic postures of father and son: the father crouching behind the high fence that surrounds the Karamazov house, trying to lure Grushenka with the bait of 3,000 rubles, and the son crouching, as if in a lair, in the adjoining garden waiting to see if the bait will be taken. A series of fences rib the back alleys of the town, and they all seem to lead to the high-fenced Karamazov garden. Alyosha has to scramble over them on two occasions in order to see Dmitry. The first time he has to tuck up his cassock and needs Dmitry's strong arm to help him over; the second time (after he has been weakened by his lack of faith) he scampers over the fence without Dmitry's[180] help, significantly at the same spot. What finally draws together the "topographical" symbolism of the town is the name of the town itself, which is mentioned only a few times. The name is Skotoprigonevsky, a place-name adaptation of the Russian word *skotoprigonny*, that is, "beast corral" or "beast pen." The Karamazov garden is the positional center of the town's corruption, and one's own corruption is measured by the distance from this center. The core of the Karamazov corruption lives in the pen: Fyodor, Smerdyakov, and Ivan; Dmitry lives just outside the garden and symbolically just outside the corruption; and Alyosha is a moving link between them, the world of the monastery and the world of the beast pen.

Dostoevsky seems to have this pattern of detail very much in mind when he brings the threatened murder—so long held in suspension—to a climax. When Dmitry leaps over the fence to kill his father, Dostoevsky is careful to mark it as precisely the place where Stinking Liza had climbed over so as to lay the visible progeny of Fyodor's sensual corruption, Smerdyakov, at his father's feet. When Marfa awakens on that fateful night to Grigory's groans, she thinks of the groans of Stinking Liza on the night she had given birth to Smerdyakov. Dostoevsky insists on linking the birth of Smerdyakov with the death of Fyodor, and his intention is clear. Smerdyakov, the visible embodiment of Fyodor's sensual corruption, returns to kill the progenitor.

Dostoevsky completes the spatial symbolism with the murder and its aftermath: all the Karamazovs in the beast pen are destroyed, and indeed destroy each other and themselves; all those outside the beast pen are saved. Dmitry leaps in and out over the high fence, saved by the forgotten softness of his heart; Alyosha is only a visitor from another world to the pen. Fyodor dies by what he had produced, and Ivan is driven crazy by what he, too, had produced, Smerdyakov's mind.[181]

The Trial

The novel ends with more than a hundred pages devoted to the trial. The long exposition at the beginning of the novel, which had set the stage for the drama of the Karamazov crime, is now balanced by the long exposition of "who did it" and why. The crime commands the attention of all Russia; it provokes curiosity, ambition, romance, and, perhaps most of all, the sacred rage of liberalism. There is something for everyone in the crime and in the trial. For the ladies in the galleries there is the piquant scandal of father and son fighting over the town wench and of a highborn woman struggling with the town wench over the town brawler. For the liberal elements from Moscow and St. Petersburg, there is the sacred cause of liberating Russia from outworn prejudices and ushering her into a new era of enlightened humanitarianism. For Fetyukovich, the defense attorney, there is the opportunity to show off his incomparable talents, for everyone is convinced that Dmitry is guilty, and the evidence is overwhelmingly against him. For the reader and for Dostoevsky, there is the awesome problem of the right of a child to raise his hand against his father, and by analogy the right of humanity to raise its hand against God.

Everyone judges according to his own measure. The ladies are convinced that Dmitry is guilty, and because he is guilty they are certain he will be acquitted. In this way the drama and excitement will be greater, and the lawyer from St. Petersburg will be better able to display his talents. Fetyukovich judges according to his measure too: what he argues for must be right. The liberals come to judge by the measure of the new humanitarianism, according to which Dmitry must be acquitted if Russia is to progress. The peasants come to judge also, but their measure is the true measure.

The legal process is essentially irrelevant to what[182] happens at the trial, to what is true, and to what influences the jury. Despite his adroitness, skill, and brilliant tactics, the defense attorney discovers no new facts; they come by themselves. Katerina's startling revelation that Dmitry wrote to her on the eve of the murder threatening to kill his father and Ivan's confession of the murder come as interruptions, and not as results of the legal process. The legal process is an obstacle to the facts, for the participants must rend the decorum of the court to have their say, and the truth is disbelieved and the lies believed. All Fetyukovich succeeds in doing is besmirching the character of every witness he examines. Katerina's confession of Dmitry's guilt is false and believed; Ivan's confession is true and disbelieved. The legal process brings forth only technique, ambition, and triviality. It is as if there were no place in the trial except for sneers, innuendoes, assassinations of character, and rhetoric. Rakitin can have his say, but Dmitry must shout in defiance of decorum to have his say. Rakitin is listened to and even applauded, but Ivan is looked upon as insane.

After the disorders, the bell ringings, the rhetoric, and showmanship, there remains the silence of the jury. We are told about their composition[7] at the beginning of the trial, and even the narrator has some doubts that the truth will be weighed wisely in such company. We hear nothing more of them until they deliver their judgment. When they speak, their words are an outrage to all present: to Fetyukovich's irresistible rhetoric, to the ladies' anticipation of a beautiful ending and to the progress of Russia toward some humanitarian dawn. The jury finds Dmitry guilty without qualification on every count. It is as if everything that had gone on had not touched them, and as if the whole trial had served no purpose. Fetyukovich had touched everyone but the jury. The judgment is final, unadorned, unwavering, positive, and brutal, and to everyone present—and perhaps to the reader— completely baffling. Nor can we congratulate them for ignoring the[183] rhetoric and sticking to the facts, for—and this must increase the outrageousness—they are wrong as to the facts. They have judged an innocent man guilty. They are wrong, and Fetyukovich is right. Whatever his motives, he comes close to understanding how the crime actually took place, who committed it, and why it was done. One can go through all the points of contention and find that the prosecutor is wrong on almost every count and Fetyukovich right. In fact, not only is Fetyukovich right with most of the facts but his final appeal is based on a position that sounds like a summation of Dostoevsky's ideas. When Fetyukovich argues that if the court sends Dmitry to prison it will only harden him into resentment and will make him feel justified in his crime, he is saying almost the same thing that Dostoevsky said in *The House of the Dead*. And when he pleads with the court to show mercy and love, he argues for the kind of forgiveness that Dostoevsky would seemingly countenance. What is wrong with his appeal? Like the Grand Inquisitor. Fetyukovich uses the words of Christ for a different end. As the Grand Inquisitor and Ivan have argued, he argues that children have a right to turn against their fathers when they feel

---

[7] Entry in *The Notebooks*: "composition of the jury: 4 civil servants, 2 merchants, and 6 petty bourgeois and peasants or the reverse."

themselves wronged. There is a difference, and it is significant: Ivan cannot live with his conclusions; Fetyukovich is untouched by his argument. In fact, Fetyukovich goes so far, in championing the rights of "wronged" children before their fathers, by calling Dmitry's alleged murder of Fyodor a parricide only by prejudice.

The peasants know better. They reflect the ancient stubborn faith of the people in their conviction that man is responsible for his acts, and that his responsibility lies in the movement of his heart. Dmitry, for them, is guilty because he had raged against his father, and because in his heart he had desired the death of his father. Dmitry recognizes the truth of their judgment, and he accepts it. He has felt the stirrings of a new man within him, and the sign of that new life, the condition of it, is the recognition of[184] his guilt. Dmitry wants to suffer, not in tribute to his strength in bearing it, but for God's sake. He accepts the suffering of the children in the burnt-out huts, whereas Ivan refuses to accept the suffering of children. Ivan uses the sufferings of children as a premise of revolt, Dmitry as a recognition of his responsibility.

Dmitry as purified by suffering seems to come to understand clearly, near the end of the novel, the insult he had offered Katerina. This is why he asks, through Alyosha, that Katerina come to his hospital room and forgive him. He knows that she has hurt him grievously and that it is her testimony that has probably condemned him to Siberia, but he has come to know that only forgiveness by her and not by him can cleanse her soul. His own readiness to be "forgiven" is a sign of the new man which has arisen within him. When she appears at the door of his hospital room—an appearance that recalls her first visit to him—she is momentarily wrenched out of the trap of self-willed hurting and being hurt by the sincerity of a changed and purified Dmitry. For a few minutes the astonished Alyosha witnesses one of those rare scenes, evocative of the moment that had flashed through the duel between the Underground Man and the prostitute, when love and sacrifice are no longer weapons for punishment but bonds for discovered souls. It is a moment when the pressure of self-conscious hate explodes into selflessness, so thin is the edge between the deepest hurt and deepest love. But only for a moment—Dostoevsky was too much of a realist for this to endure for more than a flash of the spirit. Rebuffed by Grushenka, Katerina returns with bitter satisfaction to the trap of her old self. With eyes flashing and voice strangled with resentment, she leaves the last pages of the novel approving the insult of Grushenka.

The novel begins with the hand of the child raised against the father; it ends with the cheers of children for another Karamazov. The "boys" are gathered about the coffin of Ilyusha, united in their love for him and in their[185] admiration for Alyosha. With Alyosha, they are confident in the beauty of life, the reality of immortality, and the hope in the future. Dostoevsky began *The Brothers Karamazov* as a novel

about children; he visited pedagogical institutions; his first notes on the
novel had to do with children. Despite this, the long chapters on the
boys are only vaguely connected with the narrative proper. Alyosha is
our primary link with the boys; as he is a link between the world of the
Karamazovs and the world of the monastery, so, too, is he a link
between the worlds of the adults and of the children. He suffers the
anger and physical attack of Ilyusha, the intellectual exhibitionism of
Kolya, and by suffering he quiets their anger against the world. What
we find in the children's world are the incipient passions of the adult's
world. Ilyusha's anger and shame before his father's disgrace reminds
us of Dmitry's honor; Kolya's learning reminds us of Ivan's; and his
cruelty to Perezvon, Ilyusha's dog, reminds us of Smerdyakov's cruelty.
But there is a difference. Kolya may revolt against his family, but he is
quickly won over to love and admiration; he may illustrate some of the
same hard vanity in knowledge that Ivan did, but his armor is quickly
pierced by a little love. Ilyusha may show a tendency to *nadryv*—by
attacking a crowd of boys and by attacking Alyosha so that he may be
punished. But he seeks to bear punishment for his father, whereas
Dmitry uses his honor as justification to threaten his father. One spark
of love is enough to consume the paper forts the boys have built about
themselves. Alyosha is the igniting force, for he makes their defenses
unnecessary. The boys may fight and even hate, but the instinctive
wells of love and compassion have not dried up, and they are quickly
reunited in the despair of Ilyusha over his lost dog and in the love and
faith over his dead body. The shadow of the adult world hangs over
them, but it is quickly dispelled, and Alyosha, a child himself in the
mildness and quickness of his heart, strives to keep them that way.

The fates of the brothers at the end of the novel are[186] still in
the making, pointing to the continuation of *The Brothers Karamazov*
Dostoevsky had planned. Ivan burns in the fever of a divided self;
Dmitry has taken up the cross of his guilt; Alyosha stands at the
threshold of the world in which he will reside. But perhaps the most
unfinished aspect of this last great work of Dostoevsky is the stark
choice he has dramatized in the "Legend of the Grand Inquisitor"
between the truth of the Grand Inquisitor and the truth of Christ,
between the craving of man for certitude and the terrible anxiety of a
free and conditionless faith. This is a choice that for Dostoevsky can be
made only in the lonely anguish of each man's heart, and it is a choice
that has split Dostoevsky's critics into two irreconcilable groups, each
insisting that Dostoevsky is on his side. We know on which side
Dostoevsky wanted to be, and there is nothing more we can prove. He
too, I am sure, suffered the anguish of the choice which he dramatized
so brilliantly, so convincingly, and so clearly that we too as readers
must, as we admire the drama, give assent to one or the other: Christ
or the Imitation of Christ. And it matters little what we say, for the
choice will be made without our words.[187]

3. APPENDIXES

Guide to Pronunciation of
Principal Names

Note: An Americanized version of the Russian pronunciation is given in parentheses. The transcription is in conventional English approximations and no attempt has been made to refine the transcription to approximate the Russian. Stress is indicated by underlining the stressed syllable. The names are given as they are ordinarily referred to.

Alyosha (Ahlyosha). The saintly son of Fyodor Karamazov.

Dmitry (Dmeetry). The headstrong and passionate son of Fyodor.

Fetyukovich (Fyetyukovich). Lawyer who defends Dmitry.

Fyodor (Fyodor; two syllables only). The sensualist father of the four Karamazov sons.

Grigory (Grigory). Fyodor's servant.

Grushenka. (Grooshenka). The young lady over whom Fyodor and Dmitry fight.

Ilyusha (Eelyusha). Son of Captain Snegiryov; the boy who bites Alyosha's finger.

Ivan (Eevan). The intellectual son of Fyodor.

Katerina Ivanovna (Kahtereena Eevahnuvna). The strong-willed young lady who pursues Dmitry with her love.

Khokhlakova, Mme. (Koklakova). The matron of little faith; mother of Lise.

Kolya Krasotkin (Kolya Krasotkin). The precocious boy who imitates Ivan and befriends Ilyusha.

Miusov (Myusof). The liberal who almost fought on the barricades of the French revolution of 1848.

145

Rakitin (Rakeetin). The unscrupulous novice who tempts Alyosha by taking him to Grushenka.

Smerdyakov (Smyerdyakof; three syllables). The illegitimate son of Fyodor Karamazov.

Snegiryov, Capt. (Snyegeeryof). Father of Ilyusha who indignantly refuses the money that Alyosha brings from Katerina Ivanovna.

Zossima (Zosseemah). Alyosha's Elder.

Discussion Questions on the Text

Part I

Book I: The History of the Karamazov Family

Why does Dostoevsky begin the novel with a long exposition of the history of the Karamazov family? Can you see any logic in the kind of women Fyodor Karamazov married? What kinds of traits does Ivan exhibit while he is growing up? Why did Alyosha become a novice? Why does each member of the family come back to the town?

Book II: An Unfortunate Gathering

What is the ostensible purpose for the meeting in the Elder's cell? What does the portraiture of Miusov tell us about Dostoevsky's attitudes toward liberalism? What does this scene tell us about what motivates Fyodor Karamazov's scandalous and seemingly illogical actions? Why does Dostoevsky have Dmitry Karamazov arrive late? Is his position self-contradictory as Miusov suggests? How does the Elder understand Ivan? Does it follow that if there is no immortality, all is permitted? Why does the Elder bow down to Dmitry? Summarize Alyosha's attitudes and feelings during this meeting.

Book III: The Sensualists

Where was the Karamazov house located? Give a description of it. Give the circumstances of Fyodor Karamazov's alleged rape of Stinking Liza. Summarize Dmitry's confession to Alyosha and try to extract from it what you consider to be his salient characteristics. Summarize his relations with Katerina Ivanovna—especially the fateful meeting when she comes to borrow money—and explain why Dmitry lends her the money in such a respectful way. How did Dmitry come to owe 3,000 rubles to Katerina? Why is this debt such a terrible burden to him? Recreate Smerdyakov's reasoning in maintaining that there would be no sin—or just a little sin—in cursing his true God if he were captured and his tormentors demanded this of him. What motivates this display of "reason"? Can you explain why Dostoevsky has Dmitry rush in and attack his father at this point in the novel? Is there a structural reason for it? Why is Katerina Ivanovna so excited when Alyosha conveys Dmitry's message that he is saying goodbye?

Part II

Book IV: Lacerations (Heartaches)

Give a description of Father Ferapont. What do you think is Dostoevsky's motive for describing such a monk? Summarize Alyosha's encounter with the boys, and specifically with Ilyusha. How do you explain the strange actions of Lise? Why is Alyosha attracted to her? Alyosha perceives something significant in Katerina Ivanovna's decision never to abandon Dmitry, even if he should go away with Grushenka, and in her decision to have Ivan take a message for her to Moscow. Summarize at this point Alyosha's changing attitudes and growing understanding of Katerina's motives. What is Snegiryov's laceration? Why does Alyosha come to visit Snegiryov and his son? Why does Captain Snegiryov reject the money Alyosha has brought from Katerina?

Book V: Pro and Contra

How do you explain Alyosha's confession to Lise that perhaps he doesn't believe in God? Give a characterization of Smerdyakov: his views, opinions, ambitions. Give a full analysis of Ivan's confession to Alyosha in the tavern: what does he mean by loving life more than the meaning of it, by "draining the cup" until the age of thirty? In what way does Ivan accept God? Why is it that Ivan cannot understand how one can love one's neighbor? Summarize Ivan's chamber of horrors about crimes committed against children. How does he go from these accounts to his rejection of God's world? Is there any way of justifying God's world in the face of these crimes against children? What are the conventional Christian justifications of evil in the world? Why are these inadequate for Ivan? What kind of person is the Grand Inquisitor? What is the Grand Inquisitor's argument against Christ? Why does Dostoevsky not have Christ answer the Grand Inquisitor? What is the Grand Inquisitor's conception of man? Is he right, according to you? In what way is Christ wrong, according to the Grand Inquisitor? What kind of world does the Grand Inquisitor envision? Most critics look on "The Legend of the Grand Inquisitor" as the culminating point of the novel, and even of Dostoevsky's entire work. Can you give some reasons why? What is it that men fear most, according to the Grand Inquisitor? What is it that they crave most? In what way have the Grand Inquisitor and his followers "corrected" God's work? What does Alyosha thing of the Grand Inquisitor? Are there any similarities between Ivan and the Grand Inquisitor? In the meeting between Ivan and Smerdyakov—after the Grand Inquisitor scene—in which they discuss whether Ivan is to go to Chermashnya, what relationship is there between Ivan and Smerdyakov? Who is manipulating whom? Why? What is the significance of Ivan's going to Chermashnya? For Ivan? For Smerdyakov? Why, later that evening, does Ivan have the urge to go down and beat up Smerdyakov? Why does he feel repulsion at himself for listening to his father stirring downstairs? What significance is there in the fact that Ivan changes his mind and goes to Moscow instead of Chermashnya?

Book VI: The Russian Monk

Father Zossima's words at his death bed were meant by Dostoevsky to be an answer to the Grand Inquisitor. How effective are they as an answer? What is the significance of Markel's conversion? What kind of life did Father Zossima lead in his youth? Why did he refuse to go through with the duel? Who was the mysterious visitor? What crime had he committed? Why was he afraid to confess? Were his fears justified as to what would happen if he confessed? What is the episode of the mysterious visitor and his confession supposed to illustrate? What are Father Zossima's views on sin, hell, judging others, equality of men, love, pride?

Part III

Book VII: Alyosha

What kind of miracle was expected at the death of Father Zossima? Who particularly expected a miracle? Were there natural reasons why Father Zossima's body should decompose more quickly than usually? Who was glad that a miracle did not come about? What is Alyosha's reaction to the death of Father Zossima? What does Alyosha's going to see Grushenka have to do with his disappointment over Father Zossima's death? What is the significance of the folk tale about the onion? What is the symbolic significance of the dream Alyosha has of the miracle of Cana of Galilee?

Book VIII: Dmitry

Whom does Dmitry try to borrow money from? How reasonable are his efforts? Analyze the actual circumstances, as Dostoevsky presents them, when Dmitry almost murders his father. What stays his hand? Describe Dmitry's orgy at Mokroe with Grushenka. Do you find his behavior probable after almost murdering his father? Is Dostoevsky's satire of the Poles effective?

Book IX: The Preliminary Investigation

Who discovers the murder of Fyodor Karamazov? Describe the circumstances. Where did Dmitry get the money for the Mokroe orgy? Interpret the significance of Dmitry's dream of the burned-out huts. Summarize the evidence against Dmitry at this point.

Part IV

Book X: The Boys

Give a characterization of Kolya Krasotkin. Whom among the adults does he resemble? Analyze his relations with Ilyusha. It has been suggested that the boys resemble some of the adults in many respects. Can you point out which boys resemble which adults? Why does Dostoevsky devote a whole book to the boys? What structural purpose do they serve in the novel?

Book XI: Ivan

Why does Ivan want Dmitry to escape? Summarize what happens in the three interviews between Smerdyakov and Ivan, and interpret the significance of the meetings. What do they tell us about Ivan's own awareness of his motives? Ivan bumps into a drunken peasant on his way to the third interview with Smerdyakov and leaves him in the snow to freeze. On his way back, however, he goes out of his way to find the peasant and to save him. How do you account for the change? Describe the physical appearance of the devil who appears to Ivan. What are his habits, likes, dislikes? Whose thoughts does he repeat? Why, from Ivan's point of view, is he an unattractive devil? How do we know (by what details) that Ivan has a hallucination? What kind of struggle is going on in Ivan?

Book XII: A Judicial Error

Who is interested in the trial of Dmitry? What do the ladies expect? Account for Katerina's changing testimony. Summarize the arguments of both lawyers. Does the trial get at the facts? Why does Fetyukovich call this parricide by prejudice? Why does Dostoevsky have the jury hand in a verdict so scandalously at odds with the expectations of the audience? How does he use the Bible?

Epilogue

Why does Dmitry ask Katerina to come to his hospital room? Why is she reluctant? Describe their meeting. Dostoevsky entitles the sub-chapter of this meeting "A lie becomes a truth." What does this mean? Describe the last scene of the novel, and explain why Dostoevsky has the novel end in this way.

Discussion Questions on the
Source Materials and the Critical
Articles

The Letters

1. In Letter No. 3 Dostoevsky gives his thoughts on Book V "Pro and Contra" and among other things speaks of depicting in this book the most extreme form of blasphemy. How do you reconcile this with the fact that Ivan says that he believes in God?

2. In the same letter Dostoevsky defends the realism of his creations. Comment on the realism of what is portrayed in this book.

3. In Letter No. 4 Dostoevsky comments on the Elder Zossima's answer to the Grand Inquisitor and evinces some doubt as to whether he will be able to create an answer as convincing as he would like. How well did the answer come off?

4. In Letter No. 5 Dostoevsky insists that the way the Elder Zossima expresses his opinions goes with his character. Do you agree?

5. In Letter No. 8 Dostoevsky says that Ivan was only indirectly guilty of the murder of his father, and that his guilt consisted in not having expressed his disgust before Smerdyakov at the forthcoming crime, which he clearly foresaw. Comment.

6. In the same letter he speaks of narrative reasons why the reader should know that Dmitry was innocent of the crime. What are they?

7. In Letter No. 10 Dostoevsky says of Book XI: "I consider the sixth, seventh, and eighth chapters to be the best done." Comment.

8. In the same letter he has some fears that his portrayal of Ivan's devil may be too long. What is your opinion?

9. What kind of picture emerges from these letters of Dostoevsky, the man and the writer? What traits of character, habits, concerns, fears, and hopes are discernible? Comment also on the tone he uses with various correspondents.

The Notebooks

1. Compare the notes with the relevant sections of the novel and point out significant changes and variations in content and form.

2. In Selection No. 1, "The Meeting in the Elder's Cell," Dostoevsky says "There is no difference between state and pagan codes." What does this mean?

3. In the same selection Fyodor Karamazov explains to the Elder why he plays the clown before people. Does he give an accurate analysis of his motives? Are these motives illustrated in the novel?

4. In Selection No. 3, "Ivan and Alyosha; Pro and Contra Section," Ivan speaks of counting on the baseness of his nature to carry him through life. What does he mean by this?

5. In Selection No. 4, "The Grand Inquisitor," the Inquisitor says "I love humanity more than you." This statement does not appear in the final version; is it merely a statement of what appears in the final version in different form, or does it represent an important change?

6. Can you find the following note expressed in any form in the final version of "The Grand Inquisitor": "Why have you come to interfere in our work? I'll have you burned."

7. In what form does the following question appear in the final version: "Can a free man be happy?"

8. The Grand Inquisitor says the following to Christ in the notes: "They sing of you as without sin, but I say to you that you are guilty." What is Christ guilty of, according to the Grand Inquisitor?

9. Compare the following quotation from Selection No. 5, "Ivan and Smerdyakov," with what is expressed in the novel: "And later at night, he jumps up. 'Does he really think, scoundrel, that it will be pleasant for me that my father will be killed. Yes, that's exactly what he's thinking.' (His familiarity is insulting.)

"(The important thing is not clear; bring up the important point.)

"'The devil take it! Perhaps it really will be agreeable for me. Ha! Ha! Perhaps he really thinks that I'm in it together with Dmitry? Perhaps something good will come of it. Besides it's nonsense; the scoundrel is simply afraid of everything so as not to get mixed up in it.'"

10. Explain the significance of this statement of Katerina Ivanovna from Selection No. 6, "The Trial,": "Oh, he laughed at me because of the bow down to the ground. I hated him."

Ernest Simmons, "A Historical and Analytic Introduction to *The Brothers Karamazov*"

1. Ernest Simmons says the following: "Throughout, the whole novel is pervaded with a search for faith—for God. This search for God

is the central 'idea' of the novel." If you consider this statement to be correct, elaborate it. How is this search embodied? Who embodies it? Are Fyodor, Smerdyakov, Rakitin, and others searching for God? If Dmitry and Ivan are searching for God, how does their search differ from Alyosha's?

2. Ernest Simmons says the following: "Nothing in human experience as we know it will satisfactorily explain the exaggerated motives and actions of old Karamazov, Dmitry, Ivan, Alyosha, Smerdyakov, Zossima, Grushenka, and Katerina Ivanovna." What does this mean? Does it mean that the characters are not probable? To what extent is the psychology that operates in them recognizable in our own lives?

3. Comment on this characterization of Alyosha: "The 'idea' he embodies is that of religious spirit brought into contact with sin in which faith triumphs over unbelief."

4. Ernest Simmons suggests that Dmitry might be considered the hero of the novel. Do you agree? If you do, elaborate on it. If not, suggest another character who might be considered as the hero.

5. Compare Ernest Simmons' explanation of Dmitry's love for Katerina with the explanation given by Edward Wasiolek.

6. Ernest Simmons suggests that Dmitry becomes a tragic figure at the trial. What does Simmons have in mind?

7. Comment on the following explanation of Ivan: "The 'idea' that Ivan embodies is that of the purely rational being whose reason leads him into evil and to a denial of God."

Sigmund Freud, "Dostoevsky and Parricide"

1. What, according to Freud, is the weak point of Dostoevsky's personality?

2. How did criminal tendencies in Dostoevsky find expression?

3. How does Freud explain Dostoevsky's attacks of epilepsy?

4. How, according to Freud, did Dostoevsky react to the death of his father?

5. How does Freud explain Father Zossima's bow before Dmitry when Dmitry threatens his father's life?

6. Why did Dostoevsky have such boundless sympathy for the criminal?

7. Freud sees a connection between Dostoevsky's choice of material and the psychological facts of his life. What is the connection?

8. What is the psychological process by which Dostoevsky's desire of his father's death is transformed into masochistic and destructive tendencies against himself?

9. In what way did Dostoevsky's feelings of guilt arising from his wish for his father's death influence his attitudes toward the authority of the state and toward belief in God?

10. What are Freud's basic assumptions in explaining Dostoevsky, the man, and his work? Do you agree with these assumptions?

Eliseo Vivas, "The Two Dimensions of Reality in *The Brothers Karamazov*"

1. Comment on the following: "But the error of some of the efforts to interpret the meaning of Dostoevsky's novels lies in the assumption that there are 'doctrines' or 'views' to be found in them—systematic structures of abstract thought involving major affirmations and denials—when what they contain is a dramatic organization of life, which includes characters most of whom are deeply interested in ideas."

2. Eliseo Vivas insists that Dostoevsky's ideas are dramatized and not abstractly presented. Consider some religious or philosophical idea found in *The Brothers Karamazov* and show how the idea is qualified by the person's character, motivation, intelligence, and other subjective characteristics.

3. Eliseo Vivas states the following: "Thus, it is a commonplace that Dostoevsky anticipated Freud; that he was cognizant of the fact and understood the role of the unconscious; that he had a lucid knowledge of the duality exhibited by the human psyche and of its consequences; that he understood adequately the function of dreams; that he knew how shame leads a man to frustrate the actions through which he attempts to appease it, and how pride is the expression of insecurity and shame; how cruelty constitutes self-castigation, and how injured vanity takes revenge through love." Can you find examples of these generalized insights in *The Brothers Karamazov*?

4. Eliseo Vivas gives an example of the various "modalities" of the liberal type we find in *The Brothers Karamazov*. He suggests that we can do the same for other types. In a similar way, analyze the modalities of the monks, or the passionate, headstrong types (Fyodor, Dmitry, Ilyusha, Katerina Ivanovna, Grushenka), or some other type.

5. What does Eliseo Vivas think of Freudian criticism as generally practiced? Why?

6. Do you consider this to be an accurate statement: "And intelligence by itself is the source of all evil, and ultimately of despair.
This is one of the things that Dostoevsky knew with the same
certainty that Ivan knew that he was because he thought."

7. "One device that Dostoevsky uses to illustrate the duality of the
soul of a character is to conduct the narrative on two planes."
Illustrate this generalization.

8. Compare Eliseo Vivas' analysis of Katerina and Dmitry's relations
with the analyses of Ernest Simmons and of Edward Wasiolek.

9. What did the terms "Europe" and "Russia" mean to Dostoevsky?

Albert Camus, "Ivan and Rebellion against God"

1. How do you interpret this line: "The blasphemy is reverent, since
every blasphemy is, ultimately, a participation in holiness."

2. Summarize in your own words Camus's understanding of Ivan's
rebellion against God.

3. Can you discern from Camus's tone whose side he is on: Ivan's
or God's?

4. Camus sees Ivan's rebellion as the opposition of justice and truth.
What does Camus mean by each of these terms, and does this
set of terms adequately describe Ivan's struggle?

5. What are the grounds of Ivan's rebellion against God?

6. What is the contradiction that drives Ivan mad?

7. Explain the dilemma that Ivan consciously accepts: "to be virtuous
and illogical, or logical and criminal."

8. What does it mean "to pursue metaphysical rebellion to the bitter
end?"

9. What does "becoming God" mean?

10. Camus says that Ivan chokes on this contradiction: "Long reflection on the condition of mankind as people sentenced to death
only leads to the justification of crime. Ivan simultaneously hates
the death penalty (describing an execution, he says furiously:
'His head fell, in the name of divine grace') and condones crime,
in principle."

D. H. Lawrence, "The Grand Inquisitor"

1. Who is the Grand Inquisitor for D. H. Lawrence?

2. Compare D. H. Lawrence's comments on Ivan's rebellion with
those of Albert Camus and Philip Rahv.

3. Do you agree with this: "Yet, after all, Ivan is the greatest of the three brothers, pivotal. The passionate Dmitry and the inspired Alyosha are, at last, only offsets to Ivan."

4. Whose side is D. H. Lawrence on, the Grand Inquisitor's or Christ's? How does he support his conclusion?

5. What are the limits of man's nature according to D. H. Lawrence's interpretation of Dostoevsky?

6. According to Lawrence, why does Christianity fail?

7. Comment on the following: "His wild love for Jesus is mixed with perverse and poisonous hate of Jesus: his moral hostility to the devil is mixed with secret worship of the devil."

8. Is Dostoevsky's analysis of the weakness of men and the limits of man's nature true of men today, according to Lawrence?

9. What is it that the common people never understand and that Dostoevsky understood?

10. If Christianity is the love of mankind, how has Christ failed to love mankind?

11. Why did Jesus ask too much of mankind?

12. What is "heavenly bread"? "Earthly bread"?

13. Why is Christianity an impossible ideal?

14. According to Lawrence, Jesus condemns miracles and yet believes in them himself. Comment on this seeming inconsistency.

Philip Rahv, "Sources and Significance of 'The Legend of the Grand Inquisitor'"

1. Philip Rahv says the following of "The Legend of the Grand Inquisitor": "It enriches the ideological content of the novel in which it is embedded enabling us to understand more fully the far-ranging implications of Ivan Karamazov's 'rebellion,' but it is even more meaningful in terms of Dostoevsky's development as a whole; and the figure of the Grand Inquisitor is dramatically compelling enough to stay permanently in our minds as a symbolic character-image of the dialectic of power." How does it help us understand Ivan's rebellion? In what sense is "The Legend" symbolic of "the dialectic of power"? Does it help us understand the logic of political power in twentieth-century movements?

2. Philip Rahv points to the fact that when Dostoevsky speaks in his own person—as in *The Diary of the Writer*—he is dogmatic and one-sided; but when he speaks with the voices of his created characters, he triumphs over the propagandist in himself. Rahv explains

this by the "advantage of complicity" that Dostoevsky enjoys in the dramatic situation and that he loses when he speaks in his own person. What does Rahv mean by the "advantage of complicity," and do you think it gives us an insight into Dostoevsky's creative process?

3. According to Philip Rahv, "The Legend" essentially examines the issue of freedom versus happiness. Do you agree?

4. Comment on this: "Therefore to identify Ivan wholly with the Inquisitor, as so many commentators have done, is an error, though a lesser one than that of wholly identifying Dostoevsky with him. The fact is that "The Legend" has not one but two protagonists, Jesus and the Inquisitor, and that Ivan makes no real choice between them. Jesus is freedom and transcendent truth, whereas the Inquisitor typifies the implacable logic of historical reality; but so stark a confrontation in itself demonstrates that Ivan's dilemma is absolute."

5. What are the sources in Dostoevsky's previous work of the curious identification or association he makes between socialism and Roman Catholicism? Can you make sense of this identification? What root idea did he see in both?

6. Summarize some of the sources for the theme of Christ's return to earth.

7. In what sense can we look at Dostoevsky as a religious revolutionist?

8. Philip Rahv sees a profound change in Dostoevsky's conception of man's capacity for freedom from the writing of *Notes from the Underground* to the writing of "The Legend of the Grand Inquisitor." Explain what change he sees, and defend or attack his view.

9. How is genuine freedom related to suffering for Dostoevsky?

Mark Kanzer, "A Psychological View of Alyosha's Reaction to Father Zossima's Death"

1. What is the general psychological thesis that underlies Mark Kanzer's thesis for this novel?

2. What kinds of reactions does the death of Father Zossima release in Alyosha, and what significance do these reactions have for Dr. Kanzer?

3. Do you consider Alyosha to be sexually frustrated?

4. Would you be able to explain the specific evidence Mark Kanzer uses to support his sexual thesis in some other way? How could you explain Alyosha's turning to drink, his breaking the fast, the fact

that he calls Grushenka his sister, and the other specific facts that Mark Kanzer's thesis explains?

5. How does he explain Alyosha's participation in the dream of the Cana of Galilee?

6. How does Kanzer explain Alyosha's kissing the earth after the miracle of Cana of Galilee?

7. What significance does Kanzer see in Dostoevsky's giving his epilepsy to Smerdyakov and the name of a son who had recently died to Alyosha?

8. What analogy does Kanzer see between Shakespeare's motives in writing *Hamlet* and Dostoevsky's in writing *The Brothers Karamazov?*

Ralph Matlaw, "Myth and Symbol in *The Brothers Karamazov*"

1. What is a myth?

2. Give examples of the "myth of regeneration."

3. Comment on the following: "Smerdyakov's role in the murder, then, can never be justified on purely rational grounds."

4. What are the different ways in which myth appears in the novel?

5. Ralph Matlaw shows how Dostoevsky repeats in variation the idea of resurrection in various characters. Choose another idea and trace out the repetitions and variations of the idea in the thoughts, statements, and actions of other characters.

6. Explain what is suggested in the following quotation: "The problem of Ivan's guilt is enormously complex and provides the subject for much of the book. Yet the same problem appears in its simplest form in the strangling of the goose, where the issue is perfectly clear, the guilt and moral consequences (if any) obvious."

7. Ralph Matlaw suggests that Kolya Krasotkin and Ivan Karamazov share a similar psychological mechanism. What is this mechanism?

8. Ralph Matlaw says: "One of the most fascinating repetitions of symbolic scenes involves making important metaphysical or moral statements by means of a distasteful object." Illustrate this with examples, and qualify the statement if you think it needs qualification.

9. Ralph Matlaw gives us a number of examples of descriptive details used for symbolic purposes; for example, Fyodor Karamazov's fleshy Adam's apple, Ivan's sagging right shoulder, and Alyosha's downcast eyes. Analyze the symbolic detail clustered about a character or a scene and interpret its significance.

Edward Wasiolek, "The Brothers
Karamazov: Idea and Technique"

1. In what way are children important in the novel, and how has Dostoevsky built them into the structure of the novel?

2. Edward Wasiolek suggests that the opening scene in the Elder's cell anticipates in miniature the rest of the novel. If you agree, explain what is anticipated in the opening scene.

3. In what way is Ivan related to the hate that propels Dmitry's attack of his father?

4. Does Ivan contradict himself in his views on the relationship of the Church to the lives of men?

5. Explain Katerina Ivanova's motives in the way she acts toward Dmitry. Explain Dmitry's reactions and motives.

6. What does the word *nadryv* mean and how does it help explain Katerina Ivanovna's motives? The motives of others?

7. Is the "bow" a recurrent gesture in *The Brothers Karamazov*?

8. Why does Katerina Ivanovna pursue Dmitry with her love?

9. How is the sub-plot of Katerina's tortured love for Dmitry related to the main plot of Dmitry's hatred of his father?

10. What is Ivan Karamazov's *nadryv*?

11. Is Ivan a rationalist according to Wasiolek?

12. In what peculiar way does Ivan accept God? Does this mean that he "believes in God" as we ordinarily understand that statement?

13. Summarize the Grand Inquisitor's argument against Christ. What does Wasiolek mean by the Grand Inquisitor's despoilment of Christ?

14. Can we prove whether the Grand Inquisitor or Christ is right?

15. Comment on the following: "Dostoevsky made the only case he could for Christ, and the truth of Christ he presents does not demolish the Grand Inquisitor's truth any more than the Grand Inquisitor's truth demolishes Christ's truth."

16. Is there any way of answering the Grand Inquisitor's charge that Christ did not care about the multitudes but only for the small number that were strong enough to follow him?

17. What is a "free faith" for Dostoevsky?

18. Where in the novel can we find an answer to the Grand Inquisitor?

19. Why is Ivan irritated with Smerdyakov?

20. Why does Smerdyakov want Ivan to go to Chermashnya?

21. Explain the symbolism of the place name Chermashnya.

22. Explain how Father Zossima's law "all are responsible for all" is an answer to Ivan's law "all is permitted."

23. Why is the acceptance of forgiveness the hardest and most beautiful thing for Dostoevsky?

24. Explain how the name of the town in which the Karamazov drama takes place summarizes a symbolic pattern that has been built up throughout the novel.

25. In what sense does everyone at the trial judge according to his own measure?

26. Why does Dmitry ask Katerina Ivanovna to come to his hospital room?

27. How do we account for the seemingly perverse judgments of the peasants?

Theme Topics

1. Every set of facts in a literary work of art can be interpreted according to different disciplines. Thus, Dr. Kanzer interprets the visit of Alyosha to Grushenka's apartment and his dream of the miracle of Cana of Galilee in Freudian terms. One could interpret the same facts according to different sets of terms: Christian, mythic, sociological, existential, Marxist. Take this scene or some other scene and interpret the same set of facts with two sets of terms.

2. Most critics are dissatisfied with the dramatic portraiture of Father Zossima. If you are convinced that he is an inadequately drawn figure, analyze the technical causes why this is so.

3. What is true freedom for Dostoevsky?

4. Is there a middle ground between Christ's conception of freedom and the Grand Inquisitor's?

5. If you think that Ivan's revolt against God's world is wrong, how can you justify a universe that contains the horrors that he has enumerated?

6. As a test of Dostoevsky's realism, see if you can gather from contemporary newspapers similar reports of atrocities committed against children.

7. Eliseo Vivas notes Dostoevsky's "lack of interest in nature." Assuming this to be true, characterize the kind of world we find in *The Brothers Karamazov*. What details and settings are most characteristic?

8. "The Legend of the Grand Inquisitor" presents us with a paradox in craft. It is by universal consent deeply moving, yet it is seemingly undramatic in form, consisting entirely of a long monologue. How can we account for its dramatic power?

9. Book IX, "The Preliminary Investigation," is a late addition to the novel. What, if anything, does it add to the novel?

10. Whom do you consider to be the hero of the novel?

11. Some critics consider other characters (Rakitin, for example) more repulsive than Fyodor Karamazov. If you agree, explain why Fyodor Karamazov is not the most repulsive character in the novel.

12. What are the weak points of *The Brothers Karamazov?*

13. Choose a scene or a character and explain why you consider it or him to be the best in the novel.

14. Dostoevsky began thinking and writing *The Brothers Karamazov* by considering children, and he devotes an entire book to them in the novel. What role do they play in the novel?

Theme Topics Requiring Further Reading and Research

1. Contrast Alyosha with Prince Myshkin in *The Idiot*.

2. Read George Orwell's *1984* and compare it with "The Legend of the Grand Inquisitor."

3. Compare the doctrines of Shigalyov in *The Possessed* with those of the Grand Inquisitor.

4. Compare the treatment of freedom in *Notes from the Underground* with the treatment in "The Legend of the Grand Inquisitor."

5. "The Legend of the Grand Inquisitor" can be looked upon as the culmination of Dostoevsky's work. Read a representative number

of works by Dostoevsky and explain how they anticipate the drama that takes place in "The Legend of the Grand Inquisitor."

6. Compare the rebellion of a hero in a novel of your own choosing with Ivan Karamazov's rebellion.

7. Read the entirety of Camus's *The Rebel* and discuss the chapter on Ivan, "The Rejection of Salvation," in the context of the plan of the whole work.

8. Compare Schiller's *The Robbers* with *The Brothers Karamazov*.

9. Ernest Simmons suggests that Ivan Karamazov is the "last of the doubles." Summarize the appearance of the double character in the main works of Dostoevsky that preceded *The Brothers Karamazov* and explain the ways in which Ivan is similar to or different from the other double characters.

10. Compare Ippolit in *The Idiot* with Ivan Karamazov.

11. Choose a novel of Kafka's and compare it with Dostoevsky's *The Brothers Karamazov* on some point of interest to you.

12. Eliseo Vivas, in contrast to many other critics, insists that Dostoevsky's psychological and metaphysical side is fully consistent—indeed organically related—to his art. Take some favorite idea of Dostoevsky, read a good biography and some portions of *The Diary of a Writer*, and write an essay showing how his art is or is not consistent with his ideas.

13. Choose one of the selections from "Suggestions for Further Reading" in this book and write an essay analyzing and evaluating the selection.

14. Choose a character from a contemporary novel you admire and compare the devices the author uses to make his character vivid and interesting with those that Dostoevsky uses for a character of your own choosing.

15. While writing *The Brothers Karamazov* Dostoevsky reread and annotated a copy of the book of Job. Compare Job's fate with some aspect of *The Brothers Karamazov*.

16. Read several works by Dostoevsky and analyze his treatment of women.

17. Read a good biography and relevant portions of *The Diary of a Writer;* then consider Dostoevsky's political opinions as they appear in his life and in *The Brothers Karamazov*.

Suggestions for Further Reading

A selected list of biographical and critical works is given below. The best preparation for understanding *The Brothers Karamazov* is the reading of other works by Dostoevsky. In additon to his other three great novels—*Crime and Punishment, The Idiot,* and *The Possessed*—students will want to read *The Double,* an extraordinary early work, and *Notes from the Underground,* one of the most profound intellectual documents of the last century. Both works clearly anticipate many of the problems of *The Brothers Karamazov.* Some reading from the Boris Brasol translation of Dostoevsky's *The Diary of a Writer* (New York, 1949) will provide useful first statements on problems Dostoevksy was writing about when he was beginning to think about *The Brothers Karamazov.* Finally, a good biography and a selected number of critical works may be of help in placing *The Brothers Karamazov* in the proper historical and intellectual setting and in providing a vocabulary that has been used in discussing the literary and intellectual problems *The Brothers Karamazov* raises.

For additional references to scholarly and critical material on Dostoevsky, including his other works of fiction, the student should consult Maurice Beebe and Christopher Newton, "Dostoevsky in English: A Selected Checklist of Criticism and Translations," *Modern Fiction Studies,* IV (Autumn 1958), 271–291. This may be supplemented by consulting the MLA Bibliography for the years since 1958.

Letters and Reminiscences

Hill, Elizabeth, and Doris Mudie, ed. and trans. *The Letters of Dostoevsky to his Wife.* New York: Richard R. Smith, 1930.

Koteliansky, S. S., and J. Middleton Murry, ed. and trans. *Dostoevsky: Letters and Reminiscences.* New York: Knopf, 1923.

Koteliansky, S. S., ed. and trans. *Dostoevsky Portrayed by his Wife; the Diary and Reminiscences of Mme. Dostoevsky.* New York: Dutton, 1926.

Mayne, Ethel Colburn, ed. and trans. *Letters of Fyodor Michailovitch Dostoevsky to his Family and Friends.* London: Chatto and Windus, 1914.

Biography

Carr, Edward Hallett. *Dostoevsky (1821–1881), a New Biography.* Boston and New York: Allen and Unwin, 1931.

Dostoevsky, Aimée. *Fyodor Dostoevsky, a Study.* London: Heinemann, 1921.

Magarschack, David. *Dostoevsky.* New York: Harcourt, 1961.

O'Connor, Frank. "Dostoevsky and the Unnatural Triangle," in *The Mirror in the Roadway: A Study of the Modern Novel.* New York: Knopf, 1956, pp. 199–222.

Slonim, Marc. *The Three Loves of Dostoevsky.* New York: Rinehart, 1955.

Troyat, Henry. *Firebrand; the Life of Dostoevsky.* trans. Norbert Guterman. New York: Roy Publishers, 1946.

Yarmolinsky, Avraham. *Dostoevsky, His Life and Art.* New York: Criterion Books, 1957.

Critical: Dostoevsky

Fayer, Harry Mischa. *Gide, Freedom, and Dostoevsky.* Burlington, N.H.: Lane Press, 1946.

Freud, Sigmund. "Dostoevsky and Parricide," in *F. M. Dostoevsky, Stavrogin's Confession.* trans. Virginia Woolf and S. S. Kotheliansky. New York: Lear, 1947, pp. 87–114. Also in William Phillips, ed. *Art and Psychoanalysis.* New York: Criterion Books, 1957.

Ivanov, Vyacheslav. *Freedom and the Tragic Life: A Study in Dostoevsky.* trans. Norman Cameron. New York: Noonday Paperbacks, 1957.

Kanzer, Mark. "Dostoevsky's Matricidal Impulses," *Psychoanalytic Review,* XXXV (April 1948), 115–125.

Lloyd, John Arthur Thomas. *Fyodor Dostoevsky.* New York: Scribner's, 1947.

Poggioli, Renato. "Dostoevsky or Reality and Myth," in *The Phoenix and the Spider: A Book of Essays about Some Russian Writers and Their View of the Self.* Cambridge, Mass.: Harvard, 1957, pp. 16–32.

Reik, Theodor. "The Study of Dostoevsky," in *From Thirty Years with Freud.* trans. Richard Winston. New York: Farrar and Rinehart, 1940, pp. 158–170.

Shestov, Leo. *Job's Balances.* trans. Camilla Coventry and C. A. Mc-Cartney. London: Dent, 1932.

Steiner, George. *Tolstoy or Dostoevsky; An Essay in the Old Criticism.* New York: Knopf, 1959.

Trilling, Lionel. "Manners, Morals, and the Novel," in *The Liberal Imagination.* New York: Doubleday, 1950.

Wasiolek, Edward. *Dostoevsky: The Major Fiction.* Cambridge, Mass.: M.I.T., 1964.

Wellek, Rene, ed. *Dostoevsky; a Collection of Critical Essays.* Englewood Cliffs, N.J.: Prentice-Hall, 1962.

Critical: The Brothers Karamazov

Amend, Victor E. "Theme and Form in 'The Brothers Karamazov,'" *Modern Fiction Studies,* IV (Autumn 1958), 240–252.

Bertenson, Sergei. "'The Brothers Karamazov' at the Moscow Art Theater," *American Slavic and East European Review,* XVI (1957), 74–78.

Blackmur, R. P. "Between the Numan and the Moha: Notes toward a Theory of Literature," in *The Lion and the Honeycomb.* New York: Harcourt, 1955, pp. 307–308.

Brewster, Dorothy, and Angus Burrell. *Modern Fiction.* New York: Columbia, 1937, pp. 40–64.

Guardini, Romano. "The Legend of the Grand Inquisitor," trans. Sally Cunneen, *Cross Currents,* III (Fall 1952), 58–86.

Manning, Clarence A. "The Grand Inquisitor," *American Theological Review,* XV (January 1933), 16–26.

Matlaw, Ralph E. *Notes from the Underground and the Grand Inquisitor.* New York: Dutton, 1960.

Matlaw, Ralph E. *The Brothers Karamazov; Novelistic Technique.* The Hague: Mouton, 1957.

Ramsey, Paul. "God's Grace and Man's Guilt," *Journal of Religion,* XXXI (January 1951), 21–37.

Ramsey, Paul. "No Morality without Immortality: Dostoevski and the Meaning of Atheism," *Journal of Religion,* XXXVI (April 1956), 90–108.

Sewall, Richard B. "The Brothers Karamazov," in *The Vision of Tragedy.* New Haven: Yale, 1959, pp. 106–126.

Slochower, Harry. "Incest in *The Brothers Karamazov,*" *American Imago,* XVI (1959), 127–145.

Strem, George. "The Moral World of Dostoevsky," *Russian Review,*
    XVI (1957), 15–26.

Wasiolek, Edward. "Dostoevsky's *The Brothers Karamazov,*" *Explicator,* XVI (1957), Item 7.

Weinrich, M. I. "Ideological Antecedents of *The Brothers Karamazov,*" *Modern Language Notes,* LXIV (June 1949), 400–406.